S0-AKT-139

Dear Pete —

We all try in our own ways to make our community a better place especially for those who are not as fortunate.

Frank Kosh

1/10/87

The New Corporate Philanthropy

How Society and Business Can Profit

The New Corporate Philanthropy

How Society and Business Can Profit

Frank Koch

Plenum Press · New York and London

Library of Congress Cataloging in Publication Data

Koch, Frank.
The new corporate philanthropy.

Includes bibliographical references and index.
1. Industry – Social aspects – United States. 2. Corporations – Charitable contributions – United States. I. Title.
HD60.5.U5K6 658.1'5 78-24380
ISBN 0-306-40115-0

First Printing – May 1979
Second Printing – January 1981

A Division of Plenum Publishing Corporation
227 West 17th Street, New York, N.Y. 10011

Printed in the United States of America

Foreword

Somehow it surprises me that this book wasn't written earlier, but I'm glad it wasn't. If it had been, Frank Koch probably wouldn't have sensed the vacuum that has existed, and this practical book wouldn't have come to be. I'd like to stress *practical.* The book describes in a comprehensive and—more importantly—practical way how every corporation can marshal its financial support, employee talents, and other resources to make a meaningful impact on society.

I happen to be one of those corporate executives who believes that a business has a responsibility to make such an impact. My brother Peter agrees. Our father and uncle set an example for us, and the tradition goes back to our great uncles and their uncle, Levi Strauss himself. For more than 125 years Levi Strauss & Co. has shown that social responsibility is good business and, in recent years, that it is also compatible with dynamic growth.

We are proud of that tradition and what it produced, but I think the modern era of social responsibility or corporate citizenship at Levi's got its impetus in 1968 with my association with the National Alliance of Businessmen. It was there that I saw what other companies were doing: innovative ways to train, to transport, to provide jobs. It opened my eyes to areas in which business could become involved, areas I never before thought of as business responsibilities—even areas where it could have an impact.

Until then, I think it fair to say, our own attitude was that we had a responsibility to return to society some of the rewards we received from business success. Now we believe strongly that a corporation must become actively involved in facing and solving the social problems of America. Today's corporation must develop practical means of giving human needs the same status as profit and production. This does not mean that business will not continue to assume its responsibility for making a profit for stockholders, ensuring ample income for its employees, and providing quality products for its customers, but the social forces at work in our nation today demand that the corporation make a philosophical and a material response to the other needs of the people and the community.

In the long run, this task of the corporation will be in its own best interest, since it cannot prosper as fully or as long in a society frustrated by social ills and upheaval. It's not a question of whether a business, regardless of size, can afford to undertake programs of social reform. We don't think a business can afford not to.

Just how long do you think this country can enjoy its current affluence in the face of the inequities that exist in our society? Those of us in positions of influence, large or small, must all make some active contribution to the elimination of these inequities. And, pragmatically, I'm convinced it's good business to do so.

Frank Koch is convinced of that, too, and has written this book, which makes a strong case for that view. I know how much respect our executives who have worked with him have for the practical way he has implemented his philosophy. How he has written a valuable guidebook to show others what they can do . . . and why they should do it.

The book makes frequent mention of the Commission on Private Philanthropy and Public Needs, commonly known as the Filer Commission. My membership in that group helped focus my thinking about the need for imaginative corporate giving just as NAB membership sharpened my thinking about other areas of corporate citizenship. The commission learned that corporate cash philanthropy of $1.35 billion in 1976 amounted to only about 5% of all private philanthropic giving in the United States. We learned that only 20% of the corporations that filed an income tax form claimed a charitable deduction and that the giving, which has hovered around 1% of pretax net income since 1945, is only one-fifth of the allowable IRS maximum.

Frank Koch gives convincing arguments for increasing the level of corporate giving. Equally important—maybe more so—he gives convincing arguments, and methods, for increasing the effectiveness of such philanthropy. I was pleased that he cited a number of examples from our firm's activities, but I think we, as well as all companies with an open mind to getting results, can learn much from this book.

So I urge that the pages that follow be read carefully, keeping in mind that the problems of our society are not going to disappear; rather they are going to compound at an increasing rate unless we— a "we" that includes business in a prominent role—help to solve them.

WALTER A. HAAS, JR.
Chairman of the Board
Levi Strauss & Co.

Acknowledgments

I am particularly thankful to several corporations that permitted me to initiate new approaches to corporate social responsibility through company contributions and community involvement activities. I would like to acknowledge the personal support of the chairman and president, respectively, of Syntex Corporation, Drs. George Rosenkranz and Albert Bowers; and two former executives of Syntex who founded their own companies, Dr. Alejandro Zaffaroni of Alza Corporation and Dr. Carl Djerassi of Zoecon Corporation.

Having said that, I want to state that the ideas and recommendations in this book represent my own personal views of corporate giving and should not be construed to have the endorsement of any corporation with which I have been associated.

I would also like to mention Lucien "Mike" Sichel, retired Washington vice-president of Abbott Laboratories, who provided encouragement for my ideas and values in my early years at CIBA Corporation; Milton Moskowitz, business columnist and senior editor of *Business and Society Review*, who has been generous in his recognition of my efforts in promoting corporate social responsibility; and Jing Lyman, board member of the Rosenberg Foundation, who has been most supportive of my attempts to revitalize corporate philanthropy.

The book would not have been possible without the assistance of many individuals. These include Sandra Blakeslee (addiction research and treatment); J. Moreau Brown (aid to education); Frank Cady (environment and ecology, common ground, international assistance); Nancy Freedman (better local transit); Lewis Griggs (public television); Phoebe Harlow (women's causes); Judy Horst (family planning); Karen Meyers (women's causes); Barney Olmsted (new ways to work); Bob Orser (helping nonprofits); Barbara Schilling (volunteer board members, united giving); and Wally Thompson (helping minorities).

Several others provided assistance and encouragement. John W. White of Cheshire, Connecticut, helped me to understand that finding a publisher takes almost as much energy as writing a manuscript. Perry Leftwich, a professional colleague, by heaping lavish praise on my early writing efforts, gave me the courage to plunge forward with a difficult task. Betty Mackey, my secretary for ten years, typed the manuscript and consoled me when the problems of becoming a first-time author seemed too difficult to overcome.

My acknowledgment also goes to the nonprofit organizations with which I have been associated over the past 20 years. These worthy groups and dedicated people have provided the inspiration and documentation for this book. I am pleased to spread the good news of the causes they have championed so well. They deserve to be better known and more generously supported.

Unfortunately, it is not feasible in this type of book to cover all those organizations and causes that warrant corporate support. My objective is to instruct and motivate—not to describe every area in which corporate support could be meaningful. The knowledgeable reader will notice many vital concerns (health care, youth programs, help for the elderly, assistance for the physically handicapped, rehabilitation of criminals, etc.) that are not specifically addressed in this book. Please understand that this omission is no indication of my feelings that these are not also vital areas for corporate support.

Finally, this book is dedicated to my colleagues in the business community who recognize that our present economic system can be preserved and prosper only in a just, productive, and stable society where the role of the corporation is perceived to be in essential harmony with the needs and aspirations of all citizens and the goals of other democratic institutions in our communities, in the nation, and in the world.

FRANK KOCH

Palo Alto, California

Contents

PART ONE

PART TWO

PART ONE

1

Corporate Giving: The Untapped Potential

We save ourselves, our business, only by making this society work equally well for all its members. To me that means, among other things, voluntary giving — giving knowledge, time, money, wherever we are convinced it will improve quality, correct evils, extend equity in America. The case for corporate giving is an essential part of corporate survival.

J. IRWIN MILLER, Chairman of the Executive Committee for Cummins Engine Company

Mr. Miller has always been in the forefront of those enlightened business leaders who believe that effective corporate philanthropy is an essential ingredient in overall corporate responsibility. These businessmen understand that the character and direction of our world has changed dramatically in the past few decades. Events have produced an array of economic and social problems that have precipitated in thoughtful business people a deep concern for the viability and survival of our way of life.

These changes have significantly enlarged the impact and the responsibilities of the modern corporation. Corporate isolation or lack of social vision are not practical options for the business leaders managing large businesses in the final quarter of the 20th century. Fortunately, there is a growing awareness and concern in the business community reflected in these words of Louis Lundborg, former chairman of the Bank of America:

> Happily, there are corporations whose top officers have not lost their perspective, and whose sense of sound responsibility tells them that neither the company nor its products are the final corporate goal. They see that the quality of life, the conditioning under which people live, and the things that give meaning to their lives are the ultimate concern of all organized activity, corporate or otherwise.[1]

[1]Louis B. Lundborg, *Future without Shock* (New York: W. W. Norton, 1974), p. 129.

The public has long expected the business community to play an active role in helping society to deal with some of its most pressing problems. Louis Lundborg expressed it this way:

> And what society is saying to business, in effect, is, "If you want the privilege of going on running this big, all-embracing machine, all-engulfing machine, you've got to help see to it that it produces a better quality of life for everybody."[2]

A revitalized sense of corporate mission for a more active and broader role in society can reduce the isolation of corporations and begin to turn around some of the current negative public attitudes toward business. Only 15% of those surveyed in a 1975 Harris poll expressed "a great deal of confidence" in the heads of large corporations — down from 55% in 1966. This is a shocking and dangerous situation.

It is also important to maintain and enhance in this country a pluralistic approach to our social needs, or government will inevitably be brought in to address problems if other initiatives are not forthcoming. It isn't enough to decry the expansion of governmental activity into every nook and cranny of public and private life. Surely the business community with its enormous intellectual, financial, and other resources can develop alternatives in the area of social problem-solving.

To accomplish these objectives, the business community does not have to start at ground zero. This process can start by first tapping the full potential of corporate giving. The system is in place in many of our major corporations and can be established in others. What is missing is corporate leadership, according to the late John D. Rockefeller 3rd:

> My perception is that more and more business leaders realize that times are changing and that they must begin to carefully reconsider their proper role and responsibilities in the new situation. Yet despite the growing dialogue on "corporate responsibility," my observation is that yet few business leaders have reached clear conclusions, and even fewer have taken decisive action.[3]

It is timely and opportune to change this situation. Corporate leadership shows signs of emerging. The isolation of many corporate executives seems to be abating.

I believe that corporations today cannot make intelligent decisions about their business activities without a keen awareness of what is going on in society outside of the corporation. Responsible corporate leaders must have sufficient and accurate information about the vital social, political, and economic crosscurrents in the world. With this knowledge, they can direct corporate support to the many innovative efforts aimed at important community and national needs.

This means that corporations will have to pay attention to community health problems and learn about urban decay, the deterioration of

[2]Ibid., p. 87.

[3]John D. Rockefeller 3rd., *The Second American Revolution* (New York: Harper & Row, 1973), p. 93.

the physical and social environment, the problems of housing and unemployment, educational needs, drug abuse, the aspirations of minorities and women, the social role of the arts, the problems of criminal justice, violations of human rights, and poor conditions in other countries.

It means that corporations must seek out and support those individuals and community organizations around them that have something positive and unique to offer to society: organizations and people that are really close to the groups they claim to represent, people who are able to use their minds and imagination in dealing with deep and frustrating problems, people who have learned that taking command of their own destiny is the first step in getting effective support from others, and people who are not afraid to fail and who know how to capitalize on success.

Through involement with such people, the corporation can make the greatest impact on society with the resources, human and material, at its disposal.

An exciting new partnership is waiting to be established — a partnership among thousands of corporations all over the country and the hundreds of thousands of nonprofit organizations, mostly operating on a community level, that have shown energy and initiative in dealing with pressing social problems. Individual corporations need not wait for the entire business community to decide what needs to be done or what will work. Each corporation can begin with its own ideas, interests, and resources. Corporations and community organizations can develop relationships in ways that are realistic and relevant.

There is not much need these days to point out to corporate executives that the business community does not have a generous amount of public support and credibility. The reasons are many and complex, and it is not my purpose to discuss them here. I am convinced, however, that corporations can substantially improve negative public attitudes toward business by more intelligently applying their resources to revitalized and redirected corporate giving and community involvement efforts. In some cases, this will require the establishment of new corporate programs with meaningful objectives and effective means of reaching them. In other cases, it will require the reallocation of existing resources devoted to corporate philanthropy and community relations so that corporate support can become more relevant and effective.

In 1973, I published an article, "Philanthropy: Still the Corporate Stepchild," in the spring issue of *Business and Society Review.* The article expressed disappointment in the lack of concern by business about effective corporate giving. This was the principal cause, I felt, for the very modest impact of corporate contributions on society — an impact that could be substantially increased in my view by a new approach to this potentially meaningful corporate activity.

Corporate giving can become a much more important element in private-sector philanthropy. There is not much likelihood that other sources of philanthropy can show much growth in the coming years. Individuals already account for about 80% of total private giving. With inflation and the trend of increasing taxes at all levels of government, there is little hope that individuals will be able to increase their share of support to charitable causes.

The 26,000 grant-making foundations provide about 7% of total private support, but this share is not likely to increase—in fact, it will probably decrease. In a 1977 news story in *The New York Times,* the Foundation Center stated that the nation's major foundations sustained a $3 billion reduction in the value of their assets, or 9.5%, during their latest available two fiscal years. Much of the decline, it was reported, "was attributable to fluctuations in the securities market since 1972." But there were other problems:

> Higher payout rates set by the Treasury Department prior to the passage of the Tax Reform Act of 1976 may also have had their effect as well as attempts by foundations to maintain a previous level of giving in the face of continuing needs of grantees in an inflationary environment.

The Foundation Center then predicted a likely reduction in "the amount of real support that existing foundations can provide on a continuing basis over time" to their various charitable causes.

Corporations provide only about 5% of the total amount of private support. What are the chances for an increase in the proportion of business giving?

From a theoretical point of view, the opportunity is substantial. This is based on a few facts about corporate giving:

Fact One: Only one corporation in five reports any tax-deductible contributions.

Fact Two: Total corporate contributions average 1% of pretax earnings, and the IRS permits deductions up to 5%.

Table 1. Comparison of Private and Corporate Giving

Recipients	Private giving[a]	Corporate giving[b]
Religion	47%	—
Health and welfare	24	39%
Education	13	37
Arts and humanities	6	8
Civic activities	3	11
Other	7	5
	100	100

[a] *Giving USA 1978, Annual Report* (New York: American Association of Fund-Raising Counsel, Inc., 1978), p. 6.

[b] Anne Klepper, *Annual Survey of Corporate Contributions,* 1976 (New York: The Conference Board; 1978), pp. 26, 27.

Again, theoretically, if *all* corporations would make tax-deductible contributions and they would give at the rate of 5% (rather than 1%) of pretax income, there would be a possibility of a 25 times increase in corporate giving. Obviously, this is not a practical objective. But it does suggest that there is a potential for a meaningful increase in corporate giving. No other area of private philanthropy has this potential. If corporate giving isn't the new frontier of philanthropy, there is no new frontier.

Corporate Giving Today

Corporate financial contributions to charitable organizations were $1.57 billion in 1977, an increase of 14.6% over 1976, as reported by the American Association of Fund-Raising Counsel, Inc.[4] It is estimated by some sources that another $1 billion or so of additional support comes from corporations, in the form of other cash grants, the donation of employees' services, the use of company facilities, employment programs for marginally employable people, and the like.

How does business giving compare with other sources of philanthropy? In the same report by the American Association of Fund-Raising Counsel, showing trends and statistics for the year 1977, total contributions were about $35.20 billion. This included gifts from foundations of about $2.01 billion, bequests of $2.12 billion, and gifts from living persons of $29.5 billion. So the $1.57 billion of corporate cash philanthropy amounts to about 4.5% of all private philanthropic giving in the United States.

Corporate giving goes to a wide range of causes. The allocation of corporate funds, however, does show some special characteristics. The comparison of private and corporate giving shown in Table 1 is based on reports of the Conference Board and the American Association of Fund-Raising Counsel.

About 22 cents of each corporate dollar goes to local agencies through the United Way of America or other organizations that annually raise funds for a number of participating charities. These organizations receive additional assistance from companies in the form of payroll deductions, promotional materials, and time off with pay for campaign volunteers.

Corporate giving, as shown in Table 2, has hovered around 1% of pretax net income since 1952. However, it varies widely among companies within the same industrial group, as shown in Table 3.

In 1975, the Commission on Private Philanthropy and Public Needs

[4] *Giving USA 1978, Annual Report* (New York: American Association of Fund-Raising Counsel, Inc., 1978), p. 17.

Table 2. Corporate Giving

Year	Net income before taxes (million)	Amount (million)	As % of net income before taxes
1956	$ 48,600	$ 418	0.86
1957	46,900	419	0.89
1958	41,100	395	0.96
1959	51,600	482	0.93
1960	48,500	482	0.99
1961	48,600	512	1.05
1962	53,600	595	1.11
1963	57,700	657	1.14
1964	64,700	729	1.13
1965	75,200	785	1.04
1966	80,700	805	1.00
1967	77,300	830	1.07
1968	85,600	1,005	1.17
1969	83,400	1,055	1.26
1970	71,500	797	1.11
1971	82,000	865	1.05
1972	96,200	1,009	1.05
1973	115,800	1,174	1.01
1974	126,900	1,200	0.95
1975	123,500	1,140 (est.)	0.92
1976	156,900	1,375 (est.)	0.88
1977	172,100	1,570 (est.)	0.91

[a] Sources: *Department of Commerce, Internal Revenue Service, The Conference Board, AAFRC estimates.*

came out in favor of a goal of 2% pretax income for corporate giving to philanthropy. This commission (which is also known as the Filer Commission after its chairman, John H. Filer, chairman of Aetna Life & Casualty) was created in 1973 as a privately initiated and funded citizens' panel. It had two objectives. The first was to study the roles of both philanthropic giving in the United States and the area through which giving is principally channeled, namely, the voluntary sector of American society. The second objective was to make recommendations to the

Table 3. Contributions as a Percentage of Pretax Domestic Net Income, 1975 (Insurance Companies Excluded)[a]

Classification	Top 25% of companies	All companies
Primary metal industries	1.20%	0.98%
Chemical and allied products	1.26	0.63
Fabricated metal products	3.42	1.11
Banking	2.64	1.48
Engineering and construction	4.37	0.58

[a] Anne Klepper, *Annual Survey of Corporate Contributions, 1976* (New York: The Conference Board, 1978), p. 9.

voluntary sector, to Congress, and to the American public concerning ways in which the practice of private giving can be strengthened and made more effective.

The preface of the commission's report stated the reasons for the study:

> The Commission's objectives reflect a conviction that giving and voluntary, public-oriented activity—the components of "philanthropy" as broadly defined—play a central role in American life but that the continuation of this role cannot be taken for granted. For the sector's economic durability has been brought into question by the mounting financial difficulties of many voluntary organizations and nonprofit institutions. At the same time, two of the main institutional underpinnings of philanthropic giving—private foundations and charitable tax deductions—have been politically challenged.[5]

John D. Rockefeller 3rd was largely responsible for the establishment of the commission along with several government leaders, including Wilbur D. Mills, then chairman of the House Ways and Means Committee; Secretary of the Treasury George P. Shultz; and William E. Simon, who would succeed Shultz. Participation in the commissioners' work was broad and included religious and labor leaders, former cabinet officers, minority representatives, executives of foundations and corporations, and other individuals with wide-ranging and differing viewpoints on the subject of philanthropy.

One Filer Commission study disclosed that of 1.7 million corporations that filed an income tax form in 1970, only 20% claimed a charitable deduction, only 6% gave over $500, and nearly 50% of all corporate giving came from fewer than 1,000 companies. Generally, these companies have assets of $200 million or more, and the amount contributed averages about a half million dollars.[6]

If business were to meet the Filer Commission challenge by increasing its contributions to 2% of pretax corporate income, substantial additional support would be available for the many worthwhile causes that depend on contributions. And, of course, if most corporate leaders would see the feasibility of allocating the IRS maximum of 5%, corporate giving would advance to the number two philanthropic position, second only to gifts by living individuals. Some corporations are already giving at a rate of 5% or more, including some large companies such as Cummins Engine and Dayton-Hudson.

Companies in certain industries give more at the maximum tax-deductible level of 5% than do those in other industries. In Table 4, the proportion of companies giving 5% or more ranges, within specific industries, from 1.4 to 4.9%:

[5]*Giving in America* (Washington, D.C.: Commission on Private Philanthropy and Public Needs, 1975), p. 1.

[6]Ibid., p. 21.

Table 4. Percent of Corporations with Net Income Making Contributions That Are 5% or More of Net Income by Industry, 1970[a]

Industry	Corporations
Agriculture	1.4%
Electric, gas, and sanitary service	1.6
Transportation	1.7
Services	2.1
Mining	2.2
Finance, insurance, and real estate	2.4
Communications	2.5
Retail trade	2.8
Contract construction	3.1
Wholesale trade	3.6
Manufacturing	4.9

[a] Adapted from Thomas Vasques, "Corporate Giving Measure," *Research Papers,* Vol. 3, Commission on Private Philanthropy and Public Needs (Washington, D.C.: Department of the Treasury, 1977), p. 1847.

As the Filer Commission reported: "It is ironic that the business community, which has so often expressed its wariness of Washington and the growing size of government, should fall so far short of legal limits in helping select and support publicly beneficial programs outside of government, through nonprofit charitable organizations."

The commission also reported that former President Lyndon Johnson recognized the irony of this situation when he addressed a group of business leaders in 1971:

> In spite of the fact that your federal government has seen fit to allow a charitable deduction of five percent of your profits, the record is quite clear that you business leaders still feel that the federal government can spend this money more wisely than you can.[7]

Whether chief executive officers want to increase the level of their corporate giving is another question. Certainly, however, they can increase the effectiveness of their corporate giving. Corporations are doing less than a superlative job in this regard, as most contributions executives I know heartily agree. The idea was well expressed by Norman Kurt Barnes in the conclusion to his article "Rethinking Corporate Charity"[8]:

> To suggest that companies need to put their charitable operations on a more rational basis is not, of course, to say that their managers must abandon all of the humane—and Christian—impulses that have built corporate charity up to a $1 billion level. The objective should be to combine these impulses with a more rigorous conception of corporate costs and benefits. The combination might be fantastic.

[7] Ibid., p. 56.
[8] *Fortune* (October, 1974).

It is important for corporate giving to play a wider and more meaningful role in our communities and in our society. Corporate giving and involvement have distinctive and important characteristics—some of which are unique to philanthropy:

- Corporate giving has great upside potential. If the 80% of corporations that give nothing would join the companies that do contribute, a major new resource would be tapped and its effects would be felt in every community in the land.
- Corporate giving, unlike most foundation and individual giving, can include a variety of support assistance in addition or in lieu of cash contributions.
- The energy and interests of millions of corporate employees can be tapped to support community causes. Some corporations have taken inventory of their human resources and have developed programs to encourage employees to participate in the giving and involvement process.

At what seems to be an increasing pace, the boundaries separating the proprietary interests of the corporation from its public responsibilities are becoming blurred.

A variety of precedents can be found to support a corporate concern with noneconomic consequences. Some are grounded in a philosophy of paternalism, now largely disappeared. Others are concerned with local community benefits—as, for example, support of a local hospital, which can be viewed as either an employee benefit or a community one. Companies that operate nationally can exercise a wider discretion in the selection of the objects of their bounty; a company that draws heavily on the national pool of engineering and managerial talent can more readily relate to its own welfare the contributions it makes to educational institutions.

Some corporations have developed affirmative approaches grounded in the belief that the welfare of the company is significantly tied to the welfare of the society in which it operates. Once this premise is accepted, it becomes apparent that giving alone is not sufficient. The giving must be done in ways that maximize the effectiveness of the gift. In short, the giving program should be thoughtfully developed and managed, much as is any other corporate activity. The giving function can be planned; it can have appropriate objectives; its accomplishments can be measured; and, if necessary, the effort can be redirected to improve its performance.

2

A Strategy for Corporate Giving and Community Involvement

Corporate giving should not be a form of institutional kindness, it should be a cool and reasoned investment in the future of the firm.[1]

Each corporation should develop its own strategy for corporate giving and community involvement in the same way that it develops an acquisitions strategy or product development strategy. There has to be a direction and a plan for getting there. Objectives have to be identified and the corporation must have a measuring stick to let it know when the objectives are reached.

Furthermore, the *process* of developing a corporate strategy for contributions and community involvement is, in itself, a beneficial activity. It will raise pertinent questions about the role of the corporation in society, about the corporation's goals and objectives, and about management's attitudes toward its employees, the communities in which it operates, and the major social issues of our times.

Corporations must make their philanthropy businesslike if they are to make their business philanthropic.

It's no mystery that the companies that do the best job in corporate contributions and in community relations are organized to be effective in these areas. There is no way to develop and initiate successful programs and projects without having competent people to direct these activities, without support from top management, without coordination and communication throughout the company, without an adequate budget, without sound policies and procedures, and without a sense of mission. It's surprising, therefore, that some companies still believe that effective giving and involvement can occur without proper organization, adminis-

[1]John M. McGwire and Thomas W. Fletcher, "The Emerging Public Role of the Corporation," *SRI International Business Intelligence Paper* (September 1978), p. 21.

tration, or planning. Chapter 4 explains how a company can organize for more effective giving.

The corporate contributions dollar must come up to the same measure of cost-effectiveness that is expected from the corporate dollar invested in research, marketing, production, or administration.

There is obviously no way of measuring the comparative value of a contributions dollar versus a research dollar. But the company can decide that it will make a comparable *effort* to ensure that the contributions dollar will result in the highest possible return, given all the options available. It is discouraging to see how some companies handle their contributions funds. They expend great ingenuity and effort to ensure that each research, manufacturing, marketing, and administrative dollar brings the greatest return. Then they turn around and dole out money to charitable organizations in a fashion that is ineffective and sometimes counterproductive.

Cost-effectiveness is a term that is popular in business today. It simply means that you can look at what goes into a project (input) and compare it with what comes out (output). Then, for the same given objective, the input and output of different approaches or processes can be measured. Obviously, you are looking for the most output for the least input.

Nonprofit organizations that depend on corporate support are becoming very intolerant of unbusinesslike corporate approaches to charitable giving. Corporations have the talent and resources to make cost-effective evaluations of proposals requesting contributions support. It's foolish not to make these evaluations; done carefully, they can ensure that the results will measure up to the value of the support provided.

There must be objective criteria to decide where corporate dollars should be going.

On her deathbed, Gertrude Stein was asked, "Well, Gertrude, what is the answer?" She replied to her companion, Alice Toklas, "Well, Alice, what's the question?"

I am afraid that the answers to many contribution requests are given before the right questions are asked. These are a few good questions: What do we know about this organization and its people? What are the chances that they can reach their objectives? Is there any way to measure whether or not they reach their objectives? If they do meet their objectives, will anything really change in a positive sense? Have people who are supposed to be helped by this project had a hand in deciding what should be done? Do our employees have any interest in this effort?

Directly opposed to the analytical approach is the habit of making decisions based on these sorts of statements:

> "We don't have time to evaluate the program benefits, so let's just give them what we gave last year."

"If we don't provide support, this outfit will surely go out of business." (Maybe going out of business is not a bad thing for a nonprofit organization that isn't filling a real need or can't develop community support for its way of meeting that need.)

"That's a pet charity of the president's stepmother. We can't cut them off!" (It's not the stepmother's money—it is the corporation's gift.)

"It's a great thing they are attempting so what can we lose if it doesn't fly?" (When the plane crashes, it doesn't make the donor look very smart not to have noticed the cracks in the wings.)

"We will give them seed money and hope they can somehow keep the project going after we walk away from it." (The only thing as bad as failure is a successful project or program that can't be sustained.)

"Let's find out what ABC Corporation has decided and do the same." (It is often useful to seek the advice of other funding organizations, but that should not be the sole criterion for making a decision.)

"This outfit has been around twenty-five years, it's bound to be doing a good job." (Yes, and there's a guy in New Hampshire who earns a good living making buggy whips.)

"They need some volunteers, but none of our employees are interested in community projects." (The self-fulfilling prophecy approach to employee involvement.)

"This organization wants only $100; they can't need it badly." (Have you ever been stranded in a subway without a quarter?)

"This outfit is asking for $100,000; they must be doing something important." (Price and value are not interchangeable terms.)

"This organization is in New York (or Washington, D.C.); it's bound to be better than the local group working on the same problem." (Some but not all of the country's brains and imagination are found in major population centers.)

A big step in the development of any corporate contributions program is to reach a point where subjective or irrational comments do not form the main basis for approving or denying requests from nonprofit organizations. In Chapter 5, "Proposal Evaluation: Impulse, Habit or Reason," I have outlined a practical approach to this vital aspect of company giving.

The company contributions fund should be decided in a rational and consistent manner.

The determination of the total contributions budget should be done with the same thoughtfulness that is given to other corporate budgets of a similar size or larger.

One method is to establish the annual fund by using a formula related to sales or earnings, number of employees, or any other yardstick. The most preferred formula seems to be a percentage of pretax corporate income.

This method has several benefits. It is consistent with the manner in which statistics are generally collected on corporate giving. It provides a way of comparing support of individual firms or industry or of geographical groupings of companies with the efforts of other firms and groups as well as with the maximally allowed percentage (5%) under IRS regulations. Finally, it automatically adjusts the contributions budget to the financial performance of the corporation. It reinforces the idea that the financial success of the corporation will automatically increase the dollar amount of support put into the community.

Full disclosure is as sound a policy and practice in corporate giving as it is in financial reporting.

One of the basic problems with corporate giving is the general lack of information on the subject. Even more disturbing, however, is the secrecy or lack of disclosure that surrounds the contributions policies and practices of many corporations. Such lack of disclosure is not only unnecessary but counterproductive. Unfortunately, this lack of information and disclosure even takes place *within* the corporation, where many executives and other employees have only a sketchy idea of company policies and activities.

Full corporate disclosure should include a variety of information: how much the company contributes and how it decides on the amount of the total corporate fund; what causes it supports and how much support each receives; what criteria and mechanisms are used to evaluate proposals for support; where and when proposals should be submitted and when decisions will be made; who are the key people involved in reviewing and approving support proposals; and exactly what information the company requires to make an intelligent review and decision.

In the next chapter, the corporate disclosure of the company's giving information is covered in detail.

The corporation should capitalize on its talents and resources; it should get involved in things it understands; the company should look at the social problems that have an impact on its realm of operations.

Every company is different in some respect from every other company. Each has its own personality and history just as a person does.

Its body of knowledge and expertise is unique. Its circumstances are peculiar to its own experience and environment.

The contributions and community involvement activities of the company should relate to the reality of the company, its organization, its people, its plans, and its objectives.

For most of my corporate life, I have worked for companies that have had a large stake in the pharmaceutical business. These companies have been active in scientific research, tend to be innovative, market in a rather sophisticated professional environment, and depend for their success upon the vitality of the entire health-care field.

It's not surprising, therefore, that such companies expend a portion of their contribution funds in projects and programs designed to improve health care and delivery. It is a field in which they have some special interest, experience, and know-how. It would be surprising to me if these companies suddenly saw their *primary* role as providing support for the establishment of minority banks.

The old adage that "the shoemaker should stick to his last" applies to some degree in the field of corporate philanthropy. This doesn't mean that a pharmaceutical company can't put some of its deposit funds in a minority bank (some have done so), but it does suggest that one important place to put the company's efforts is in areas where it has the most experience and resources.

Get your employees involved in corporate contributions; get your contributions program involved in things that interest and affect your employees.

A corporation is a pyramidal structure. At the top is the management group that directs the activities of the company; below top management is the larger middle-management and supervisory group; and the largest segment is the rank-and-file of employees in staff and operating groups throughout the corporation. One of the most productive ideas to be implemented is to involve the greatest number of employees at all levels.

Matching gift programs can ensure that employees at all locations will be able to designate (by their own gifts) where some of the company's funds are placed. Social-service leaves and community funds in support of employee involvement are other ways that employees at all company locations can increase their participation in community affairs.

A great untapped resource is waiting to be activated in every corporation that has not yet reorganized its contributions and community programs to promote the maximum involvement of its own employees. This resource can bring substantial new energies and talents into the community and, in the process, can enhance the employee's loyalty to and respect for the company. The importance of broad employee involvement and examples of how some companies are achieving it are covered in Chapter 6.

The corporation should get involved in the communities it knows, with the people it knows best, and with the needs that have the best chance of being fulfilled and are important goals of the community.

It is important to devote a good portion of the corporate contributions fund to local efforts in and around the plant and office locations of the company. Companies are more familiar with the local people and with the organizations that are trying to meet the needs of the people in the community. The problems in the local community are generally manageable, and the efforts of one company can have an impact. The possibility of employee involvement is also maximized. Finally, the company can monitor better the results of the company's support and involvement.

The corporation won't be "copping out" or ignoring the broad social issues. It will be attempting to deal with these problems in a realistic way on a community level. It will be trying to prevent a problem from developing instead of simply dealing with the symptoms of a problem after it is firmly entrenched.

Practically every major social issue can be addressed on the community level: drug abuse, inadequate housing, health care, child care, discrimination, poor education, pollution, crime, and unemployment. Companies don't have to go charging into unfamiliar territory to address the social ills of our time. In most communities, they exist in one form or another just outside the factory gates and corporate offices.

All the action shouldn't emanate from corporate headquarters; effective company giving should take place in all major company locations.

Forward-looking company policies and active leadership should come from corporate headquarters. Giving and community involvement at the headquarters should provide a model for subsidiaries and divisions at other locations. Corporate-contributions management should also encourage and facilitate purposeful philanthropy as well as employee involvement throughout the company.

The corporation's total contribution fund can be allocated to ensure that all plant locations have the resources to meet their responsibilities in their communities. Such allocations can be based on one or more factors, such as the size of the local operation, the number of employees, or the sales and production levels.

The objective is to provide sufficient funds to the local unit to enable it to respond to most of the requests it receives without "bucking" them to corporate headquarters. It is ridiculous to review requests from *all* locations at corporate headquarters. It is also inefficient and ineffective. Managers in the local unit are in a better position to judge local needs accurately.

Occasionally, however, a special funding request to a local unit should be passed on to the corporate headquarters for handling or for a recommendation. It may involve a request for an amount of money that is substantially beyond the capability of the local unit to provide, or the activities of the requesting organization may have an impact beyond the local community.

All possible corporate resources should be inventoried; there are many different ways that assistance can be provided.

Too many corporate assistance programs are based on the assumption that money is the *only* thing that the company can provide. This may be true for a foundation, but it is certainly a narrow way for a corporation to look upon its giving potential.

Corporations have people with all sorts of knowledge and skills. Corporations have facilities. Corporations have supplies and equipment. Corporations have products, services, and many other resources.

If these resources are identified in an organized fashion, a great deal of additional worthwhile help can be provided to nonprofit organizations and the community. Chapter 7 describes a variety of ways that corporations can provide support other than making a cash contribution or in addition to contributing money.

Corporate policy should permit continuing support to established causes while funding some new initiatives.

It's a fact of corporate giving that most of the monies distributed will go to established programs that have been providing benefits for the community year after year. For that reason, it is important that the corporation maintain its support of worthy organizations over the long haul. If for one reason or another it has to stop or interrupt that support, the corporation should advise the nonprofit organization as much in advance as possible to soften the loss of the company's funding.

If the company's support is being given for a specific period, this should be made clear. Some pledges are made over a period of several years. In such cases, it might be wise to scale down the contribution from the highest amount in the first year to the lowest in the final year. Foundations have used this technique to accustom nonprofit groups not to depend entirely upon one grant-maker's support. Corporations can use the same technique in making large gifts that might tend to establish dependency on the company's philanthropy.

I have heard some corporate executives remark that all company grants should be one-time "seed-money" contributions to new organizations, projects, or programs. I don't agree. Seed-money contributions are sometimes the correct approach if the new organization, project, or program can obtain broad support after a successful launching. The existence of such broad-base support cannot be assumed. There is no point in helping to launch some worthy cause that will wither and die immediately after it blooms.

The corporation should not be afraid of creative risk-taking; if the potential benefits are significant, the odds, although high, may be reasonable.

Entrepreneurs are risk-takers. They like long odds with the potential of rich rewards if they are successful. Most corporate executives understand intelligent risk-taking and have no difficulty in employing that concept in research, marketing, finance, and production. They often freeze up, however, when the opportunity for *social* risk-taking presents itself.

In the contributions area, this situation arises when someone from the community comes forward with an exciting and innovative idea. It is clear that if the concept works, it can be a dramatic step toward solving a difficult community problem or it can capitalize on a significant opportunity.

The tendency in many corporations is to back away from this sort of involvement because it *may* fail—and it's safer to put all contributions into the most predictable organizations and causes. That's a mistake. Some part of the corporation's support portfolio should always be in high-risk, high-potential investments. There are examples of creative risk-taking that paid dividends in Part Two of this book.

Helping others to help themselves is the best kind of corporate support to provide.

In the 1975 annual report of the Lilly Endowment, Landrum R. Bolling, president of the foundation at that time, made some remarks about self-help development that are relevant and timely: "Gifts that undermine self-respect, that create dependence, or that promote futile, temporizing half-measures in dealing with deep-seated problems may be, at worst, positively harmful—or, at best, a waste of time and money."

Contributions that are meaningful, he said, are those that "help people help themselves." He said that Lilly Endowment has come to see the special importance of programs and projects that give promise of furthering the capabilities of people to handle their own professional and vocational responsibilities and to cope with community problems.

An excellent book has been written about the tremendous power in people, which, unfortunately, is a much underutilized asset in our society. The book is *Peoplepower,* written by Morgan J. Doughton, and published by Media America, Inc., in 1976. Doughton is particularly critical of government support efforts that have "prescribed for the poor a dependency survival kit requiring and offering minimal challenges to their self-help and mutual assistance." He calls for a "quiet revolution of releasing the promise in people, through revitalized small-group processes based upon responsibilities for the people, carried out through and representing the invention of myriad forms of effective mutual assistance." Self-help development should be a key element in the corporate contribution's strategy, and there are examples in *Peoplepower* and in this book of self-help projects and programs that are assisting people to take charge of their own lives.

The corporation should not participate in the movement of rising but unrealizable expectations; it's better to do nothing than to help people fail.

Major corporations are large and resourceful organizations employing talented and energetic people, and such companies have demonstrated their capabilities in many ways. But it is vitally important for corporations to know what they *cannot* accomplish or should not even attempt to accomplish.

The 1960s saw corporations thrust in the spotlight with a mandate from the White House to solve every major social problem, including discrimination, urban decay, poor mass transportation, inadequate housing, and environmental pollution. The error of corporate leaders in those years was to think that corporations had some ready solutions for these complex and long-standing problems. Now corporate managements are wiser, but frequently this wisdom is not reflected in the corporate contributions program. Contributions by some firms are still creating and supporting expectations that have no hope of being satisfied.

Should the company establish a foundation? What are the advantages of a company-sponsored foundation compared to direct corporate giving?

The Foundation Center estimates that there are about 1,500 company foundations.[2] The Foundation Center also says that about 275 of *Fortune's* 500 largest industrial firms have their own foundations.

Many corporate contributions are therefore given through tax-exempt and legally independent foundations receiving money from a single company, and sometimes from individuals closely associated with it. The Conference Board estimates that nearly 60% of business giving in the 1960s was accomplished through business foundations. This percentage has diminished since the Tax Reform Act of 1969, which imposed many new requirements on all foundations. A Filer Commission study of 800 companies indicated that 35% of total corporate giving came from company-sponsored foundations in 1974.

There were two reasons for the early growth of the business foundation. The first relates to the excess-profits tax on corporations instituted during World War II and the Korean War. By establishing a company foundation, corporations reduced the amount of taxes paid and at the same time retained some control over the funds placed in the foundation. More than half of the company foundations were established in these periods of national emergency.

[2]R. Palmer Baker, Jr., and J. Edward Shillingburg, "Corporate Charitable Contributions," *Research Papers,* The Commission on Private Philanthropy and Public Needs (Washington, D.C.: Department of the Treasury, 1977), p. 1859.

The other reason for the emergence of the business foundation was that it provided some flexibility and stability in corporate giving. When earnings are higher, the corporation can place a larger amount of funding in the foundation to balance against the years when earnings are lower. As far as recipients of corporate philanthropy are concerned, this approach also insulated them somewhat from the ups and downs of the business cycle.

Each company will have to review its own objectives and consult its attorneys and tax experts to determine if the formation of a foundation is the best way for the corporation to manage its contributions activities. Additional information on this subject can be obtained from the Council On Foundations, Inc., 888 Seventh Avenue, New York, NY 10019. The Conference Board also published in 1970 a booklet, "20 Company-Sponsored Foundations," which describes the program and policies of a selection of these Foundations.

Is the United Way the only way? How much of the contributions budget should be allocated to united giving?

The concept of united giving has been around for a long time. Scott Cutlip tells us that the first united giving campaign took place in Liverpool, England, in 1873. Clergymen from the city emigrated, Cutlip said, and by 1887 the first united campaign in the United States was initiated in Denver.[3]

An idea that lasts that long is bound to be worthwhile. I believe that is true about united giving despite criticism directed at this approach from some charities not involved in united giving and some minority organizations that do not feel that they are getting their fair share of the monies raised in united-giving campaigns.

According to the American Association of Fund-Raising Council, there were 2,354 United Way campaigns across the United States and Canada in 1975, which raised a total of $1.1 billion. Payroll-deduction gifts by employees accounted for 62% of the total; corporate gifts amounted to 29%; and the remaining 9% came from individuals giving at home and from foundation gifts.

United giving is a big operation. AAFRS reports that United Way allocations of fund-raising receipts provided for direct services to 34 million families and that some 20 million volunteers were involved in recent campaigns.

It is clear from these statistics that united giving is dependent for its success upon business firms that donate and that encourage their employees to donate. This is not surprising, as the united-giving concept has been embraced by business firms since its inception.

[3]Scott Cutlip, *Fund Raising in the United States,* (New Brunswick, N.J.: Rutgers University Press, 1965).

United campaigns have an established and useful place in corporate giving. Although worthwhile, however, they should not be the only approach to corporate giving on a community level, particularly for large corporations with extensive interests and resources. The reasons for this assessment and some other conclusions about united giving are outlined in Chapter 10.

Corporations should encourage and assist nonprofit organizations to be more effectively managed.

In the past 20 years, I have encountered a substantial number of nonprofit agencies that needed management assistance—some desperately. I have observed organizations with fund-raising crises, cash-flow problems, low staff morale, high staff turnover, board–staff conflicts, and unreliable financial records. I once thought that the only thing a company could do when confronted with a prospective donee with one or more of these problems was to turn down its request for a cash contribution—even though the proposed project or program had worthwhile potential. More recently, I have discovered an alternative approach, which is described in Chapter 8, "Helping Nonprofits to Be Managed More Effectively."

My experiences and what I have learned about the efforts of other corporations as well as the emergence of groups specifically designed to deal with the management problems of nonprofit organizations have given me some optimism about the productive things that can happen from these efforts. It is an area that every corporation should consider in organizing its contributions program.

3

Corporate Disclosure: Let the Sun Shine In

The fact is that there is very little sunshine in the world of corporate philanthropy. There is a shroud of mystery over the philanthropic efforts of most corporations. Many corporate executives act like foundation executives did 20 years ago—in despair because their good deeds go unnoticed and in fear that too much exposure will send a hoard of grant seekers down on them like avenging angels.[1]

In an article in *Grantsmanship Center News*, "Exploring the Elusive World of Corporate Giving," Jack Shakely said that the lack of information on corporate giving both collectively and individually is one of the principal roadblocks to improved performance in this important section of philanthropy.

I agree with Shakely, because this lack of disclosure creates several problems:

1. It reinforces the attitude within corporations that company giving doesn't require the same level of competent managerial skill that is devoted to other aspects of the business.
2. It inhibits the development of effective corporate giving policies and practices and the involvement of employees in community action.
3. It makes it difficult for nonprofit organizations seeking support to determine whether their projects and programs are appropriate for specific corporations.
4. Although a favorable public response to corporate giving should not be the major rationale for such activity, it is certainly a worthwhile by-product. Lack of disclosure of company contribu-

[1]Jack Shakely, "Exploring the Elusive World of Corporate Giving," *The Grantsmanship Center News* (July–September 1977):49.

tions to many worthwhile causes keeps the community from responding and supporting these company efforts.

Grant Seekers Need to Know

One of the incredible things about corporate giving is how little information most firms provide to nonprofit organizations that are seeking company support. This must be the "mushroom" theory: *things grow best in the dark.* Clearly it does not work that way. No firm would purchase an expensive piece of equipment without putting out detailed specifications on what the company wants. But frequently that is what is done in the contributions area. No specifications are put out, and the company naively waits for grant seekers to come up with worthwhile proposals without company input. It does not take much effort to inform grant seekers about what interests the company.

Organizations requesting corporate contributions should know (1) areas that the company supports; (2) the level of support provided; (3) when the contributions budget is prepared and approved; (4) to whom the proposal should be forwarded; (5) the approximate time it will take to review proposals and to reach a decision; and (6) the criteria used to evaluate proposals. It is important that these guidelines be written and updated when policies or procedures change.

Support Areas

This part of the guidelines can be as brief or detailed as the company wants. Here is an example of one firm's statement:

> We will contribute locally where we have special interest, knowledge and involvement. We will consider projects and programs involving the environment, minority needs, special education, community health services, international programs, art, and cultural acitvities. Support will generally go to proven organizations or new programs that can result in meaningful responses to social problems.

Some companies like to tell people specifically what they do *not* care to support:

- The company does not contribute to sectarian or denominational groups unless their services are offered on a nondiscriminatory basis.
- Contributions are not made directly to individuals—only to organizations or to individuals through a nonprofit organization.
- The company does not contribute to profit-making organizations.

- Requests for goodwill ads in programs are discouraged. If the organization is deserving of support, the company would prefer to consider a direct contribution.

Contribution Amounts

It is important for the requesting organization to find out, preferably at its initial contact, the range of contribution amounts usually approved by the grantmaking organization. This information can be presented in the following manner:

Dollar amount of gift	Percentage of total gifts	Percentage of total dollars
0– 99	8	5
100– 499	22	7
500– 999	25	12
1,000–1,999	14	15
2,000–4,999	16	17
5,000–9,999	11	19
10,000–and above	4	25

Budget Schedule

It is important for grant seekers to know when the company develops its contributions budget so that proposals for major new programs and projects can be submitted in time to be reviewed as part of the total contributions effort for the coming year. Otherwise funding for new programs and projects is possible only by tapping the unallocated portion of the contributions budget.

Contribution Contact

Since corporate contributions are handled in various company departments (public relations, personnel, corporate secretary's office, etc.), it is helpful to tell the grant seeker where the proposal should be directed.

In a small or medium-sized company with one location, generally there will be only one contact point. In other corporations, large divisions or subsidiaries may have their own contributions program. Each of these should be listed in the guidelines with an explanation of the type of requests that are appropriate for each organization unit. For example, in one company, research grants are the responsibility of the research division, and these proposals should be directed to the contributions administrator in that division.

Decision Making

Grant seekers should know how often the firm's contributions committee meets, who is on the committee, and when a decision should be forthcoming. If there is a delay in reaching a decision, an estimate should be given of when it may be reached. Nonprofit organizations frequently are operating on a month-to-month basis, and the timing of funding is extremely important.

Criteria

Finally, the grant seeker should be given a list of the criteria used to evaluate proposals. Each company will have its own list, depending upon its particular circumstances. A list that I have developed and used is included in Chapter 5.

Shareholders Need to Know

While he was researching his article on corporate giving, Jack Shakely studied about 100 corporate annual reports. His comment:

> First, not one corporation in five makes any mention whatsoever of its corporate philanthropy in its annual report. Of the hundred or so I studied, only a handful noted specific areas of interest and only one (Equitable) mentioned the exact dollar amount given away. Not one mentioned who the potential grant seeker should contact.[2]

This is a situation that can be changed. It is a simple matter to add a brief section on "Corporate Giving" or "Corporate Responsibility" to the annual report. The annual report is the corporate publication that gets the widest distribution, not only to shareholders but to the media, to government and community leaders, and to others interested in the company. It is shortsighted of management not to use this vehicle to communicate important aspects of company giving and related activities that are of interest to the readers of the annual report.

One good example of a company communicating information on corporate contributions is the 1977 annual report of the Clorox Company. The report contained a two-page spread on "Corporate Social Responsibility," which included this information on corporate giving:

> Last year, Clorox contributed $350,000 to more than 400 deserving organ-

[2]Ibid., p. 46.

izations, programs and activities in the communities in which it operates. The Company's contributions fall into five major categories—health, welfare and youth, education, civic and cultural. During the year, Clorox received nearly 1,100 requests for financial assistance. Eligible requests are reviewed by the Company's Corporate Contributions Committee. This five-member committee represents a cross section of Company functions and departments. Clorox's present contributions budget represents about one-half of one percent of the Company's 1977 pre-tax income, and is expected to be increased gradually as earnings permit.

The spread also included sections on minority economic development, community involvement, affirmative action (including a table giving 1976–1977 statistics on employment of minorities and women at various job levels), government affairs, and economic education.

One possible reason for the present lack of disclosure by many firms may be the concern that shareholders will not approve of such activities. This concern does not appear to be based on the actual experience of companies that do disclose corporate giving information to their shareholders. The shareholders, in fact, seem to be more understanding than some managements in sensing that this type of activity is important to long-range corporate success and survival in our society. For example, in 1978, stockholders of IBM cast 98% of their voted shares against a proposal that would have adversely affected charitable contributions.

Corporate Disclosure at Atlantic Richfield

In recent years, some corporations have moved effectively in the direction of supplying information to the public on the scope and character of their corporate giving and other corporate responsibility efforts.

One of the most outstanding efforts has been the two major reports of Atlantic Richfield Company in 1976 and 1977, entitled *Participation I* and *Participation II.* They are a frank and open expression of the status of corporate responsibility activities within the Atlantic Richfield Company. Unlike many other reports, these do not feel the compulsion to paint all corporate efforts in radiant colors. This corporation is strong enough and honest enough to admit that not everything it tries to do is spontaneously successful. In fact, sometimes it fails. This candor goes a long way in establishing credibility for Atlantic Richfield because the public sees it as a refreshing reversal from the usual corporate pablum spooned out in institutional advertisements celebrating this or that corporate achievement.

In the introduction of *Participation II,* this candor is evident in the words of Thornton F. Bradshaw, president of Atlantic Richfield:

> A fair question at this point is what have we learned about the essential nature of corporate social responsibility? How can it be reduced to concrete realities to be counted and stacked in satisfying bar charts and graphs? The truth is, it cannot. No objective standards that we know can adequately justify spending $15,000 to help convert an abandoned church into an activities center for a deprived neighborhood; $10,000 to help a Boy Scout Council expand its campground; or $300,000 to sustain the Aspen Institute for Humanistic Studies. Yet Atlantic Richfield does them. Why? Because they go with the territory. As every shareholder, and indeed, every American, understands, we are not living in conventional times. And so, if this company chose to act as corporations once did—hewing close to business and disregarding larger obligations—its actions would be rejected because they did not look beyond the dollar signs to see the people. Atlantic Richfield obviously is limited in what it can do in a social way. Quite as obviously, we have not jeopardized those limits by anything we have done in the last 24 months. But we are doing what we feel is prudent and effective and honestly acknowledges some of our obligations to a social and economic system that has made it possible for us to prosper and grow. This is and will continue to be the standard by which we gauge this effort.

Following this introduction, the publication explains Atlantic Richfield's corporate responsibility philosophy and describes many of the efforts that flowed from this philosophy. These include programs in transportation and in the environment, company assistance in the communities where ARCO is located, support of cultural activities, aid to education, assistance for minorities and women, and some examples of how ARCO employees are involved in the social concerns of the company.

The most intriguing aspect of *Participation I* and *Participation II*, however, is the critique of Atlantic Richfield's social responsibilities by Milton Moskowitz—an independent authority in this field, a business columnist, and senior editor of *Business and Society Review.* In the introduction to *Participation II,* President Bradshaw said that the company had "again retained Moskowitz to assess our 'bottom line' in a social sense, and we renewed our agreement *to publish his critique without change,* except on matters of fact."

In the critique, Moskowitz said that

> the corporate tone established by Anderson (chairman of ARCO) and Bradshaw is of a different timbre. There is little screeching about the virtues of free enterprise and the evils of socialism. Instead, there is a quiet attempt to address some important social issues in a manner that avoids being parochial.

Moskowitz then presented an Atlantic Richfield social responsibility balance sheet covering urban mass transportation, oil refinery pollution, surface coal mining in Montana, hydrogen sulfide leaks from a Texas oil well, oil tanker safety, charitable contributions, and company affirmative action involving minorities and women. The assets and liabilities are listed in detail and with much frankness, followed by this conclusion from Moskowitz:

> The final verdict has yet to be rendered. As the youngest of the petroleum giants, Atlantic Richfield is making some new tracks in the energy industry. The danger is that as it adds girth, it will revert to type, become remote from human needs, seeking growth for growth's sake and serving basically its own wants. ARCO is at least aware of these pitfalls. It appears to have the sensitivity to recognize that if it succumbs to old line industrial braggadocio, all will have been for naught. And it is this sensitivity, coupled with the enormous economic power at its disposal, that makes Atlantic Richfield an interesting company to watch.

Information on Atlantic Richfield's policies and programs in social responsibility, including corporate contributions, can be obtained from Atlantic Richfield Company, Public Relations Department, P.O. Box 2679 T.A., Los Angeles, CA 90051.

Other corporations may not yet be ready to disclose their social responsibility and corporate contributions performance in as detailed and objective manner as ARCO, but more information is being put out by a number of firms:

IBM and Corporate Responsibility. A 44-page booklet covering the company's social-responsibility efforts in equal-opportunity programs, aid to education, education and training of minorities and women, pollution control, international corporate responsibility, youth programs, support of the arts, human use of company technology, health services, criminal justice, transportation, urban development, population studies, and agriculture. Published in 1972 by IBM Communications Department, Armonk, NY 10504.

Bank of America Foundation Annual Report. Explains guidelines for support and areas where assistance is provided, including health services, United Way and other federated campaigns, social-service programs, aid to education, civic and cultural causes, and international projects. Lists each foundation grant and includes foundation financial statements. Bank of America Foundation, Box 37000, San Francisco, CA 94137.

1978 Public Responsibility Report: There's No Substitute for Commitment. A 20-page booklet published by Celanese corporation. It states that the twin objectives are to make a profit and to pursue the common good through individual and corporate good citizenship. It describes progress in political action, equal employment, health and environment, energy conservation, contributions, and safety. The report says that Celanese contributes about $1.3 million annually to charitable, cultural, civic, educational, and medical projects in communities where its employees live and work. Copies are available from Corporate Communities Department, Celanese Corporation, 1211 Avenue of the Americas, New York, NY 10036.

Corporate Social Responsibility: The Avon Commitment. Published in 1977, this 23-page booklet describes corporate goals and progress in five areas of social responsibility: employment policies, minority economic development, consumer relations, community relations, and contributions. Contact Community Affairs Department, Avon Products, Inc., 9 West 57 Street, New York, NY 10019.

The Other Dimensions of Business. Exxon brochure published in 1977. One of the best corporate reports, it lists all company grants of $5,000 or more. Public Affairs Department, Exxon Corporation, 1251 Avenue of the Americas, New York, NY 10020.

Mobil and Society: Moving in the Right Direction. An undated report of 20 pages that catalogs some of the more significant programs of the company and the Mobil Foundation, including equal opportunity, hometown involvement, support of the arts, employee involvement, overseas projects, consumer aids, and conservation. Public Relations Department, Mobil Oil Corporation, 150 East 42 Street, New York, NY 10017.

Social Progress Plan. A Quaker Oats 14-page report covering food and nutrition, employment opportunities, minority enterprise, environment, urban affairs, education, drug abuse, youth programs, and health care. Corporate Affairs Department, Quaker Oats Company, Merchandise Mart Plaza, Chicago, Il 60654.

Corporate Social Responsibility. A Ralston Purina Company 1977 report of 44 pages summarizing company and employee efforts in summer-job placement, urban development, contributions, energy conservation, and equal-opportunity employment. Contact Urban Programs Department, Ralston Purina Company, Checkerboard Square, St. Louis, MO 63188.

Corporate Responsibility. SmithKline Corporation 10-page booklet describes a number of social goals to which the company is committed, including equal employment opportunity, environmental protection, drug abuse prevention, aid to education, and corporate contributions. Contact Public Affairs Department, SmithKline Corporation, 1500 Spring Garden Street, Philadelphia, PA 19101.

A Report on Social Responsibility. Aetna Life and Casualty 28-page brochure covering equal employment opportunity, urban revitalization, neighborhood development, and corporate giving. Includes list of recipients of Aetna grants. Corporate Communications Department, Aetna Life and casualty, 151 Farmington Avenue, Hartford, CT 06156.

Union Carbide Profile: Special Report on Social Progress. A 33-page 1974 report on the findings of the company's reappraisal of its corporate citizenship activities, including its accomplishments and shortcomings. Corporate Communications Department, Union Carbide Corporation, 270 Park Avenue, New York, NY 10017.

1977 Contributions to Charitable and Educational Organizations. Standard Oil Company of California 15-page booklet that lists those organizations to which the company contributed $1,000 or more during the year. Categories include general public interest, civic, cultural, health and social welfare, international relations, student aid, aid to institutions, aid to basic research, and instructional aids. Both domestic and foreign donations are covered. Published in 1978 by Corporate Communications Department, Standard Oil Company of California, 225 Bush Street, San Francisco, CA 94104.

A Company That Cares. A 10-page brochure distributed in 1977 covering Johnson & Johnson's efforts in consumer health information, sports and recreation, environmental programs, the arts, disaster relief, medical research and education, child health, aid to education, energy conservation, and related programs. Public Relations Department, Johnson & Johnson, 501 George Street, New Brunswick, NJ 08903.

Social Responsibility Report. Control Data Corporation 14-page brochure published in 1978 on equal employment opportunity, child development programs, native American projects, urban redevelopment, consumer credit education, and minority business support. Public Affairs Department, Control Data Corporation, 8100-34th Avenue South, Minneapolis, MN 55420.

Pattern for Giving. A 36-page report published in 1977 describing the philanthropic activities of the Shell Companies Foundation in united giving, health care, support of the arts, aid to education, minority support, and community welfare. Community Relations Department, Shell Oil Company, P.O. Box 2463, Houston TX 77001.

Social Responsibility. Levi Strauss 16-page brochure published in 1977 covering the organization of the company's community affairs department and programs in corporate contributions, minority economic development, child day-care, and employee involvement in the community. Community Relations Department, Levi Strauss & Company, 2 Embarcadero Center, San Francisco, CA 94106.

Because We Live Here. Continental Illinois National Bank and Trust Co. A 48-page brochure published in 1977 covering educational support, consumer guidance, affirmative action employment, youth summer jobs, employment of the handicapped, community development, minority business enterprise, low- and middle-income housing, health services, and civic and cultural support. Corporate Communications Division, Continental Illinois National Bank & Trust Co., 231 South LaSalle Street, Chicago IL 60693.

Corporate Social Involvement. A 20-page report of United California Bank's social involvement policy, including social responsibility programs, employee involvement, and support of worthy educational and community causes. Public Affairs Department, United California Bank, 707 Wilshire Boulevard, Los Angeles, CA 90017.

In addition to the publications listed above, which cover a range of corporate social-responsibility policies and activities, there are other publications that address specific areas, such as equal employment opportunity, energy, health, and environment. The Bank of America has published a *Bibliography on Corporate Responsibility for Social Problems,* which provides the essential details on worthwhile publications and other references. The 1977 edition is 78 pages and can be obtained for $2.00 to cover handling and mailing from Editorial Services, Bank of America, P.O. 37000, San Francisco, CA 94137.

Syntex Communications Efforts

At our company, Syntex, we have communicated information about corporate giving in a number of ways. Since 1971 we have had a "Corporate Responsibility" section in the annual report to shareholders. Early in that year, we also decided to publish a 10-page special issue of our company newspaper, *The Syntex Reporter*, outlining our corporate-responsibility philosophy and summarizing what the company and its employees were doing in community action. In 1973, we repeated the idea with a 12-page issue devoted to "Syntex and the Environment."

We printed several thousand extra copies of both issues and distributed them to community leaders and the local media, as well as to people and organizations interested in corporate responsibility efforts. As a direct result of the publication of these two issues, the company received honor awards in 1971 and 1973 from *Environment Monthly,* then a leading environmental publication.

We did another interesting thing in communicating information on corporate contributions. I had an idea for telling the community about some of the efforts we were making in supporting local nonprofit organizations and causes. I was concerned that it not turn out to be a self-serving corporate communication, so I discussed it with Perry Leftwich at the Palo Also advertising and design agency that has assisted our public relations department for a number of years. He came up with a great concept for a newspaper advertisement that included information on 20 local community organizations that the company was supporting. The copy for that advertisement was tremendous. Here is what it said:

Twenty Non-Profit Organizations That Can Show Us All a Profit

> Here are twenty attractive investments, right here in the Palo Alto area, with the promise of unusual returns in 1974. These organizations handle a variety of community problems, creatively and constructively. That's why Syntex helps support them. Along with the United Way and about fifty other non-profit organizations here and in other parts of the Bay Area. Why not join us with your support, too? An investment in their work is, we think, a good investment in a better society. And we all profit from that.

The advertisement was published in the January 31, 1974, edition of the *Palo Alto Times* and also in the *Stanford Daily.* The response was remarkable, particularly from the mayor of Palo Alto, who was then Kirke Comstock: "How proud I am to be mayor of a city where outstanding organizations like yours are located. Congratulations!" Many of the organizations listed in the ad wrote to express their appreciation. We also got a favorable response from employees, including one written message congratulating the company for "an elegant and masterly piece of public relations" and remarking that it was "another example of the kind of good judgment and good taste that makes me proud of Syntex."

Companies that want to initiate efforts to improve the effectiveness of their contributions programs should pay attention to the way they communicate in this area and review how much effective information they make available to employees, shareholders, and community leaders and to those people and organizations seeking their company's support. It doesn't take much in the way of budget to make improvements in this area—mainly a determination to do better and the persistence to improve steadily the entire communications process.

4

Organizing for Effective Giving

Far too few companies have taken the time or trouble to properly evaluate their company contribution problem or to formulate a sound and workable program to meet this problem.[1]

It is discouraging that Leo Shapiro's remarks in his book, *Company Giving,* published 19 years ago, continue to be an accurate description of the manner in which many companies approach corporate contributions activity.

Corporations should approach corporate giving in the same methodical way that they deal with other business problems or opportunities. They should decide what they want to accomplish (set objectives) and then they should develop a plan to mobilize their resources (people, financial, and other) to ensure that the desired objectives are achieved successfully.

The first step is to develop specific and meaningful objectives—and this is as important in corporate giving as in any other part of the business. Without contributions objectives, it is impossible to develop a plan of action or to evaluate performance. Every corporation will have to develop its own particular list of objectives. It is something that needs to be done before starting a new program or attempting to revitalize an existing one.

The following is an example of the contributions objectives of a typical corporation:

1. Allocate 2% of the corporation's pretax net profits to the direct support of charitable causes, and increase this amount over the next 10 years to 5%.
2. In addition to cash grants, provide other types of worthwhile support, including the use of company facilities, company serv-

[1]Leo J. Shapiro, *Company Giving* (Chicago: Survey Press, 1960), p. 98.

ices such as printing and design, donated company products, and the volunteer efforts of company employees.
3. Provide support to a range of social causes, such as improved health services, environmental improvement, minority advancement, support of the arts, international projects, educational needs, urban revitalization, and community betterment.
4. Organize the contributions program so that it is imaginatively directed and efficiently operated.
5. Utilize an objective method of evaluation in determining where the company's support will be allocated.
6. Increase employee involvement through matching contributions (representing about 20% of total budget) and encouragement of employee participation in community causes.
7. Allocate corporate giving resources so that all plant and office locations can participate in contributions and community involvement.
8. Provide information on corporate giving policies and practices to employees, shareholders, and community leaders and particularly to organizations seeking company support.

Contributions Administrator

The most important person in the implementing process is the one selected to administer the program. In large corporations, this should be a full-time responsibility. In other companies, the responsibility should be assigned to an executive who directs a related function, such as public or community relations.

The person handling the contribution's function should be selected carefully. This is not a place to semiretire an executive "who likes people" but who may have no talent for managing the program.

These are some of the qualifications to look for:

1. Competent administrative and communications skills
2. Strong social awareness
3. Desire to become involved in worthwhile causes
4. Innovative thinking
5. Ability to relate to diverse groups outside of the corporation

If there is no individual within the company with these qualifications, an administrator of a local community foundation or the executive director of a successful nonprofit organization might be offered this corporate position, especially if he or she is familiar with business operations to some degree.

Whether the position is filled from inside or outside, the position should be established at a high enough staff level (manager or director) to ensure that the program will have sufficient visibility and that the administrator will receive the needed support throughout the organization.

Contributions Committee

A contributions committee will usually prove to be a helpful adjunct to the work of the administrator. A membership of four to six people should be sufficient. The basis of selection will vary with the organizational structure and the availability of individuals with special skills or interests. Frequently, selecting an individual from each of the major management functions, or from each of the major operating departments or divisions, will be an appropriate method. It may be desirable to rotate the membership.

The usual responsibilities of a contributions committee are to (1) recommend contribution policies; (2) approve the annual budget; and (3) evaluate requests not specifically budgeted or in excess of the amount budgeted.

The committee should meet at least monthly to ensure that requests are reviewed without unnecessary delay. At each meeting, the contributions administrator should provide recommendations on the requests that are being considered, as well as a report of funds expended in the previous month and for the year to date.

Procedures for Decision Making

The company should be able to deal with requests in an expeditious manner. If financial limits have been established through a budgeting process, and if the program has been adequately defined by objectives and guidelines, major delays or other managerial inefficiencies can most often be traced to a failure to establish a clear and effective decision-making process, including an appropriate delegation of authority to approve requests and recommendations.

A helpful analogy in this connection is the use of a system of approvals similar to that commonly employed in the processing of capital appropriations, with the limits of final authority clearly identified for each level. Rarely will it be necessary to employ more than three or four levels, even in the largest organizations.

First-level approvals will be made by the administrator; approvals involving larger amounts or programs will be made by the contributions committee; and the largest contributions and most significant programs will require the approval of top management or the board of directors. A plan of delegation suitable for most organizations is outlined below.

LEVEL 1 The contributions administrator is authorized to handle the following requests without other review or approval: (1) requests that have already been budgeted, and (2) individual requests below a specified amount, such as $100 or $500, which in total do not exceed the amount allocated for general purposes for the period.

LEVEL 2 The contributions committee is authorized to review and approve: (1) unbudgeted requests and (2) requests for approved contributions that overrun the budgeted amount. In both cases, the authority is limited to an established maximum and to the availability of budgeted but unallocated funds.

LEVEL 3 Requests for major gifts. Under a level-three division of authority, final approval, rejection, or modification is a top-management decision. Under a four-level plan, authority to approve gifts above a predetermined amount is reserved to the board of directors. The amount to be set depends on company size and other considerations. For example, in some companies final approval of top management might be set at $25,000, with amounts above that figure going to the board for consideration.

The Contributions Budget

To provide effective management of corporate contributions, a top-level decision is required to determine the amount, or level, of contributions before the machinery of administration is set in motion. Setting a dollar amount annually (or a fixed amount for some other budgetary or accounting period) has the disadvantage of being a repetitive act, and the risk is that the amount may come to be set routinely, with diminished attention to community need and corporate ability. However, this may be the only practical solution for a company whose earnings fluctuate widely.

Most companies will find that it is better to establish a formula for giving, based on corporate pretax earnings. The national average currently stands at about 1%; amounts up to 5% are deductible for federal income tax purposes (and therefore cost the average company about one-half the dollar amount, in terms of after-tax income). Some companies already give the allowed maximum; many other companies, on thoughtful self-examination, could probably do the same.

A special help in developing your formula is the *Annual Survey of Company Contributions,* published by the Conference Board, 845 Third Avenue, New York, NY 10022. This survey report breaks down corporate giving in a number of interesting ways: by industry classification; by company size measured in assets, pretax income, and number of employees; and by areas of giving, such as health, education, culture, and community welfare.

Establishing a formula accomplishes several things. First, it is a standing commitment to allocate a specific amount of corporate resources to charitable causes. Basing it on pretax profits ensures that the corporate contributions fund will benefit directly from increases in corporate earnings. It also prevents a situation where a 10% shortfall in profits might result in a 50% decrease in contributions.

Determining the corporate share establishes the overall amount of corporate giving for a designated period. A formalized budgeting process then allocates these funds and provides the control necessary for the effective management of the function.

Some activities will probably have been identified as suitable for the continuing support of the corporation. Some programs will be recognized as winding up, and others will have been encountered while still in the planning stages. Finally, some worthwhile projects will arise each year of which the corporation will have no advance knowledge. It is good practice to reserve a portion of the funds for contingencies, overruns, and new projects. Experience suggests that 10% of the funds should be reserved for this purpose.

In the course of budget development, proposals should be reviewed in channels. That is to say, proposals made by the administrator involving an amount of money in excess of his delegated authority should be reviewed by the contributions committee, and those above the level of delegated authority of the committee should be reviewed by higher management. As a final step, the total amount involved in recommended projects should be compared with the amount determined as the corporate share for the period, and the proposals should be adjusted so that the total allocation does not exceed the predetermined corporate share.

Record Keeping

There are three elements of a simple but effective record-keeping system: (1) a contributions register; (2) a card file; and (3) a file of correspondence and other materials on each organization receiving a company contribution.

Received	Action taken	Organization	Allocated	Unallo-cated	Matching gifts	Total
4/1	4/2	Urban Coalition	4,000			4,000
4/1	4/5	Stanford University			50	50
4/1	4/6	Junior Achievement	100			100
4/2	4/8	Nature Conservancy	500			500
4/2	4/8	United Negro College Fund	1,000	250		1,250
4/2	4/9	Community Child Care		500		500
		April contributions	18,400	1,705	480	20,585
		January—March	82,000	3,015	1,800	86,815
		Year to date	100,400	4,720	2,280	107,400

Figure 1. Contributions register.

The contributions register is a simple notebook, (Figure 1). As each request is received, it is logged by recording the date and the name of the organization requesting assistance. When action is taken, the date and the amount of the contribution are noted as an allocated or unallocated item in the budget. Each month, the amounts are totaled; then that

FRONT

Council on Economic Education
250 Columbus Avenue
San Francisco, California 94133
(415) 989-7506

Contact: Bill Miller, West Coast Director

IRS Tax Ded.: Yes
Calif. Tax Ded.: Yes

Employee Contact: John Smart, Board of Trustees of California Chapter

REVERSE

Oct. 6, 1970	$ 250	Brochure Printing
Apr. 18, 1972	1,000	General Support
Sept. 6, 1973	1,000	" "
Aug. 21, 1975	1,000	" "
Sept. 20, 1975	1,250	" "
Sept. 12, 1976	1,250	" "

Figure 2. Contributions file cards.

month's figures are added to the previous totals to show the results for the year to date. This register provides a record of each request, and whether it was approved or denied; indicates how long the company is taking to handle each request; and helps to ensure that actual contributions will match up with the budget.

A 3″ × 5″ card should be kept on each organization to whom the company has contributed (Figure 2). On one side, include the organization's name, address, and telephone number as well as the contact person. Also indicate the organization's tax-deductible status, both federal and state if your state has a corporate income tax. If there is an employee who serves as a contact with the organization, this person should be listed to remind the contributions administrator to keep that employee informed of all contact with the organization. On the reverse side of the card, list each contribution, giving the date, the amount, and the purpose of the gift. Filed alphabetically, these cards provide a quick and easy reference system to the organizations supported and the contributions made over the years.

Contributions Etiquette

It is plain courtesy to make grant decisions in a reasonable period of time. If it is an item already allocated in the budget, forward the check and the covering letter no later than two weeks after receipt of the request. If the proposal has to be sent to the contributions, management, or executive committee or to the board of directors, advise the requesting organization that this is being done and tell them approximately when a decision will be reached. A postal card or a phone call is all that is necessary as a response.

Candor is another important quality. There is nothing worse than to give a requesting organization the feeling that you are supportive of its request when the chances of a corporate donation are slim. When a proposal isn't suitable for your company, don't hesitate to say so right away.

I remember one instance where a talented young man came to me requesting a large grant to bail out a performing arts organization that was in deep financial trouble. I told him that we would not put our contribution dollars into such a hopeless task. I urged him to explore a job opening then available with a local municipal arts organization. He got the job and thanked me for an honest piece of advice.

If a company can't help the requesting organization directly, it may be able to suggest other local corporations, foundations, or individuals that might be in a better position to provide support. This information is very much appreciated by organizations seeking support.

Annual Contributions Report to Management

At the end of each year, a report should be prepared for management and the company's board of directors. It should include both the total dollar contributions for the year compared to the budget and the actual contributions as a percentage of pretax income compared to the formula, if such a formula is used.

The amounts contributed during the year should be broken down by the areas supported: aid to education, health services, community welfare, environmental projects, the arts, international projects, etc. This breakdown will ensure that you are adequately supporting the various organizations that are important to the company.

The report should include highlights of the important new projects funded as well as feedback from the organizations that have benefited from company contributions. Finally, it can include recommendations for changes in contributions policies, objectives, or strategies.

5

Proposal Evaluation: Impulse, Habit, or Reason

The indispensable ingredient of a good proposal is a good idea. There is no substitute for it.[1]

In her book *Grants,* Virginia White devotes a chapter to the important work of writing a grant proposal. She offers sound advice to organizations seeking financial support. Most decisions by corporations and other grant-making institutions will be based primarily on the information supplied by the organization requesting support. The computer-related saying "Garbage in—garbage out" applies. If the grant-making organization does not receive adequate information, the probability is increased dramatically that the evaluation process will be less objective than it should be.

It is important, therefore, that organizations seeking corporate contributions have an accurate picture of the nature and extent of the information they want to convey to the institution being approached. Although the essential aspect, as Virginia White has said, is a good idea:

> The most beautifully prepared application will not turn a pedestrian idea into an inspired one. . . . The best idea in the world, inadequately described or unimaginatively presented, can be misinterpreted or even overlooked.[2]

The most practical question, then, is "If there is a good idea, how can it be best presented?" One approach was presented in an article by Norton J. Kiritz in *The Grantsmanship Center News.*[3]

Kiritz suggests that the proposal contain seven components: (1) an

[1]Virginia P. White, *Grants* (New York: Plenum Press, 1975), p. 225.
[2]Ibid., p. 226.
[3]Norton J. Kiritz, "Program Planning and Proposal Writing," *The Grantsmanship Center News* (June–July 1974): 11–14.

introduction; (2) a need or problem assessment; (3) program objectives; (4) program methods; (5) an evaluation plan; (6) a future funding plan; and (7) the budget.

The purpose of the *introduction,* according to Kiritz is to establish credibility in the eyes of the funding source. He suggests that this can be accomplished by answering a few questions: How did the organization get started? How long has it been around? What are some of the organization's significant accomplishments? What are the organization's goals? What support is received from other organizations and individuals?

The *need or problem assessment* is the place to "zero in on the specific problem or problems that you want to solve through the program you are proposing." Kiritz advises the requesting organization to "make sure that what you want to do is workable—that it can be done within a reasonable time, by you, and with a reasonable amount of money."

Kiritz states that it is important in defining *program objectives* to distinguish between methods and objectives: "One common problem in many proposals is a failure to distinguish between means and ends—a failure to distinguish between methods and objectives." If an organization is trying to obtain employment for minority workers, for example, it isn't enough to state as an objective that the organization will counsel a certain number of minority job seekers each month. Rather the objective would be to obtain *permanent employment* for x number of minority individuals each period. Counseling is a means; the objective must be employment.

It is important, according to Kiritz, to state how the objectives will be reached, that is, the *methods* to be utilized. The organization not only has to describe these methods but also has to explain why these particular methods were selected.

The *evaluation* is important—it will indicate how the success or failure of the program will be determined. This can be accomplished, however, only if the objectives are measurable.

Kiritz also feels that potential contributors should know how the organization will obtain *future funding* when the requested grant runs out. This is probably applicable more to government funding than to private foundation or corporate grant-making. It is important, however, if the proposal request is for a "seed-money" grant that the organization explain how the program will be sustained. Kiritz says that "a plan to generate funds through the project itself—such as fees for services, subscriptions for publications, etc.—is an excellent plan." I agree but such a plan is not often feasible.

The final component of the proposal is the *budget,* where all of the costs are given. They include personnel costs (wages and fringe benefits), consultants and contract services (bookkeeping, legal, fund-raising, etc.), space costs, equipment purchases or rental, consumable supplies, travel expense, utilities (telephone, heat, light), insurance, printing, etc.

In addition to these specifics outlined by Kiritz, the requesting organization might also want to consider providing information on the individuals who will be involved in the program or project, including their professional qualifications; how long it will take to complete the project or program; and where it will take place.

If an organization uses this format for its proposal, adapting it to its particular circumstances, it will provide the essential information on which an objective evaluation of the proposal can be made.

Well, if we assume that the grant-making organization has received the right information, can we then assume that the evaluation will be objective and the decision correct? My experience is that one cannot make this assumption.

Let's go back to the computer analogy. Let's assume that all the necessary information has been fed into the memory bank of the computer. Does this by itself mean that a correct solution to a problem will be forthcoming? Not exactly. The person using the computer has to know how to use the data in the computer. In certain circumstances, some data are more important and relevant than others. The computer has to be "programmed" to produce the best use of the stored information.

This means that the grant-making organization has to program itself: it must develop a clear idea of its own objectives in giving, its own interests and priorities, its own resources, and other factors. This introspection can generate specific evaluation guidelines that will enable the company to avoid reliance on subjective reactions or personal preferences.

Formal criteria should be developed to provide a basis for continuous, relevant, and consistent judgments, as free as possible of individual preferences or prejudices. Developing criteria is a largely individual matter, given the differences in corporate situations and opportunities. When formulated, they should be reduced to explicit written statements; otherwise different individuals will interpret the criteria differently. And while not all criteria will be applicable in every situation, an effort should be made to develop a comprehensive set. The considerations set out below should be of assistance in this process:

1. Is the organization working in areas of critical social need and importance? (Those that were doing a great job 25 years ago may be tilting at windmills today.)
2. What is the basic approach of the project or program for which funding has been requested? Is it creative or innovative or does it just continue or extend what is already known and established?
3. Does the project or program get at the root causes of the problem or merely deal with the symptoms?
4. What is the target population? To what extent can it benefit

from the program or project? What provisions have been made for the target population to participate in planning and execution?

5. If successful, will the project or program make the people involved more or less dependent upon the corporation and others? What are the chances that the group can be partially or totally self-sufficient if the company's initial support is provided?
6. Will a successful solution permit this project or program to be implemented in other geographical areas where the same need exists?
7. What is the current operating budget of the organization? What is the projected cost of the proposed program or project? Has any provision been made for an independent audit of expenditures if it is a large project or program?
8. What percentage of the funds collected is spent on administrative and fund-raising activities? (If it's over 25%, watch out!)
9. How long has the requesting organization been in existence? What has been its overall performance?
10. Can the organization provide evidence that it is a tax-exempt organization?
11. What are other companies, foundations, and individuals contributing?
12. Can and should the organization be more properly obtaining funds from other sources? Many groups do their own fund raising when they should belong in a group effort such as the United Way. (If so, and you nudge them, they may apply for United Way funding.)
13. Is this need better served by private giving or by tax-generated funds?
14. What is the probability that the organization will reach its funding goal? Is there reason for the company to make a pledge based on the organization's ability to achieve its overall funding goal?
15. Would it be appropriate to offer a contribution on the condition that an equal sum be matched from some other source?
16. What is the capacity of the corporation's gift or pledge to influence others to contribute to the project—or to launch a new project that could quickly gain wide and substantial support?
17. Is the organization requesting cash or "in kind" support? Is it requesting cash for some service or product that the company can supply directly?
18. Will the contribution advance the community relations and public relations of the company?
19. Can the company identify its contribution with a particular

project or program, or will it go into a general fund? (If the company is looking for visibility, the latter is usually not the way to go.)

20. Does the project or program duplicate or counteract efforts of another organization or institution? (If there are two organizations trying to accomplish the same goals, maybe you can pledge support if they agree to a marriage.)
21. If the gift is for a building fund, is there an adequate provision for any resulting increase in the organization's operating overhead?
22. Is it a continuing or one-time contribution? Balance should be maintained between that portion of the company contributions budget that is devoted to continuing versus one-time contributions to ensure that there is flexibility in the program.
23. Does the organization provide a service that is available to company employees, such as family counseling, child care, adult education, or cultural programs?
24. How many employees does the company have in the community served by the requesting organization?
25. What role do the company's employees play in the soliciting organization?
26. If the requesting group is a national or an international organization, does it have a regional operation where contact can be maintained on a local level?
27. Are there any potential legal restrictions or tax problems that should be cleared up before making a contribution?
28. Is the organization attempting to influence legislation by propaganda or otherwise?
29. Who are the people on the organization's board of directors? Is it a working board or a cosmetic one? Is it representative of the broad interests and constituency that the organization claims to serve?
30. Who are the key staff people? What are their professional backgrounds and qualifications? Will additional staff be required for the proposed new program or project?
31. Are there reputable and knowledgeable people willing to provide an endorsement of the aims and activities of the soliciting organization?
32. By what criteria will the success or failure of the project or program be measured? Can the company conveniently monitor the success or failure of the organization's effort?
33. Has the organization documented its needs, its objectives, and its capabilities in a clear and concise proposal?

6

Employee Involvement: A Rich but Underutilized Resource

When I go through one of our plants, and see everybody excited about the new team project, and hear how they feel as individuals about their company and how the Levi Strauss Foundation is helping out in town with a project that the Community Involvement Team is working on, I just know they feel good about their jobs and themselves, and so do I.[1]

Fostering employee involvement in corporate giving and community action programs should be a major objective of every company's efforts. The reason is simple. People are important. Often their talents and assistance are more helpful than a cash contribution. It is unfortunate that when we think of philanthropy, we usually think of someone writing a check for a worthy cause. Most voluntary donations in our society, in fact, are people donating *themselves,* their time, their energy, their enthusiasm to an organization or to a cause that they feel is very important.

The scale of this voluntary effort is enormous, as calculated in a study by Harold Wolozin of the University of Massachusetts in 1975.[2] A uniform wage rate of $4.76 in current dollars was applied to all organized volunteer job activities. This formula disclosed that the total dollar value of organized volunteer services was almost $34 billion in 1974! This amount was $9 million more than the total of all tax-deductible contributions to charitable causes in the same year. Also interesting was the study's conclusion that the value of such organized voluntary activity increased by 500% between 1965 and 1974.

Wolozin also pointed out that "If the volunteer services contributed

[1]"It's Everybody's Responsibility," *Social Responsibility* (San Francisco: Levi Strauss & Company, 1977), p. 10.

[2]Harold Wolozin, *The Value of Volunteer Services in the United States* (Washington, D.C.: ACTION, 1975), p. 4.

through organizations—organized volunteer work—were to be imputed on the Gross National Product, its services component would be increased by more than 6%."

Giving USA reported that

> the role of the volunteer is increasing in America and for the most part the reason is simple: Volunteer help keeps administrative costs down and at the same time the volunteer achieved a feeling of fulfillment and of being involved.[3]

Giving USA also reported:

- Twenty-four percent of the adult population in the nation, or 37 million people, donated part of their time and their efforts to volunteer work.
- Thirty percent of those surveyed donated nearly 3 hours per month—or well over 35 hours each year—to keep the volunteer spirit alive.
- Women made up 59% of the volunteers.
- The biggest single group change was among retirees, whose total number and participation had more than doubled in a 10-year period.
- The Office of Domestic and Anti-Poverty programs listed a total of 235,227 volunteers involved with various domestic programs financed by federal dollars.
- More than 135,000 persons over the age of 60 have volunteered for the foster grandparents program to help children with special needs on a person-to-person basis.
- The volunteer strength of 20 national health agencies in 1976 was almost 20 million people.

The United Way of America is the leading nondenominational organization in terms of volunteer support. It had 20 million volunteers involved in the processes of direct service, fund raising, communications, allocations, and program planning of its 1976 campaign. Many of these United Way volunteers are corporate loaned executives. This is understandable since the concept of united giving emanated from the needs, requirements, and community interests of business and industry. Since the United Way is the largest annual fund-raising effort in the United States, with a substantial amount of the $1.1 billion raised coming from employee and company gifts, Chapter 10 will discuss united giving from a corporate and community perspective.

It is encouraging that the concept of personal involvement is already recognized and practiced at the higher levels in the corporate communi-

[3]*Giving USA 1977, Annual Report* (New York: The American Association of Fund-Raising Counsels, Inc., 1977), p. 51.

ty. A Conference Board report on corporate leadership in philanthropy indicated that 92% of the chairmen and presidents of major corporations were associated with one or more philanthropic organizations and were devoting a weekly average of about three hours of company time and three hours of their own time to these efforts.[4]

There is a need, however, as a Committee for Economic Development statement has pointed out, for top management to

> provide stronger leadership within many corporations to develop the policies and climate that would stimulate employees, especially young managers, to apply their interests and skills to relevant social as well as conventional matters.

The statement makes another important observation, that

> the additional duty could be more widely and explicitly recognized as a normal, rather than extracurricular, part of managerial responsibilities and as *an essential ingredient for managers aiming to equip themselves for broader executive responsibility.*[5] (Italics added)

Corporations employ millions of people in cities, in suburban and rural areas in every part of the country—and in other countries as well. There is great leverage here. There is the potential for a great multiplier effect when corporations maximize employee participation at every level in every location.

Employee involvement can be encouraged and initiated in a number of ways. Employees can be brought into the evaluation and decision-making process of corporate giving. Companies can support the community involvement of individual employees and groups of employees; support employee gifts with matching company contributions; provide scholarships for the children of employees; and maintain communications programs to keep employees informed of company support programs.

Contributions Committee Membership

The contributions committee is a key place to get more employees involved in the process of corporate giving. In Chapter 4, the role of the contributions committee was discussed. In selecting committee members, it is a good idea to choose a group that includes representatives of the major activities of the company, such as manufacturing, administration, marketing, research, and so forth. It might also be worthwhile to

[4]James F. Harris and Anne Klepper, "Corporate Philanthropic Public Service Activities," *Research Papers*, The Commission on Private Philanthropy and Public Needs (Washington, D.C.: Department of the Treasury, 1977), p. 1749.

[5]*Social Responsibilities of Business Corporations* (New York: Committee for Economic Development, 1971), p. 4.

include employees representing various levels, such as top and middle management and even the rank-and-file. Such a diversely organized committee will ensure that a broad base of employees has a say in contributions policies and decisions. It will also serve as an effective first line of communication throughout the company in respect to the firm's efforts in contributions and community involvement.

Start a Fund for Community Service

In 1972, IBM started a program that enables employees to obtain company support for volunteer service programs in local communities across the country. The only condition: the employee has to be active in the community organization to get the money. IBM's aim was to stimulate more volunteer action by its employees. Most of the grants range from $100 to $1,000. IBM wants these funds to go where they can make a real difference—not where these dollars will only displace regular contributions from other sources.

By the end of 1975, the fund had responded to requests for assistance from more than 8,000 employees and retired IBM-ers involved in more than 4,000 community projects. To get the funds, the employee writes a request describing the organization, the community project, the amount required, and the extent of the employee's involvement. Only two approvals are required: one from the employee's manager and one additional approval. A great majority of the employee requests have been approved.

Inquiries about this program should be addressed to Fund For Community Service, International Business Machines Corporation, Old Orchard Road, Armonk, NY 10504.

Begin a Faculty Loan Program

This is another innovative IBM program. It provides paid leaves for professional employees to teach for one full academic year at colleges and universities with large enrollments of minority and disadvantaged students. IBM introduced the program at 18 black colleges for the 1971–1972 school year. Since then, the program has been expanded to include colleges serving American Indians, Mexican-Americans, and economically depressed Appalachia.

Faculty loan volunteers stay on IBM salary and full company benefits. The company pays relocation expenses and temporary living costs while the volunteers are away from home. In one year, 34 IBM employees were teaching at 34 different schools. They have introduced new courses, built campus radio stations and engineering laboratories, established student chapters of technical societies, and developed computer techniques for classroom instruction.

For more information about this program, write to Coordinator, Faculty Loan Program, International Business Machines Corporation, Old Orchard Road, Armonk, NY 10504.

Levi Strauss Employee Involvement

One corporation, Levi Strauss, has developed two ways to involve employees in company giving and community action.

Company contributions are disbursed through the Levi Strauss Foundation. Allocation of more than half of the foundation's funds is recommended to the foundation's directors by a rotating employee advisory committee. This committee is composed of eight employees of the home office who work on a volunteer basis with the community affairs department, where most of the 100 or more requests per month are received and initially reviewed. The committee represents a cross-section of employees, from different divisions, sexes, and races. It meets every six weeks and has a real impact on what gets funded. One committee member said that "In the two and a half years that I've been on the committee, they've never rejected a recommendation that we have made."

The advisory committee gives priority to requests that emanate from or directly serve communities where Levi Strauss is located. This procedure leads to the second way that the company has developed in order to increase employee involvement: Levi's Community Involvement Teams.

Employees in nearly 50 plants and distribution centers across the United States volunteer their time to identify local needs and initiate participation among other employees in implementing programs to help solve local needs. These teams raise thousands of dollars each year to donate to nonprofit organizations for assistance with programs that they feel merit support. Frequently the Levi Strauss Foundation supports with grants the programs in which teams and local plant managements have been involved.

These Community Involvement Teams provide employees with a means to identify community needs and to implement programs to assist in meeting those needs. Often the teams have served as catalysts to get other community groups and potential funding sources involved in projects initiated by the teams. The activities of these Levi Strauss employee groups around the country are diverse and meaningful:

- In Albuquerque, New Mexico, the team donated a sewing machine to a group of women making quilts for people in wheelchairs.

- In Wichita, Kansas, the team repaired and insulated homes of elderly and disadvantaged citizens.
- In Charleston, South Carolina, the team donated clothing and purchased a refrigerator for an employee whose house burned down.
- In El Paso, Texas, the team helped start a motor repair school for participants in a local drug abuse program.
- In Valdosta, Georgia, the team helped restore a historic cemetery.
- In Champaign, Illinois, the team purchased communication monitors for the local fire department.

In 1975, Community Involvement Teams in 45 Levi Strauss facilities worked at least 31,701 volunteer hours on 288 community service projects. The teams also raised $91,600. For more information, contact Community Relations Department, Levi Strauss & Co., 2 Embarcadero Center, San Francisco, CA 94106.

Organize a Social-Service Leave Program

Xerox Corporation started a program in 1972 so that employees could take time off from work to do something for the community and for society, on a full-time basis, for a period of time—and do it at full pay, with full benefits, with full assurance of a job and a warm welcome when the employee returned to Xerox.

The Social Service Leave Program makes *people* talent available for work on social problems in the recognition that quite often people are an even greater resource than dollars. Equally important is the belief that after such leave, employees have a heightened awareness of and concern for social problems, which they will extend to other Xerox employees upon their return.

Leave takers in 1972 and 1973 took on many projects: counseling youth in a Mexican-American area of Los Angeles; creating a model classroom for teaching mentally retarded preschoolers; marketing services for the Interracial Council for Business Opportunity; and editing a newspaper about equal rights for women.

Xerox employees feel that the program is an important thing for the company to be doing; even those who are not active participants themselves take pride and satisfaction in it.

For more information, write Xerox Corporation, High Ridge Park, Stamford, CT 06904, or read the detailed description of the Xerox Social Service Leave Program in the book *Corporate Social Responsiveness,* by Robert Ackerman and Raymond Baner, distributed by Reston Publishing Company, Inc., in 1976. Another source is the booklet "Policies on Leaves for Political and Social Action," published in 1972 by The Conference Board, 845 Third Avenue, New York, NY 10022.

Get Employees Involved in the Involvement Corps

This is another interesting approach that was originated by a group of corporate executives in 1968. It began with corporations in the San Francisco Bay Area, Los Angeles, Portland (Oregon), and Denver. In 1973, it expanded to several other cities and now includes corporate volunteer projects at more than 50 corporations.

The program involves five elements: a sponsoring corporation, a volunteer corporate task force, a community need and self-help project, a trained coordinator or community involvement team, and a continuing program of maintenance and support by Involvement Corps staff.

The corporation contracts with the Involvement Corps (a non-profit corporation), pays a consulting fee, and underwrites any direct expenses. The employee task force selects a project that the company and the Involvement Corps staff feel is worthy and appropriate. The task force assembles a resource pool available to help the project achieve its objectives through a common interest in sharing their skills and spare time with the project.

The project attempts to identify with a specific social concern, such as health care, community development, ecology, youth guidance, drug rehabilitation, remedial education, housing, mental health, or elderly care and companionship. Each project is reviewed by the Involvement Corps staff to ensure that it meets basic minimum requirements:

1. Its goals are defined.
2. It has substance.
3. Its needs can be met by volunteers.
4. It can utilize the resources of the corporation and its employees.

The coordinator or community involvement team identifies the skills, resources, and interests of the employees, communicates the project's needs to them, identifies the variety of ways in which they can serve the project, and gives them volunteer assignments. The coordinator is the liaison with the Involvement Corps staff, the employees, and the corporation.

In 1977, Involvement Corps programs in California used 1,700 volunteers from 11 corporations. They were responsible for 28,000 hours of service to over 50 community organizations. The volunteers also provided $98,000 in materials and services to the community. The following are some examples of Involvement Corps projects:

Ampex Corporation *Service League of San Mateo County* provides rehabilitative and welfare services to per-

	sons incarcerated in the county jail and their families.
Crocker Bank	*Alma,* multipurpose center in Los Angeles for the developmentally disabled.
Crown-Zellerbach	*Meals on Wheels* provides hot meals for shut-ins in San Francisco.
Foremost-McKesson	*Friends Outside* provides emergency and long-term support services to families of prison inmates.
Lloyds Bank	*Los Angeles Free Clinic* provides medical, dental, job placement, psychological counseling, and legal aid services.

Corporations have identified ways in which an active Involvement Corps task force has been of tangible benefit to the company:

1. Greater company visibility within the community
2. Increased interaction among employees, resulting in stronger corporate identification
3. Management and employee development through participation
4. Provision of the opportunity for employees to develop "people" skills

More information about this community–company–employee partnership is available from the Involvement Corps, 1366 Las Canoas Road, Pacific Palisades, CA 90272.

Matching Employee Gifts

In Chapter 11, there is a description of the program matching employee gifts to educational institutions that was started in the General Electric Company over two decades ago. A more recent approach to matching gifts is the practice of many firms in matching employee contributions to United Way campaigns.

In 1977, the Bank of America broadened its employee gift-matching program to include cultural groups. It will match any employee contribution from $25 to $7,500 to museums, dance companies, symphony orchestras, historical societies, libraries, and public television stations.

Corporations should pay increasing attention to this part of the contribution program. Matching gifts provide several benefits. They enable the employee to decide where certain corporate contributions funds are to be allocated. They provide an incentive for employees to make meaningful contributions.

In addition to the Bank of America approach, there are other ways that corporations could increase matching gifts. The company could develop a list of charitable organizations that would qualify for a matching company gift. At distant plant locations, local managers could be given the option of adding local organizations to the qualifying list.

Corporate matching gifts are often only a small percentage of the total amounts contributed each year by corporations. It would be feasible and worthwhile if 20–25% of total corporate gifts were a result of matching employee gifts. This would ensure that a larger number of employees are playing a meaningful role in allocating corporate contributions. It could also stimulate additional giving by both corporations and individuals in the business world.

Scholarships for Children of Employees

One way for a company to increase employee involvement in contributions programs is to set up college scholarships for the children of its employees. It is possible to do this with a tax-deductible contribution, provided certain IRS conditions are met. Seven mandatory requirements and a percentage test requirement are stated in the Revenue Procedure 76-47 (IRS private letter ruling 9/22/77, Document 7751048).

An effective method of setting up such scholarships is through the National Merit Scholarship Corporation. The company and the NMSC agree on a minimum and a maximum scholarship award. This agreement is necessary since the awards, after being made on academic ability, are related to financial need.

The company announces the scholarship competition, including test dates, and distributes applications to all employees. The forms are returned to the company, then sent to the NMSC, which notifies the sponsoring company of the names of the winners and the recommended amount of the awards.

Using the NMSC has several advantages. The company does not have to do any testing or financial evaluations, and the scholarship awards are based solely on merit. For information about an employee scholarship program, contact National Merit Scholarship Corporation, 990 Grove Street, Evanston, IL 60201.

Employee Contributions Fund

One of the oldest yet most effective approaches to employee involvement is the "Bucks of the Month Club" (BOMC) of Lockheed Corporation. It started during World War II, when Lockheed and its employees were barraged with a number of worthy appeals from charitable groups.

The employees decided to organize their own contributions fund by deducting 25 cents a week from their paychecks. The monies were then accumulated in a central fund and disbursed by a committee at each major plant location.

The committee in the Sunnyvale, California, plant is composed of six people: two hourly-paid employees named by the union; two salaried employees named by the Lockheed Management Association; and two employees named by the Employees Recreational Association. In addition to handling the payroll deduction, Lockheed provides office space and a full-time secretary for the committee and permits the members to perform committee work on company time.

Lockheed has about 20,000 employees in the San Francisco Bay Area, and 95% participate in the program. The average employee deduction is in the range of $2–$4 per week or $100–$200 annually. This program generates a substantial amount of contributions from this one company installation—about $9 million in the past 30 years.

The United Way gets from one-third to one-half of the BOMC Funds. Another 20% of the collections is set aside for direct financial aid to Lockheed employees. This allocation is acceptable to the Internal Revenue Service, providing the employee share of BOMC disbursements is not a major share of total contributions.

Lockheed also has its own company contributions program, which is completely separate from BOMC. Lockheed does not match BOMC contributions to the United Way or to educational institutions, but the company does make a direct contribution to the United Way as well as to other nonprofit organizations.

If a company employs a large number of people, a substantial fund can be accumulated in this type of program. It does require some company support, but basically it is a program by and for employees. The company, of course, gets a substantial amount of credit in the community for the contributions made by its employees.

Keeping Employees Informed

No matter what system is used for company and employee contributions, it is important that all people in the organization be kept informed of contributions and community involvement activities. Unfortunately, this is not always done. Jack Shakely of the Grantsmanship Center has said that "most corporation employees don't know what their own corporation is doing, and whatever sense of pride or goodwill that employees might have felt is lost."[6]

This need not be the case. Usually, there is a regular company publication that can be used to announce the various grants that are made and to explain changes in policies and guidelines related to contributions and community action. The annual report, which most employees read, is another place for this information to be covered. Employees should have access to such information so that their active cooperation and involvement can be maintained.

Employee involvement is one of the most productive ways for a company to improve its corporate giving and other support activities. Corporations employ millions of talented and concerned people. When corporations tap the enthusiasm of this multitude of people, some dramatic things happen. Levi Strauss, Xerox, IBM, and other enlightened corporations have demonstrated that employee involvement works for the community and also has a positive effect on employee morale.

[6]Jack Shakely, "Exploring the Elusive World of Corporate Giving" *The Grantsmanship News,* (July–September 1977): 48.

7

Fifteen Ways to Provide Valuable Support without Making a Cash Contribution

With the application of a little imagination, there are many possibilities for business to collaborate with nonprofit groups beyond funding.[1]

For every dollar corporations donate to nonprofit organizations, it is estimated that they give another dollar's worth of "in-kind" support in the form of goods or services. This is a unique aspect of corporate philanthropy as contrasted to giving by foundations.

This substantial amount of noncash support is possible because corporations have many resources, including products; facilities; equipment and supplies; promotional, legal, and financial talent; design and printing services; and so forth.

It is important for nonprofit organizations to realize that a cash gift is not the only type of support that they may obtain from a business organization. If they limit their requests to cash alone, they may be passing up a variety of things that can be as valuable as (or even more valuable than) a cash contribution.

If there are a variety of ways in which a business can help, some kind of support is much more likely. This permits a nonprofit group to be more flexible in terms of asking for assistance and allows the company greater latitude in terms of deciding in what specific manner it chooses to provide support.

It is important for each company to take an inventory of the resources at its disposal.

Furthermore, it might also be a very good idea for each community

[1]John D. Rockefeller 3rd. *The Second American Revolution* (New York: Harper & Row, 1973), p. 124.

organization to make a complete list of things that it needs so it will not overlook potential assistance from business organizations.

One: Purchasing Power

One day I was visited by Judy Horst, a young woman who had done some freelance writing and photography for the company. She said that she was organizing a Big Sisters chapter in our area. She had come up with a novel fund-raising idea but also a snag. Her idea was to produce for sale a handsome calendar featuring dramatic color photographs of San Francisco. She and some other photographers would donate the pictures, and someone else had agreed to donate the design work. She had commitments from several stores to purchase quantities of the calendars for resale to the public. What she couldn't find was a printer who would do the job without a large advance payment.

Several days later, I heard that one of our marketing groups was gearing up for an important national meeting. When I asked them if they could use an attractice promotional handout, I got an enthusiastic response. The marketing people agreed to purchase several thousand calendars with the corporate logotype tastefully imprinted on the cover. The company's commitment encouraged the printer to produce the calendars without a cash advance. The whole project, including the commercial sale of the calendars, was carried out successfully. The Big Sisters chapter achieved its fund-raising objective and decided to make the calendar an annual fund-raising project.

Two: Employee Access

A company can be looked upon as a collection of individual employees. Carrying this concept a bit further, these individuals can be viewed as potential volunteers, advocates, clients, members, or contributors. Some nonprofit groups have been aware of this concept for some time and have taken advantage of it. There are a number of ways in which this can be accomplished:

1. Informational materials can be supplied by the charitable organization for display on company bulletin boards.
2. Permission can be obtained from some corporations to set up tables in company cafeterias or other locations to inform or solicit employee participation. The League of Women Voters has increased voter registration in this manner.
3. In special cases, payroll deductions may be arranged for some types of appeals, but this procedure is usually restricted to the United Way or similar broad-based campaigns.

4. Arrangements can sometimes be made through the company personnel department or employee recreation association to sell tickets to events sponsored by community performing-arts and other organizations.
5. If an employee is filling a unique role in a community organization, the editor of the company newsletter or magazine might be inclined to write an article on the employee's involvement, bringing the nonprofit organization to the attention of all the firm's employees.
6. In large companies with many employees, voluntary blood donations can be arranged, with mobile units that can be set up on the firm's premises.

Three: Surplus Equipment and Supplies

Companies often have surplus equipment and supplies that can be used by nonprofit groups. Often the equipment has been fully depreciated, so the company is prepared to give it away. Community groups needing office furniture or equipment should contact the purchasing agent or office services manager of local firms. A good idea is to look for companies that are moving to a new location or have put up new facilities. This often means that some office furniture and equipment may be discarded.

Companies that have surplus equipment or supplies can quickly find a community group that will take the material by putting a notice in the classified section of the local newspaper. We once disposed of 5,000 odd-shaped but usable mailing envelopes in this manner.

Here is a list of surplus or obsolete items that charitable organizations might possibly obtain from businesses: desks, chairs, tables, typewriters, calculators and other office machines, floor coverings, draperies, lumber and other building materials, tools and shop equipment, laboratory apparatus, paper, envelopes, other office supplies, file cabinets, and lighting fixtures.

Four: Publicity Help

Just about every nonprofit organization from the community variety to national groups uses newspapers, magazines, radio, and television to publicize its activities and to attract financial support, members, and volunteers, as well as to maintain its identity as an effective institution. Except for the major state and national groups, these organizations generally do not have professional public relations or media expertise. Any company that has a public relations department or retains an outside agency can offer free publicity support to nonprofit groups in terms of developing and placing articles or new items in the media.

An approach we tried in 1977 was to organize a workshop on public relations, publicity, and communications for the member agencies of the United Way of Santa Clara County. This United Way has about 85 member agencies, and most of them sent staff people or volunteers to attend the one-day workshop in our conference center. It was a successful event organized by my Syntex colleague, Russ Wilks.

Five: Promotional Materials and Services

Producing and distributing promotional materials are essential activities of most charitable organizations. Corporations have creative talent in their advertising, sales promotion, and public relations departments, including copywriters, photographers, and designers. With these resources, a company can offer to develop a brochure, a poster, or a mailing piece.

Since these services don't usually involve significant out-of-pocket costs, providing such assistance is normally not costly to the company. Also, the company's creative people enjoy working on something different, and it gives them an opportunity to get involved in a community project. Finally, in some of the smaller communities, the high level of creative talent in the company may not be commercially available in the area.

Here are two examples of creative services provided by our firm:

- Preparing the copy for a brochure distributed by a children's health-care organization to acquaint the public and referral agencies with the diagnostic and treatment services offered by the organization, and to assist in fund raising and in the recruitment of volunteers.
- Designing a brochure for a nonprofit minority employment service. The brochure was printed by another local company, Hewlett-Packard Corporation. Its distribution increased awareness of the employment service within the minority community as well as in the business community. It gave strong impetus to fund-raising efforts and increased the number of applicants seeking employment counseling and placement.

Six: Printing Services

Some large firms have their own in-house printing facility. It is worthwhile for these firms to do some printing of mailers, posters, brochures, and other types of materials for community organizations.

The cost of doing this in the company print shop is usually less than the same job done by a commercial printer. Let's say a community group gets a $100 estimate from a local commercial printer and asks for a donation from the company to cover the cost. If the company print shop can do the job for $75, it makes more sense to donate the printing than to make a cash contribution.

A potential benefit to the company is that most community groups are usually delighted to give credit for the donation right in the printed piece: "This brochure printed as a community service by XYZ Corporation." This message reaches all the people reading the printed material and is an effective and long-lasting public relations message for the company.

Usually the company print shop cannot meet the same deadlines as commercial printers. It is necessary for the community group to contact the company well in advance of the date that it will require the printed material. This will give the company time to evaluate the request, to determine if the print shop can fit the project into its working schedule, and to obtain an estimate of the in-house cost of printing the item.

Obviously, if the company's estimate is higher than an estimate by a reliable commercial printer, it would be better to offer to contribute the funds to have the work done outside. Even in this case, however, it is usually feasible to have the company obtain credit by requesting a line in the printed item: "Cost of printing donated by XYZ Corporation."

It is remarkable how many printed pieces are used by nonprofit groups. Here is a list of some items printed by our company:

1. One issue of a sixteen-page newsletter and calendar, "West Coast Dance," published and distributed by a regional dance organization. Editorial costs of the publication were covered by a grant from the California Arts Commission.
2. A brochure for a nonprofit organization dedicated to helping unemployed professionals get back to work as productive members of society. It was used to recruit individuals in need of its counseling and related services and to obtain the support of employers and government agencies.
3. A brochure distributed by a county arts council to acquaint the public with the instructional and artistic programs available in the county and to solicit individual and business memberships.
4. Programs for performances of a community chamber orchestra and opera company.
5. A public relations brochure for a mental health organization that provides diagnostic and treatment services to those disabled by mental retardation, epilepsy, cerebral palsy, and other neurological handicaps.

6. A large poster–mailer for a community environmental group working to maintain open space in the foothills of the Santa Cruz mountains in northern California. The poster–mailer was the principal element in a campaign to increase the membership of the organization.
7. An eight-page coloring book used by environmental volunteers to develop student ecological awareness in the elementary schools of the community. The books were sold for one dollar each, and the funds were used to cover the administrative costs of the program.

Seven: Mailing Services

Some companies have office service departments that can handle large third-class mailings. This would be a helpful service for an organization making a broad appeal through the mails to people in homes or businesses.

Eight: Products

Companies that manufacture consumer products can provide useful items to charitable organizations to be used as prizes or giveaways at special meetings or fund-raising events. The visibility of this type of "in-kind" support is high, and the company's support is direct and meaningful.

Nine: Fund Raising

Corporate executives are generally familiar with fund-raising. They also usually have good contacts in other corporations and in the community where they live. Sometimes they know prominent people who serve on foundation boards. An executive's contribution as a fund raiser may be the best contribution that the community group can ask for.

Ten: Loaned Executives

The United Way has depended substantially on loaned business executives for its campaign talent. This approach has worked well for several reasons. The United Way cannot afford to maintain a large professional staff, which would be utilized only in the several active months of the campaign each year. Large companies can sometimes afford to loan a talented executive for the period of the campaign. Not only does this loan provide added talent and leadership to the campaign, but it promotes communication between the organization and the participating companies.

Eleven: Financial Services

All nonprofit groups have to set up a system to maintain their financial records. This system can be simple or complex, depending upon the size of the organization, the size of the staff, and the reporting requirements of federal and or state agencies. Most companies have a financial department that could offer some professional assistance in this area.

Twelve: Legal and Tax Services

Many laws and regulations covering nonprofit organizations are being proposed and implemented on federal, state, and local levels. These pertain to accepted ways of soliciting gifts, restrictions on lobbying activity, tax status, and so forth. Although companies are not nonprofit (by design anyhow) and company attorneys are not usually experts in the nonprofit field, they can usually provide some assistance even if it is only to refer the organization to an attorney who is familiar with these laws and regulations.

Thirteen: Loan Money

There are some situations where it is more appropriate for a company to consider a loan than an outright contribution. Occasionally, a nonprofit organization that receives government or foundation funding finds itself between grants or for some other reason is short of cash. Providing the company can be assured that the regular funds will be forthcoming, it could make a short-term, low-interest loan. One word of caution: Don't make any loan that you can't afford to write off as a bad debt or a contribution if things don't work out as planned.

Fourteen: Company Facilities

If a company has facilities for meetings, it can offer the use of its auditorium or conference rooms to local groups. Depending upon the company's preferences, it can do this on a regular basis or limit such activity to special meetings, fund-raising events, and so forth. Nonprofit groups generally do not have facilities for holding large membership meetings or special events. Sometimes they don't have adequate facilities for staff or board meetings. If a company can provide these facilities, it is offering a worthwhile service that will naturally result in greater involvement of the company and its employees with many fine community organizations.

At Syntex, the use of company facilities has been a major aspect of the company's community relations since the early 1970s. At that time, the company opened a major complex of new facilities in Palo Alto, California, that included a conference center and food service facility. The center has a 150-seat auditorium, six conference rooms of varying sizes, and a large reception area. Before the center was opened, it was decided to make the conference center available to community organizations when not scheduled for company use.

Although the facilities are extensively used by company groups for meetings and conferences, it has been possible to accommodate the needs of many outside organizations. Most company usage is during normal working hours, while community groups have their meetings and events in the evenings or on weekends. During 1977, outside organizations used these company facilities for 103 meetings involving almost 8,000 people, under the direction of my associate, Rita Donovan.

Some of the meetings and events that have taken place in these facilities have been a community child-care conference, a meeting of city housing officials, an affirmative action conference, a community-college film series, a meeting of industrial nurses, a session of the county human-relations commission, two university alumni-club annual meetings, a flower and garden show, a symphony fund-raising event, a high-school PTA program, a chamber-of-commerce board meeting, a hospital staff meeting, a little league luncheon, and a fund-raising event for a state environmental organization.

This direct involvement in community meetings and events elicited a favorable reaction:

- The one-day housing seminar was a big success. About 25 people attended the meeting, including city council members, Planning Commissioners, public officials, representatives of various housing organizations, assistants to state legislators, and a building contractor. The environment was greatly conducive to a relaxed but productive discussion of housing issues in Palo Alto.—*City Planning Director*

- I wish to express my thanks for such a marvelous setting for our workshop. The conference room was spacious, the seats were comfortable, workspace was adequate, the acoustics were ideal, the atmosphere was both pleasing and receptive.—*Association of Industrial Nurses*

- We would like to express our appreciation for the use of the Gallery for our Volunteer Recognition event. The art display was particularly enjoyable. It was neighborly of the company to make its facilities available.—*County Service League*
- Our sincere appreciation for allowing us the use of your wonderful facilities. Convenient, comfortable and stocked with useful equipment—what a treat.—*ZPG–California*
- The reception and dinner were a great success. Almost 100 people attended and there were numerous expressions of admiration for the surroundings and for the general manner in which the whole occasion was carried off.—*Department of Economics, Stanford University*
- The benefit wine tasting was a huge success. Our travel fund has been substantially enhanced.—*California Youth Symphony*

One continuing use of our facilities began in 1976, when we were approached by Foothill Junior College in neighboring Los Altos Hills to make its educational services more widely available to the community. It was instituting a number of classes to be held at off-campus locations throughout the school district, including other public buildings, businesses, and churches.

Our training specialist, Roy Blitzer, got management's approval to try the idea, and he selected nine business, guidance, language, statistical, and chemistry courses that might be of interest to our employees, although the courses were open to all in the community. The program was a success and was repeated in 1977 with two new courses added—biology and word processing—and three discontinued.

One potentially interesting use of our facilities never quite made it. The local Lions Club organizes an annual Concours d'Elégance of classic vintage automobiles. The event is a fundraiser to obtain contributions for local charities. It appeared to be a great idea since our employees would undoubtedly enjoy it as well as the car buffs and Lions Club members that traditionally attended. Everything was checking out well until we rode one of the vintage cars onto our lawn area. The narrow wheels sank into the grass. We couldn't figure out a way to prevent the cars from tearing up our lawn, so the Lions Club has to find another location. I am glad that we checked out this request thoroughly. If we had gone ahead and damaged company property causing some unnecessary company expense, I am sure it would have cooled our management somewhat toward the use of our facilities by outside organizations.

Fifteen: Provide Land for a Garden

With the increasing cost of food and a renewed interest in gardening, companies with vacant land can do a good turn for their employees and neighbors. The firm can set aside some of its open land for a vegetable garden. This doesn't have to be a large parcel, particularly if the gardeners use some of the intensive gardening techniques that require very little growing area to produce a lot of vegetables. Chapter 19 explains the history of a garden on our company's land that utilizes the biodynamic/French-intensive system of horticulture.

8

Helping Nonprofits to Be Managed More Effectively

Americans of all ages, all stations in life, and all types of disposition are forever forming associations. There are not only commercial and industrial associations in which all take part, but others of a thousand different types—religious, moral, serious, futile, very general and very limited, immensely large and very minute.[1]

According to an article by Eli Ginzberg in *Scientific American* in 1976, 5 million people were employed by what Tocqueville in 1835 called "associations" and that we now call *nonprofit institutions.* Employment generated by purchases made by these nonprofits amounts to an additional 1.5 million jobs. This means that 8% of the United States work force in 1973 was employed by or as a result of nonprofit organizations.[2] The Filer Commission, calling this the "third" sector—after government and business—reported that "One out of every ten service workers in the United States is employed by a nonprofit organization, one out of every six professional workers. One ninth of all property is owned by voluntary organizations."[3]

The National Center for Voluntary Action reports that approximately 37 million Americans provided volunteer time to not-for-profit organizations in 1974.[4] The nonprofit sector—which are the various organizations in this country that provide some of our more important social services, help us look after our health, entertain and educate us, protect our environment, and in general, look for our welfare—is huge.

[1]Alexis de Toqueville, *Democracy in America* (New York: Harper & Row, 1966), p. 485.
[2]Eli Ginzberg, "The Pluralistic Economy of the U.S." *Scientific American* (December 1976): 26.
[3]*Giving in America,* (Washington, D.C.: Commission on Private Philanthropy and Public Needs, 1975), p. 11.
[4]*American Volunteer* (Washington, D.C.: ACTION, 1974).

Unfortunately, many nonprofits are run by talented and well-intentioned people who may know little about actually managing an organization. In his book *The Unconscious Conspiracy: Why Leaders Can't Lead,* Warren Bennis said that "Many an institution is very well managed and poorly led."[5] I would reverse his statement to reflect the leadership style of too many nonprofit organizations: "Many are very well led but poorly managed."

Recently, however, attitudes about the accountability of charitable organizations have changed. Nonprofit agencies are becoming increasingly aware of the need to be "professional." They have come to learn that mismanagement or "unmanagement" can discourage donors and cripple their program. Because of the decline in the market value of stock portfolios, the retrenchment of government funding, and changing tax laws, there is less money available to charitable organizations. Following the example of business, nonprofit organizations are increasingly seeking, and finding, management assistance to help them make their money go farther.

While successful businesses obviously stress managerial efficiency and effectiveness in their own shop, until recently most corporations did not have stringent management-related requirements for the agencies that they funded. Partly as a result of the growing professionalism of corporate contributions programs, companies are becoming more and more rigorous with regard to the management capabilities of the agencies that they fund.

Management Workshops for Nonprofits

I first became involved in an attempt to solve some of the management problems of nonprofit agencies in 1975, when our company made a small general-support grant to the Support Center, a nonprofit organization, with offices in Washington, D.C., and San Francisco, that helps other nonprofit agencies increase their management capabilities and thus become more efficient and effective. Our initial involvement was stimulated by the fact that Robert D. Berkowitz, now a group controller at Syntex, was a Support Center board member in Washington, D.C.

Bob Orser, who was then the president of the Support Center, working in the San Francisco office, approached us with a proposal that our firm and the San Mateo Foundation (a community foundation serving our area) jointly fund a series of seven one-half-day management workshops for nonprofit agencies in San Mateo and Santa Clara counties. Both of us agreed to fund the project, and the half-day workshops were held April through July in 1976. They were attended by over

[5]Warren Bennis, *The Unconscious Conspiracy: Why Leaders Don't Lead* (New York: Amacon, 1976) p. 27.

50 community groups representing interest areas ranging from ecology to scouting to quality of working life. There were well over 250 attendees at the workshops, with an average workshop size of about 35.

These seven workshops went beyond teaching particular skills to particular individuals. They also gave everyone involved with a community organization—volunteers, staff, boards of directors, and other community leaders—exposure to high-caliber, concerned "experts," so that each could have an understanding of accounting, program planning, office management, personnel policies, public relations, and board staff relations.

Each half-day workshop featured two or three resource people. Two partners from a local accounting firm that works primarily with nonprofit organizations led presentations on accounting and taxes. A community leader with a clear understanding of how a "good board of directors" functions spoke on the formation, duties, and care and feeding of boards. Bill Somerville, executive director of the San Mateo Foundation, and I spoke on how to get in-kind donations (not just money) from potential donors.

The participants filled out evaluation questionnaires after each workshop, and a follow-up questionnaire was sent out three months after the workshop series was over. The consensus was that the workshop series had been an extremely valuable experience for most of the people who attended. For instance, one group took the planning information and for the first time was able to get its board and staff together for long-range planning. Other groups have utilized resource persons for assistance in legal, public relations, accounting, and staff relations.

Although the company and the San Mateo Foundation provided financial assistance to subsidize the workshop series, each participant was charged a fee of $15 per workshop. Syntex also assisted in designing the workshop brochure and provided our conference center for six of the seven workshops. The popularity and effectiveness of these workshops have encouraged the development of a number of other management-training workshops since then.

In June of 1977, Bob Orser left the Support Center to form the Management Center, which is another tax-exempt organization that helps other nonprofit organizations increase their management capabilities.

The popularity and success of the Syntex–San Mateo Foundation workshops encouraged the Levi Strauss Foundation to ask the Management Center to plan and implement several two-day management workshops, one for 35 executive directors of nonprofit agencies in New Mexico and one for a similar group of 32 from Amarillo, Texas, which were held in Mescalero, New Mexico, in late 1977.

The success of the original program also led to a workshop for 30 nonprofit agencies in Boise, Idaho, early in 1978. Several corporations joined area foundations and individual donors in providing financial support: Mountain Bell, Idaho Bank & Trust, Hewlett-Packard, Boise Cascade, Idaho First National Bank, and First Security Bank.

Management Support and Technical Assistance Organizations

In the past several years, a number of organizations have been established around the country to provide management support and technical assistance to nonprofit groups. They are a relatively new phenomenon, developed as a corollary to the new realization that nonprofit organizations can and should be well managed, efficient, and effective. Some of these provide "hands-on," direct delivery of in-service training and consulting to organizations on specific organizational needs. Others provide technical assistance, such as publications, workshops, and other information and services.

The Support Center

One of the oldest and best-known management support organizations is the Support Center. The people who founded and direct this organization have long understood that the nonprofit sector is a multibillion dollar "industry" providing essential social services. They also know that the nonprofit organizations in this industry often fail to reach their objectives for reasons that usually have little to do with the merits of the services provided or the justice of their causes.

Jonathan B. Cook, managing director of the center, says that his group has identified nine reasons for this perplexing situation:

1. The chief executives of nonprofit organizations are usually program experts (social workers, artists, educators, etc.), rather than trained experts in organizational management.
2. Personal and ego-related factors play a large role in the formation of nonprofit organizations and in their working styles.
3. Many people in nonprofit organizations feel hostility toward big business and the management tools that it uses.
4. Many nonprofit organizations have very small staffs.
5. The reward systems in the nonprofit sector encourage emphasis on public relations and fund raising rather than on good management and program results.
6. The experts in each nonprofit field—the nonprofit organizations themselves—do not participate in the resource alloca-

tion process, except when they are seeking their own grants.

7. Funding sources sometimes follow "fads" and seek innovation, excitement, and affiliation rather than cost-effective impact.
8. Useful evaluation of nonprofit programs is substantially more difficult than computing the financial return on business investments.
9. The nonprofit sector does not have management resources available to it comparable to those that exist in the business world: accounting firms, management consultants, business schools, the brokerage industry, trade associations, information services, etc.

"The Support Center," Cook says, "is a response to these problems." He points out that the center has five program goals:

1. To provide client organizations with a full range of cost-effective management support services.
2. To provide technical assistance in management to broad segments of the nonprofit community through such activities as seminars, workshops, publications, and special projects.
3. To contribute to the effectiveness of other organizations that provide management support to nonprofit organizations.
4. To provide leadership and advocacy for a more effective, better-managed nonprofit sector.
5. To contribute to the effectiveness of the resource allocation and grant-making processes in the nonprofit sector.

In reaching for these broad goals, the Support Center has played an effective and pioneering role. It has

1. Become the most comprehensive source of readily retrievable skill and information on the management of nonprofit organizations.
2. Developed the largest management support organization in the country in terms of size of professional staff and years of management-support consulting experience.
3. Developed an approach to the management of nonprofits that is realistic (in that it takes into account the fact that most nonprofit administrators are not trained in management) and systematic (in that it addresses all the management aspects of running an organization efficiently).
4. Provided direct management support to over 400 organizations and indirect assistance—through workshops and publications—to thousands more.
5. Pioneered the use of comprehensive consulting process techniques—intake, screening, work plans, integration of manage-

ment disciplines, quality control, and follow-up—in the provision of ongoing management support to the nonprofit sector.

6. Conducted nationwide research into the management assistance resources available to nonprofits.
7. Instituted continuing analysis of the merits of alternative models of service delivery.
8. Helped numerous other organizations enter the management support field without "reinventing the wheel."
9. Conducted (with the assistance of interested foundations and corporations) national conferences on management support in 1974, 1976, and 1977, the latest of which resulted in extensive information and resource sharing as well as in plans that will increase the efficiency and effectiveness of all participants—including the Support Center.
10. Received financial support from over 40 separate foundations and corporations—a broad base of funding.

The center has developed and distributed a number of publications, including "You Don't Know What You Got Until You Lose It: An Introduction to Accounting, Budgeting, and Tax Planning for Small, Nonprofit Organizations and Community Groups"; "Give Us a Dollar . . . We'll Give You Change: A Guide to Soliciting Contributions from Middle and Upper-Income Individuals"; and "National Directory of Management Support Organizations." The Center is working on a "Management and Planning Guide for Nonprofit Organizations." The Support Center is located at 1424 Sixteenth Street, N.W., Suite 201, Washington, D.C. 20036.

The Management Center

The work of the Management Center is funded entirely by contributions and grants from corporations, foundations, and individuals. Some of this funding (including ours) is general support. Other Management Center funding is restricted to specific projects. Still other Management Center funding is in support of consulting work with specific agencies. In this case, the funder is involved in determining which agencies will get the assistance.

Here are a few examples of support provided to nonprofits by the Management Center:

1. Provided individual consultation in such areas as bookkeeping and accounting, financial development, program planning, and staff development and utilization to a number of San Francisco Bay Area nonprofit agencies.

2. Provided staff assistance to a planning committee forming an MSO in the Los Angeles area. That committee includes representatives from the Atlantic Richfield Foundation, Dart Industries, and United California Bank. The Management Center's work with this committee is being funded by contributions from the Atlantic Richfield Foundation and United California Bank.
3. Offered a course on fund raising to 35 executive directors of nonprofit agencies in the San Francisco Bay Area. They are currently planning other similar courses, as well as more intensive management workshops for nonprofit agency executive directors and board members.

The Management Center is located at 150 Post Street, San Francisco, CA 94108.

The Grantsmanship Center

In Los Angeles, The Grantsmanship Center provides an array of information and services to nonprofit organizations all over the country. It produces an every-other-month publication, *Grantsmanship Center News,* which contains articles, book reviews, news items, and detailed information about the grant-making rules and activities of governmental agencies, foundations, and corporations. Subscriptions are $15 for one year, $27 for two years, and $38 for three years. The address is 1015 West Olympic Boulevard, Los Angeles, CA 90015.

The center also offers small-group workshops for nonprofit private and public agencies designed to improve the participants' funding and program-planning skills. Over 6,000 organizations have participated in these workshops since the first one was held in Los Angeles in 1972. In the 12 months preceding July 1, 1978, the center conducted workshops in 54 cities in 29 states plus the District of Columbia and Puerto Rico. Two comments from workshop participants are worth recounting. A staff member of the Legal Services Corporation of Virginia said, "The greatest contribution to me was the realization that getting the money means very little if the money is not going to be spent in a productive way." A representative of a small municipal agency said, "What amazes me (considering how hard up we all are for funding) is that more agencies aren't sending their staffs to this valuable training program."

The last comment provokes the question: Why not? Surely many nonprofit organizations aren't aware that this sort of help is available. Others may know about it but may not be in a financial position to send a staff or board member to such a workshop. (The five-day Grantsmanship Center workshops cost $325 per participant, for example.) Corporations can help in both respects by being aware of workshops and other support programs for nonprofits and by recommending that nonprofits participate when corporate executives feel it would be useful. Going one step further, corporations can provide funds to nonprofits so that staff or volunteers can attend such programs.

Other Support Organizations

There are numerous other organizations that can provide some type of assistance to nonprofit groups—on a national, regional, or local level. I'll briefly describe some of them to provide an idea of the scope of services available to nonprofits:

Accounting Aid Society has its headquarters in Detroit (232 W. Grand River, Detroit, MI 48226) and offices in other cities. AAS provides incorporation and tax-exempt application assistance, implementation of accounting systems, and management consultation services.

Appalachia Community Development Corporation serves community centers, crafts organizations, health councils, and other community organizations, primarily in southwest Virginia, east Tennessee, and southeastern Kentucky. It provides financial, legal, administrative, planning and training assistance. ACDC, P.O. Box 432, Appalachia, VA 24216.

Association of Volunteer Bureaus, Inc., serves local volunteer bureaus and community voluntary action centers with assistance in board development, staff and volunteer management, and office systems. AVB, 801 N. Fairfax Street, Alexandria, VA 22314.

Center for Community Change serves community organizations throughout the country by providing general and technical assistance in organizational development, management, and people power and also publishes information about government programs from a community perspective. CCC, 1000 Wisconsin Avenue, N.W., Washington, DC 20016.

Consultants in Community Development serves nonprofits and local government agencies in the Southwest by providing consulting and training in communications, planning, problem solving, organizational development, and general management. CCD, Box 1051, Norman, OK 73070.

Independent Community Consultants serves social-change and community-development nonprofit and government agencies principally in the Southwest, the Midwest, and the

South. Services include planning, fund-raising plans, organizational evaluation, and training of staff, board members, and volunteers. ICC, P.O. Box 141, Hampton, AR 71744.

Metropolitan Cultural Alliance serves artistic and cultural organizations in the Boston area through workshops on nonprofit management, a monthly newsletter, central financial reporting services, an employment listing service, and a matching membership program for corporate support. MCA, 250 Boylston Street, Boston, MA 02116.

National Council of La Raza serves Mexican-American and other Hispanic organizations throughout the country by providing technical assistance, research, training, and management service. NCLR, 1725 Eye Street, N.W., Washington, DC 20006.

National Information Center on Volunteerism serves nonprofit organizations countrywide by providing assistance in financial, legal, board, and membership development and in administration. NICV, P.O. Box 4179, Boulder, CO 80306.

Northern Rockies Action Group serves native American citizens' organizations dealing with resource issues in Idaho, Wyoming, and Montana by providing training in communications, fundraising, community organizing, and organizational development. NRAG, 9 Placer, Helena, MT 59601.

Philadelphia Clearinghouse for Community Funding Resources serves grass-roots community organizations in the metropolitan Philadelphia area by providing financial, legal, and administrative counseling, workshops, and information services. PCCFR, 112 Race Street, Philadelphia, PA 19102.

Public Interest Public Relations serves a wide variety of public interest organizations throughout the country by developing and implementing direct-mail communications and board development programs. PIPR, 50 West 57 Street, New York, NY 10024.

Society of Retired Executives provides volunteers to work with nonprofit organizations in the Indianapolis metropolitan area in the areas of finance, legal, and administration as well as board, staff, and volunteer development. SRE, 320 North Meridan, Suite 510, Indianapolis, IN 46204.

Volunteer Lawyers for the Arts serves nonprofit arts organizations in New York State by providing legal counseling, including a legal referral service, and publishes *Arts and the*

Law eight times a year. VLA, 36 West 44 Street, New York, NY 10036.

Women's Action Alliance provides assistance in fund raising, project organization, publicity, and conference planning. It also publishes "How to Make the Media Work for You," "Getting Your Share" (an introduction to fundraising), and other useful materials. WAA, 370 Lexington Avenue, New York, NY 10017.

The Youth Project assists low-income and minority community-based citizen-action organizations throughout the country, including financial, legal, administrative, and fund-raising services and counsel. YP, 149 Ninth Street, San Francisco, CA 94103.

Business Can Provide Volunteers to Nonprofit Agencies

Corporate employees can help community agencies increase their management capabilities by joining nonprofit organizations' boards of directors, or they can volunteer their services in other ways. Corporate employees are often sought for such positions precisely because of their management know-how, although this specific need may not always be made explicit by the asking agency.

To the extent that the volunteer recognizes and values good management in his or her company—and to the extent that the company recognizes and values the involvement of employees in the life of the community—the volunteer's contribution as a business person in the nonprofit agency will be the more rewarding and the more effective. The role of a business executive on the board of a nonprofit organization can be an important contribution, and for that reason it will be discussed in detail in the next chapter.

Volunteer Urban Consulting Group

In New York, the Volunteer Urban Consulting Group (300 East 42 Street, 10017) has mobilized companies to provide effective volunteers to assist nonprofit organizations. Founded in 1969, the group now has a distinguished advisory council and board of directors that includes: Norborne Berkeley, Jr., president of Chemical Bank; Thornton F. Bradshaw, president of Atlantic Richfield; Albert V. Casey, chairman and president of American Airlines; William Chaney, president of Avon Products; Albert H. Gordon, chairman of Kidder, Peabody; Dan W. Lufkin of Donaldson, Lufkin & Jenrette; John F. McGillicuddy, president of Manufacturers Hanover Trust; Charles C. Townsend, Jr., managing director of Morgan Stanley; Marvin S. Traub, president of Bloomingdale's; John C. Whitehead, senior partner, Goldman Sachs; Byron R. Wine, partner, Weiss, Peck & Greer; and several dozen other well-known business figures.

The origins of the Volunteer Urban Consulting Group go back to the late 1960s, when members of the Harvard Business School Club of greater New York decided that their members could make a substantial contribution to the community by sharing their knowledge and experience. Their first efforts were in the area of minority economic development. Early in the 1970s, the volunteer base of the organization was extended to include alumni of other business schools, such as Adelphi University, University of Chicago, MIT, the University of Michigan, Stanford University, the University of Virginia, and the University of Pennsylvania.

In 1973, VUCG began providing consulting services to nonprofit organizations in New York City and in 1975 undertook assignments for two municipal agencies. It now employs six professionals, four of whom have MBAs. The budget is about $360,000, funded by federal and state sources and contributions from foundations, individuals, and corporations.

VUCG has found a viable way to combine the talents of a small, highly professional staff with hundreds of business and professional volunteers. Consulting services are offered in accounting, financial planning and budgeting, personnel and organizational planning, real estate, insurance, internal operations and systems, and recruitment of board members. VUCG serves as an effective liaison between the nonprofit group with a specific management problem and the business and professional people interested in using their knowledge and skills on a volunteer basis to assist a worthwhile community organization.

VUCG maintains a well-screened and up-to-date resource bank of volunteers; it locates and screens prospective clients to determine if they can be assisted by VUCG services; and it oversees project management, which is critical to the success of the management consulting process. In the first three years, 443 volunteers contributed almost 10,000 hours of consulting time to 122 nonprofit clients.

The volunteers come from three major sources: business school alumni clubs, professional associations, and business firms. The professional associations include the Art Directors Club of New York, the Association of Internal Management Consultants, the New York State Society of Certified Public Accountants, and the Young Presidents Organization of New York City.

VUCG's success with volunteers from alumni clubs and professional associations is due to several factors. It ensures a certain standard of achievement and education. Members of such groups are often the leaders of corporations and professional firms. Executives also seem to respond well to activities affiliated with their own university or professional experience.

In recent years, VUCG has asked local corporations and firms to become "volunteer companies" that can be called upon on an "as-needed" basis to recruit volunteers with specific skills. Volunteer companies have provided volunteers with talents not previously available from the talent bank. They have also been able to recruit three- or four-member teams from the same firm, which facilitates volunteer effort and interaction.

About 25 "volunteer companies" have a relationship with VUCG, which includes regular reinforcement of volunteer involvement within the firm. Avon Products, American Express, Burlington Industries, CBS, Equitable Life, Pfizer, Supermarkets General, and Union Carbide comprise the corporate group. Bankers Trust, Chemical Bank, Citibank, Chase Manhattan, Morgan Guaranty, and Manufacturers Hanover Trust are the commercial banks involved. Ernst & Ernst, Arthur Andersen, Price Waterhouse, and Peat Marwick Mitchell & Co. are the accounting firms. Booz, Allen & Hamilton and Cresap, McCormick & Paget cover the consulting field. The retailers are Macy's and Bloomingdale's. Cravath, Swaine & Moore and Cleary, Gottlieb, Steen & Hamilton are the law firms. A. G. Becker, Bache, and Goldman Sachs are the investment banking houses. It is an impressive group of corporate and professional firms.

One of the strengths of VUCG is its client selection process. As a first step, it asks a prospective client to put a request in writing outlining the scope of the problem and the need for assistance. Often the group in the most trouble cannot articulate its problem. VUCG will, in such cases, agree to discuss the problem, but a written request must follow because the discipline of putting a request in writing is a good indication of how serious a group is about its need for help, according to VUCG.

Often what is articulated is only a symptom of a more serious problem; for example, a request to design a new accounting system might really be a sign of an inadequate financial officer. VUCG finds that getting to the real issue is a skill that comes with experience.

Another key question is whether the VUCG staff and volunteers possess the knowledge to find a solution to the problem. VUCG can solve management problems, but the organization does not become involved in fund raising or program-related problems because its volunteers are not specialized in these areas and there are other organizations devoted to working on these problems.

VUCG has learned that the team approach is the most effective. Volunteers enjoy and learn from exchanging information and discussing management problems with one another. Also, when volunteers work as a team, "peer pressure" encourages team members to fulfill their commitments to the assignment. Finally, a team effort ensures that one member will be available if another member is preoccupied or out of town.

If volunteers aren't doing their job, they are quickly encouraged to resign, and because of the team approach, little momentum is lost by the departure of one volunteer. Progress is tracked on a weekly basis. It is important that project recommendations that are accepted be implemented because VUCG volunteers have lost their willingness to be assigned to a new client when they are not able to see a project through to completion.

VUCG has also established a board candidate service to provide longer-term assistance to its nonprofit clients. It did this after finding out that few business persons were involved on the boards of many of the nonprofit organizations that they were assisting. The pilot phase of the service was a compilation of the résumés of 80 business men and women who were interested in serving on nonprofit boards. The résumé summarized the candidates' educational backgrounds, skills, and interests.

The résumés in book form were distributed to over 400 nonprofit organizations. The "courting" process was left to the nonprofit organization. During the first years of the program. VUCG candidates joined 26 boards of nonprofit organizations.

In an article in the *Harvard Business Review* describing the activities of the Volunteer Urban Consulting Group, the authors said that "organizations like the Volunteer Urban Consulting Group can be created in other localities to bring the skills and knowledge of the corporate community to worthy nonprofit organizations."[6] The authors explained that similar programs

> can be attached to a community foundation, a chamber of commerce . . . or they can be left independent like VUCG—as long as the financial security and credibility of an established organization is built into a new effort.

The authors also said that "a company or a group of companies could run such a program." I would add that the United Way is also a good place for this type of effort to be organized and implemented.

Institute for Not-for-Profit Management

Another approach to improving the management of nonprofit organizations began in 1975 with some discussions between representatives of several community foundations and several major corporations

[6]Richard A. Mittenthal and Brooke W. Mahoney, "Getting Management Help to the Nonprofit Sector," *Harvard Business Review* (September – October 1977): 103.

in New York City. The purpose was to explore ways in which the foundations and corporations could most effectively contribute toward improving the delivery of services of the nonprofit sector, while at the same time reducing the agencies' operating costs. Participating in the discussions were representatives from the Greater New York Fund, New York Community Trust, Citibank, Exxon, Morgan Guaranty, and RCA Corporation.

Out of these discussions came a plan to develop, in conjunction with Columbia University, an intensive, advanced-level educational program designed to maximize the management skills of the chief operating officers of nonprofit private organizations. Columbia agreed to institutionalize the course if an initial set of pilot sessions proved successful. The pilot courses would be supported financially by the foundations and corporations.

Columbia established the Institute for Not-for-Profit Management as a vehicle for conducting the pilot programs. The institute was organized as a joint effort of the Columbia University Graduate School of Business, the School of Social Work, and the Division of Health Sciences. Dr. Thomas P. Ference, director of the master's degree program for executives in the Graduate School of Business was named director of the institute.

Each course spans a four-month period and opens and closes with a week-long program at Columbia's residence conference center, Arden House. The central themes of the seminar course are (1) the strategic planning process; (2) accounting, budgeting, and finance; (3) administration and management; and (4) program service delivery. An important feature of the course is the preparation by each participant of a comprehensive strategic plan for his or her agency.

Each participants in the pilot courses was required to have an undergraduate degree or the equivalent in a field related to his or her current position, and the participant's agency had to have an annual budget of $500,000 or more. Also the agency's board of directors had to endorse the participant's involvement. Each agency paid a fee of $250 per participant, with the remaining cost of the program covered by the sponsoring foundations and corporations. Although the tuition for future seminars has not been set, an estimate by Columbia is that it would be approximately $3,000. Because of this substantial cost, it would be appropriate for foundations and corporations to offer scholarship assistance to enable qualified candidates to benefit from the program if it becomes institutionalized at Columbia.

The first class of 50 participants completed the course in 1977, and these individuals have returned to their organizations. A preliminary evaluation of these graduates indicates a favorable response to the program. After a second class of students completes the course, a comprehensive evaluation will be made by Columbia and the sponsoring organizations to determine the viability of continuing the course.

Good management helps nonprofit organizations meet their goals of improving society and helping people. Management expertise has long been considered a necessity in the profit-making sector. In a time of public skepticism, tightened tax rules, inflation, competition, and rising administrative costs, the nonprofit sector must learn how to manage all its resources more efficiently and effectively. We in the corporate sector should do everything we can to help them do just that.

9

How Corporate Executives Can Be More Effective Board Members of Nonprofit Organizations

America's corporate chiefs lead and participate in a wide variety of philanthropic causes and devote a substantial amount of time to public service activities. They serve as chairmen or members of innumerable boards, fund-raising drives, planning and financial committees.[1]

In the Filer Commission study by Harris and Klepper, the extensive involvement of top corporate executives in a variety of philanthropic and public service activities is well documented. Responses to a questionnaire by 384 chairman or company presidents showed that 92% were involved with at least one philanthropic organization during the previous year—55% were involved with 5 or more organizations and 12% with 10–25 organizations!

These top executives supplied more than nominal influence. The survey disclosed that each gave an average of three hours of their company's time and three hours of their own time to these efforts each week. Although there are no comparable statistics for other business executives at upper and middle management levels, the pattern demonstrated by these chief executive officers is undoubtedly characteristic of involvement by other company executives.

This wealth of personal talent and energy is a rich source of support for nonprofit organizations. Many are already profiting from this source; others are learning to tap it. My purpose is not to document the former or to explain the mechanics of the latter. I do feel that there is a need, however, to improve the effectiveness of the involvement, present

[1]James F. Harris and Anne Klepper, "Corporate Philanthropic Public Service Activities," *Research Papers*, The Commission on Private Philanthropy and Public Needs (Washington, D.C.: Department of the Treasury, 1977), p. 1749.

and future, of business executives in the many worthy organizations where their time and expertise can be beneficial.

Corporate executives are generally thoughtful about their involvement on nonprofit boards. Many serve happily and effectively. For others, however, it can be a frustrating experience. It pays, therefore, for business executives to respond to invitations to join or continue their appointments on nonprofit boards with a sensible appraisal of the organization's needs and their own talents and availability. This appraisal isn't that difficult, and it will help ensure that there will be a happy and productive relationship on both sides. The purpose of the following pages is to assist the business executive to make an appraisal that will lead to a thoughtful rather than a spontaneous involvement.

Nonprofit corporations embrace a wide range of organizational styles, sizes, goals, and budgets. Each, however, has a board of directors—required by law to be responsible for the management of the enterprise. This collective board bears ultimate responsibility and authority for the management of the organization. The *individual* board member has personal responsibility but *no* authority—other than that specifically delegated by the by-laws, or by the full board, to his or her office or committee. Individual board members contribute their decision-making and policy-making skills through the committee and board structure.

Some nonprofit boards have as few as 3 members, some as many as 90. Some boards draw all their members from the same social stratum of the community, while others strive for diversity of cultural, economic, and educational backgrounds. Effective board membership is achieved through interaction with, and performance through, one's group of fellow board members. Therefore, for greatest individual effectiveness, it is of utmost importance to choose the right board, and the right organization, for *you*.

Take Time to Choose

The time to take time is between the question "Will you serve on our board?" and your answer. No amount of time invested after an impulsive "yes" will be as wisely spent as the time you spend right now. No longer is it enough to ask: Is it a good cause? Am I usually free on Wednesday? What is my relationship to this person who is making the request?

If you are considering, and are being considered for, a new job, there are things you need to know; about the organization, about their expectations of you in the new job, and about your expectations of them as an employer. What you know about looking for a job applies to your position as a potential board member.

"Will you serve on our board?" often comes first by telephone. Ask then for a meeting, or job interview, as a follow-up. Arrange to see the board president, the executive director, and a member of the nominating committee—together, if you can. These people are crucial to the agency's present function and future success, and they have the information you need to make the right decision. Take time for questions—*lots* of questions—and don't be surprised if your questions stimulate these three to talk about things they have never discussed with each other before.

At that meeting, talk about the organization, the board, and the staff. Use the questions suggested in this chapter to generate others of your own. If the answers excite your interest, explore in greater depth. If the answers indicate a mismatch, say "no" and look elsewhere to apply your time and talents.

The Candidate

Before the meeting take a look at yourself. Remember that when you decide to volunteer your time and talent, your choice of jobs is virtually limitless. The right choice starts with self-knowledge:

> Have you time—real time—to take on something extra? For two or three months? Or two or three years? Does your company encourage you to volunteer their time? Does your family? Do you seek new challenges? Or new friends? Do you need to make connections with influential people? Which people? Have you a deep commitment to a particular cause? Do you prefer structured situations where everyone knows his job and plays his role? Do you seek new problems or do you have your problem quota? What are your strengths? Weaknesses? Interests? Skills?

The average board meets monthly, for from one to three hours. In addition, board members participate in the work of committees. Planning sessions, budget sessions, program presentations, evaluations of the executive director—all may at some time have to take precedence over your golf match, family outing, or paperwork pile at the office. You will make this happen only if your membership on a particular board complements and enhances other facets of your life. It is your responsibility and privilege to help this happen by choosing the right volunteer role.

Volunteers are paid. In lieu of cash, volunteers are paid in challenge, recognition, camaraderie, good feelings that come from serving, contributing, learning. Find the job that will best satisfy you and best utilize your talents and energies in the service of your community.

The Organization

> Why is it in operation? What service does it deliver? To whom? How? Through what staff? What is the program? Has it changed over the past years? Is it in the process of change? How is its effectiveness evaluated? What are the short-term and the long-term plans?

Effective board members are advocates—for the agency, the service, and the client. If you don't care about what this group cares about, stop right here. If you *know* that all children belong at home with their mothers, the board of the local day-care center is probably not for you. Answers to these questions also indicate the agency's approach to management, nonprofits often being short on long-range planning, long on crisis management.

> Who's involved now? Can you see organization charts of board and staff? Who's on the board? How long has each one served? How many board meetings? How long do they last? How many members attend? Which ones? What do board members do? How much time does it take? What are the background and training of the executive director? Of other professional staff? Is there a bookkeeper? An auditor? A legal adviser?

Answers to these questions tell you something of the attitude present board members take toward their responsibilities. For example, it is not uncommon for a penny-wise board to hire an underpaid and underqualified executive director and neglect to provide for bookkeeping and professional audit. If, in addition, its members do not regularly attend meetings—BEWARE.

> What about money? Can you see the last public financial statement? The latest financial report? How broad is the base of support? How close are income and expense to the amounts budgeted for the same period? Is there a finance committee? A budget committee? A fund-raising committee? Who knows the answers to the financial questions that you ask? Who raises the money? What percentage of board members contribute dollars? Who loses sleep when income falls short of outgo?

Nonprofits *always* need money. Success in the marketplace of service brings more clients, more need for service, more expense, and more need for more money. Client fees and other direct reimbursements, even when they exist, usually play a minor role.

Government agencies, foundations, corporations, and individuals care about effective and accountable use of their contributions. Businesslike systems, controls, and approaches to money promote donor confidence. The same safeguards promote peace of mind for the board member who treats his responsibility seriously and professionally.

You are not unique if you "will do anything for the cause except ask for money," but the typical nonprofit cannot afford more than one or two of you. People give money to causes they believe in but usually not until they are asked by someone they know *personally*. You need to be honest with yourself on this point before you sign up as an asker or a nonasker. Boards composed of nonaskers can operate effectively as introducers or door openers—but only if they recognize that this is their style and compensate by hiring effective askers to follow through.

How Things Work

Board management is a legitimate and important board function. Considerable time may be required to formulate, and to review regularly, policies and procedures pertaining to board function, structure, identification of leadership, and renewal through new-member selection. A scheduled biennial *ad hoc* committee review of board effectiveness is a wise—but not a common—approach.

Many groups, however, mistake board *housekeeping* for board *management*. They enjoy spending considerable time and energy in discussion of meeting dates and sites, plaques for presentation to outgoing officers, and the pecking order of officers, committees, and staff. Groups that spend their time on board housekeeping often are the same groups that spend their time on operational details—to the neglect of policy, planning, and evaluation.

These questions may stimulate lively discussion, differences of opinion, or total disinterest:

> Are the by-laws up-to-date? Are they available and used for ready reference? Do they provide for rotating board? What are the procedures for identifying and recruiting new board members? Officers? Committee chairmen? Do officers, committees, and members have a clear understanding of their responsibilities and functions? Does the board formulate policy (personnel, financial, program, public relations, administrative) through committees? Must all committee members be board members? Can the system tolerate divergence of viewpoint and opinion? Is there honest, open communication between members? Are the service and commitment of board members regularly evaluated?

The board makes policy and engages staff (paid or unpaid) to operate within that policy. This broad oversimplification provides enormous potential for differing board and executive styles. While many styles can be successful, a given individual usually responds better to one than to another.

It may be your style and your expectation to attend a meeting, review the data that are laid out before you, and come to an informed decision based on those data, your expertise, and the expertise and opinions of others at the meeting. If so, you will be ineffective if you are expected to (but not specifically told to) collect the data (e.g., do the wage survey) in advance of the meeting. Many a business executive is disappointed in his or her nonprofit board membership because "no one does anything," never recognizing that he or she is the someone expected to do the doing.

It may be your style to paint policy with a broad brush, leaving skilled subordinates to fill out the details and procedures. If so, you will be ineffective where the staff does not have the skill or where the board chooses to devote its time to operational details in lieu of policy.

The important ingredient is that whoever is expected to perform a particular function knows of, and accepts, his responsibility. "Someone will," "someone should," and "wasn't someone supposed to" are the danger signals in groups where too little attention is paid to this principle. However, the board staff questions are not so much a search for danger signals as a search for information that will help you to explore how things work and how your style might effectively mesh with theirs:

> What are the procedures for hiring, firing, and evaluating the performance of the executive director? Who runs the show? The board? The president? The executive director? Does the board rubber-stamp staff decisions? Does the executive director have the authority and the responsibility to operate within board policies? Who determines the board-meeting agenda? Who staffs the board? Do members do their own typing, data collection, research? Who *identifies the need* for policies, plans, and decisions? Who *makes* policies, plans, decisions? Do board members function as program volunteers as well as policy makers? Do they understand the difference? Who rough-drafts the budget? Writes proposals? Speaks to service clubs? Understands program budgeting? Addresses the fund-raising envelopes? Keeps the records? Does authority equal responsibility right down the line?

The Job

Boards need members with well-known and influential names, with business talents, with money, and with time and energy. These are legitimate needs that can be acknowledged and discussed. If the nominating committee has done its homework, they will have high hopes for your performance in some specific area.

Too often, however, business people are asked to serve in vague, unexpressed anticipation that their business skills will automatically sharpen the agency's approach to finance, cash flow, public relations, personnel, planning, or administration. After short acquaintance, they perceive the unbusinesslike approach of the group, conclude that everyone else likes it that way, and find important reasons to start missing board and committee meetings. These ineffective board members are the victims of poor communication—and so, ultimately, are the agency and its clients.

The first meeting is the time for frank and detailed discussion of the job that you are being asked to do. These questions can help that happen—if you persist:

What are present board strengths and weaknesses? What job(s) needs doing? What talents or skills or influence is the agency seeking? To augment an existing capability? Or to fill a gap? Do they need your name? Your connections? Your secretary? Your knowledge? Your money? Your time? Have they done their homework? Are their expectations realistic?

To Serve or Not to Serve

In some distant Utopia there may be right and wrong answers to the questions you ask. For contemporary purposes, use the answers to develop an understanding of what, why, when, where, and how you are being asked to contribute. Thus armed with an understanding of yourself and of the organization, you can make a decision as to the probability of your success and satisfaction in this job—by client, community, and agency standards, as well as by your own.

Remember that at the time of decision you may have an additional option. Your research may indicate a potentially good match—but you're not quite sure. Your self-inventory may reveal that you have short-term time available—not long-term. A regular diet of lengthy board meetings may be the only negative finding—along with many positives.

If any of these apply, you might explore the possibility of committee, rather than board, membership. Many organizations require that only chairmen of committees be members of the board—and welcome outside expertise and representation in the work of standing or *ad hoc* committees. Such an arrangement provides an opportunity to contribute and participate with a lesser time commitment, and it is often useful as a kind of trial marriage.

Once you find the right job and agree to serve on the board, there are some basic guidelines for effective membership—whatever the size and complexity of the organization. The order of presentation here does not imply order of importance, nor is the preceding discussion intended to imply that the guidelines apply only to new board members. They should be of use, and in use, throughout the full term—and can be of particular use to the board member nearing completion of a first term. At that time, he or she would do well to evaluate service and commitment in the light of these guidelines before deciding whether to accept a second term.

1. *Plan to attend every meeting of the board and of the committees to which you are assigned.* This allows leeway for genuine, inevitable emergencies. Keep those to a minimum, however, because the board needs your presence—empty chairs make no contribution—and because you need to be present. While responsibility for management rests on the full board, liability for mismanagement rests on the full board as well as on each of its individual members.

2. *Bring your business skills and knowledge to the meetings.* The business of the not-for-profit corporation is the business of delivering service to the client. From the symphony orchestra to the neighborhood self-help organization, the common denominator for all board members is their responsibility: to donors—for effective and accountable use of dollars; to clients—for delivery of needed and relevant service. The board of directors is obligated to ensure the best use of dollars in the best interests of the client. Fringe benefits and uncertain liabilities there may well be, but the prime commitment of the individual member must be to the business of accountability and service delivery. What you know about business applies to nonprofits, where client service is the bottom line.

3. *Join the board.* Too often a board member complains: "*They* spend too much meeting time on details"; "*They* don't know where the money will come from"; "*They* haven't done anything about it yet." Until "*they*" become "*we*," the speaker is not a member of the board.

4. *Be prepared to speak and to listen.* Boards vary in their approaches to meetings. Some pay close attention to Robert's Rules, while others rely on group process and consensus. For the group members to apply their varied knowledge and points of view effectively to the making of carefully considered decisions, each must both contribute to, and learn from, the others.

5. *Be aware of multiple roles.* Board members of most organizations fulfill up to four separate roles: (a) *Committee members*—who deal with facts, data, details, and research, which result in policy recommendations for full board approval of referral to committee for more details and reconsideration. (b) *Board members*—who collectively make management and policy decisions on the advice and recommendation of committees; these decisions direct the actions of the staff, and individual members exercise a voice here in the group decisions. (c) *Advisers*—who, upon request, consult with professional staff in the member's area of particular knowledge and skill. (d) *Unpaid staff* (program volunteers)—who perform line functions, under the supervision of the executive director; in many organizations board members perform as program volunteers and must pay careful attention at such times to the changes in the lines of authority and responsibility.

6. *Plan to learn.* Whatever business, social, or board skills the new member may bring, there is a lot to learn. Just for starters, he or she needs intimate knowledge of the organization's staff, program, facilities, finances, service scope, and effectiveness, procedures, and policies. In addition, there is need to know where the agency fits in its community: to understand the extent of the need for its services, the alternative sources of such services, and the political and social forces affecting the client population. For greater effectiveness, the board member must expand his or her understanding beyond the immediate community (for example, political and social forces affecting the client population). If the

organization that the board member belongs to serves youth, knowledge of state and federal legislation relating to delinquency diversion and prevention; national trends in teen birth, marriage, suicide, school dropout, and unemployment rates; current psychological and sociological thought relating to youth—all are important. Imagine, if you will, a bank manager who knows only the procedures, interest rates, and client needs within his own community.

7. *Face up to your responsibility.* Acceptance of board membership assumes acceptance of responsibility for the total enterprise. Subsumed within this responsibility and too seldom noted are (a) responsibility for regular financial contributions—generous in relation to your personal pattern of giving; (b) responsibility for providing leadership—important for every board member, crucial for officers and committee chairman; (c) responsibility for advocacy—weaving your social concern into the entire fabric of your life; (d) responsibility for client service—as the end product of every decision, every action, every meeting; and (e) responsibility for fiscal health—the ultimate burden of top management, without which there is no service.

The responsibilities of your board membership must be high on your list of priorities. Once you take the time to choose the right board for you—and to understand your role as a member of that board—you will increase your effective service to board, client, community, and self.

10

United Giving: The Only Way to Fly?

The executives of medium and large businesses have tremendous power, collectively, over the success or failure of United Way fund raising all over the country.[1]

The Conference Board has reported that about one-quarter of corporate donations go to federated campaigns such as the United Way. This percentage does not include corporate contributions to federated campaigns supporting the arts, education, and other areas. There are no accurate figures for total corporate giving through *all* federated drives, but it clearly represents a substantial portion of overall business support to nonprofit organizations. As such, it automatically requires adequate discussion in a book devoted to corporate giving. Apart from this aspect, there is a growing amount of attention being focused on united giving —and particularly on the United Way because as the American Association of Fund-Raising Counsel points out, it is "the largest fund-raising campaign in North America."[2]

This attention has been generated from various sources: from national health agencies that say they are excluded from the United Way funding mechanism; from minority and other community organizations that feel that local United Ways are dominated by traditional agencies; and from some employers (governmental, nonprofit, and business) that are uneasy about the virtual payroll deduction monopoly that United Way has achieved. The latter uneasiness, I must add, is tempered by the realization of the substantial benefits of united giving to the corporation and to the community.

[1]David Horton Smith, "The Role of the United Way in Philanthropy," *Research Papers,* The Commission on Private Philanthropy and Public Needs (Washington, D.C.: Department of the Treasury, 1977), p. 1355.

[2]*Giving USA 1977, Annual Report,* (New York: American Association of Fund-Raising Counsel, Inc., 1977), p. 39.

It is an effective manner for many employers, large and small, to support a wide diversity of worthwhile nonprofit organizations and causes on a community level. It provides a screening function for those employers that do not have the ability to evaluate for themselves the worth of many diverse community organizations. It provides a mechanism to encourage and involve employees in community service and community support. It also provides an opportunity for business firms to make their own united giving contributions on a matching basis —thereby giving employees a voice in saying where some corporate support dollars will be allocated. Finally, the average expense of United Way fund raising is less than 5% of the amount raised—making it in the minds of the employers a cost-effective manner of collecting funds for charitable purposes.

Nevertheless, companies should realize that it is generally not feasible to fulfill their corporate giving responsibilities by providing *all* their support to community organizations through the United Way. There are several reasons.

Although the local member agencies of United Way are numerous (about 37,000) and most have a history of providing necessary and effective services, there are many nonprofit charitable organizations that do not, for one reason or another, obtain support through United Way campaigns. The Internal Revenue Service listed 691,000 tax-exempt organizations in June 1975, about half of which are religious organizations. The Filer Commission states that "counting local chapters of regional or national groups, there may be as many as six million private voluntary organizations in the United States."[3] Although the United Way is a large and productive force in the funding of the voluntary sector, there is no way that it can meet the needs of all community organizations.

Also, some new community organizations may not be able to qualify immediately for participation in the United Way or may elect, for valid reasons, not to join a united giving effort. In the case of the former situation, a corporate gift may permit the organization to develop its program and achieve a track record that will qualify it to be accepted for inclusion in a united giving campaign. In the latter situation, the corporation should evaluate the organization, its needs, and its objectives, as well as its reasons for electing not to become involved in united giving. Such an evaluation could result in a decision to fund the organization directly.

In discussing united giving, however, it is important to make some distinctions. While many may read united giving as United Way, the two are not synonymous. In fact, while United Way is the most broadly based

[3]*Giving in America,* (Washington, D.C.: Commission on Private Philanthropy and Public Needs, 1975), p. 36.

of the federated fund drives, Combined Health Agencies Drive (CHAD) has had its successes and its headlines; National Catholic Charities and the United Jewish Appeal have a long and solid history; and the National Black United Fund, founded in 1974, reported eight strong and functioning affiliates raising approximately $600,000 in 1975.

Another valid point worth mentioning is that although the business community was responsible for the creation of the united giving concept and has supported this idea generously and enthusiastically for many years, its support of united giving is not restricted to the United Way. Two examples might suffice. George G. Kirstein pointed out in his book *Better Giving* that in 1974 a number of firms, including RCA, Reader's Digest, Prudential Life, Bristol-Myers, and Corning Glass, formed the National Corporate Fund for Dance with a proposed first-year budget of $300,000.[4] It is necessary to mention, however, that this effort envisions company support primarily, and employee giving is not now a major objective—although it could be in the future.

Fund appeals have long been originated by federations, associations, and national organizations as well as by individual institutions or agencies. Apart from the technicalities of internal structure, gifts to, for example, the United Negro College Fund, National Merit Scholarship Corporation, United Way, and locally based community foundations offer a specific and common advantage to the donor. In each instance, the donor supports a broadly identified area of concern, while delegating in varying degrees the responsibility for study, investigation, and decision as to the relative merits of individual service agencies or units.

Many corporations support, for example, the concept of scholarship aid for bright and motivated college-bound teenagers. Most, however, don't have or want to have the staff necessary to set up and maintain a program for the identification and selection of the most worthy scholarship candidates. They delegate responsibility for that process to the National Merit Scholarship Corporation. That delegation enables the corporate contribution to have greater impact on this area of concern than if each corporation were to invite direct applications for scholarship aid from individual students or institutions.

Somewhere a balance must be achieved between the determination to make informed and responsible donor decisions and the corporate investment in personnel and time necessary for the investigation of all programs seeking business support. The decision to disburse some percentage of the contributions budget to united appeals makes it possible to increase proportionately the corporate effort devoted to the consideration of other solicitations.

Possible postures range from "Sorry, but we give *only* to United

[4]George G. Kirstein, *Better Giving* (Boston: Houghton Mifflin, 1975), p. 56.

Way," to "We make a careful investigation including an on-site visit to every requesting organization." While the one extreme delegates all responsibility for the selection of specific donees, the opposite extreme most probably represents an unwarranted effort for most companies. Given the wide range of corporate postures along this continuum, the Harris and Klepper report for the Filer Commission indicates that United Way and other federated fund drives received almost 27% of all corporate contributions in 1972.[5] (By 1976, it was down to 22%.)

What about the United Way?

The United Way of America is big business—generally acknowledged to have been born of frustration in the business community besieged by a multiplicity of fund-seeking drives. Whether the first united campaign took place in Denver in 1887—or in Cleveland at the turn of the century—the concept of a combined agency campaign took root and grew.

National Executive Director of United Way of America, William Aramony, reports a growth from 39 organizations in 1919 to 1,000 in 1947 to 2,307 in 1976. Campaign contributions in 1976 (United States and Canada) were $1.2 billion. Over 37 million individuals, groups, and corporations contributed to that total—which in turn provided for direct services to 30 million families through over 37,000 service agencies. Some 20 million volunteers were involved in the total process—from fund raising through communications, program planning, and allocations to the provision of direct services.

Harris and Klepper reported to the Filer Commission that corporations contributed 41% of the United Way of America campaign funds in 1954, but by 1973 this percentage had decreased to 28%. Gifts by employees, however, have shown an opposite trend, going from 30% in 1954 to 61% in 1973. This statistic refers to payroll-deduction contributions at the place of work.[6]

One thousand of the nation's largest corporations surveyed for the Harris and Klepper report (457 responding) indicated that

- 99% made company contributions.
- 97% had employee solicitation programs.
- 79% loaned employees to United Way campaigns: one out of every two chairmen or presidents served as United Way board or

[5]James F. Harris and Anne Klepper, "Corporate Philanthropic Public Service Activities," *Research Papers*, The Commission on Private Philanthropy and Public Needs (Washington, D.C.: Department of the Treasury, 1977), p. 1761.
[6]Ibid., p. 1764.

committee members, and up to 10% of company employees were actively involved in soliciting for local campaigns.

Nonparticipating agencies sometimes see the United Way as an exclusive and excluding "they"—dedicated to maintaining the status quo; unresponsive to emerging needs and service providers; and aggressively monopolistic in their drive for increased dollars. In some instances, critics have set up competing systems; in others, they have taken their grievances to the courts and to the media.

Corporations see the United Way as a means of allocating contributions to community service; of involving employees at all levels in a group effort for community service; and of responding to a cause in which many employees have a personal stake through their involvement—either as volunteers or as recipients of service—with one or more of the agencies represented in the federation. However, the procedure is certainly not painless, involving, as it does, countless hidden costs in released time; accounting and payroll; and the meetings, planning sessions, pep talks, goals, and deadlines that constitute an in-house campaign.

Employee Participation and Attitudes

Corporate employees see the United Way in the context of their personal relationship with community service agencies. That is, an individual employee with ties to a United Way member agency has a different view from that of the employee whose agency or cause is not, for whatever reason, affiliated with the United Way.

There is some evidence that the well-motivated concern of some employers for the demonstrated needs of local agencies as well as the natural competition of in-house campaigns has made some solicitation efforts less than voluntary—and in some unfortunate cases almost mandatory.

There are obviously some gray areas between "encouragement" and "pressure," but it is vitally important that the company facilitation of employee giving should in *no way* abridge the individual's right of free choice in the selection of those causes that he or she wishes to support. As Richard Carter has written, each person should have the right, "after private negotiations with his conscience, to give time and money to any cause that pleases him," as well as the right "to withhold support from any cause in which he lacks personal interest."[7]

Problems in this area can be avoided by not permitting supervisors to solicit employees directly reporting to them and by withholding information from superiors on whether employees working for them made

[7]Richard Carter, *The Gentle Legions* (New York: Doubleday, 1961), p. 273.

contributions or not—and on the amount of pledges or gifts. It is not difficult to do this. In our company, only *one* individual in the financial department receives the pledge cards from all employees—and this person cannot share this information with any other employee, including company officers. Also payroll deductions are a confidential matter between the employee and the personnel department.

It is not surprising, however, even with these precautions, that the corporation cannot please all its employees through its United Way policy, any more than it can address all the community's needs for service through its own United Way contribution.

When a company sets out to decide the amount of its own contribution to United Way, it is important to ask to what degree the member agencies represent the needs of the community—qualitatively and quantitatively. In some communities, generally towns and smaller cities, the member agencies might well reflect the principal needs of the community. In urban areas, they would tend, for various reasons, not to reflect the priorities of all of the diverse groups in the city. A local plant subsidiary's budget, therefore, might allocate 50% of its funds to united giving, while a corporate headquarter's allocation for united giving might be 10% or less of the budget.

To determine what percentage of its contributions budget shall be earmarked for the local United Way contribution, the corporation should take a close look at its local United Way and the agencies that receive United Way funding.

The 1970s movement toward standardized use of the name *United Way* by the agencies affiliated with the United Way of America tends to obscure the very real differences that may exist between one such local affiliate and its neighbor. Corporations should therefore familiarize themselves with characteristics and policies—and loci of power and influence—within their local United Way. They might investigate:

1. The mechanism for identification and selection of agency admission, review, and allocation committee members.
2. The percentage of community agencies that are United Way member agencies.
3. The percentage of a member agency's budget supported by its United Way allocation.
4. The average age of member agency organizations.
5. The rate at which new agencies have been admitted to membership.
6. The percentage of total allocations made to female-serving as compared to male-serving agencies or to organizations that support the needs and aspirations of minorities.
7. The percentage of representation of minorities or women on review and allocation committees.

8. The fund-raising restraints, if any, that are imposed on member agencies.

In this way, the corporation can assess the role that the particular United Way affiliate plays in its community as a guide to determining its policy for providing company financial support and access to employee giving.

Payroll Deductions: One Appeal for All

Payroll deduction as a methodology for collection and "one campaign to serve all needs" as a slogan are popularly associated with United Way. They rate a separate section here because they are, in fact, fund-raising techniques. Although the techniques are the children of United Way, they are coveted by others.

No wonder that having devised, sold, and thrived upon the payroll-deduction technique, United Way is anxious to protect its territory. No wonder, too, that others long for access to this apparently surefire means of increasing contributions.

I find it uncomfortable to have noncorporate groups feuding over rights to corporate procedures. Are we willing to allow one or more opportunities for charitable payroll deductions? Have the computer and its systems room for more data? Can we devise new systems? Do we want to? These are corporate decisions—to be influenced by community needs, certainly, but also by employee attitudes and the intelligent use of company resources.

The concept of one campaign to satisfy all community needs is unrealistic today. I believe that this can be acknowledged without denigrating the value of United Way volunteer involvement and its agency review and allocation process.

The idea that one contribution can satisfy corporate responsibility to the community is as appealing to the corporation now as when it was first conceived. Present-day realities, however, make it less and less tenable to the thoughtful corporate philanthropist.

The one-campaign-for-all concept requires corporate decisions well beyond the choice of Federated Campaign A, B, or C. Given the cost of the present United Way in-plant campaign, is the corporation willing or able to multiply that cost by a multiple of similar federated funds? How much employee on-the-job time and energy can be diverted to charitable activity? How can that corporate time best be used in the service of the community? If there is to be more than one in-house campaign, how can the present model be adapted to serve the needs of the corporation as well as those of the community?

What of the Future?

In this chapter, I have often opted to pose what I consider to be the right questions—for which I don't always presume to have the answers. I do hope that some corporations will experiment and adapt their united giving goals and procedures to provide some data on what is possible and workable in the way of improvements. In the meantime, we can all be assured that united giving will continue and (I hope) improve. Here is my cloudy view of the future.

On a national level, organizations such as the United Negro College Fund, National Merit Scholarship Corporation, National Corporate Fund for Dance, and others will provide additional alternatives for corporate giving.

On the local-community level, federated combined fund drives will continue. It seems most likely, in fact, that they will proliferate. In addition, they may evolve new patterns—as witness the 1960s growth in the number of community foundations. Designed to accumulate endowment funds for the benefit of the community, some few of these foundations have recently adapted their structure so as to administer corporate giving programs—a role historically seen as that of the United Way.

Corporations would do well, particularly at the local level, to assess their commitment to change, to innovation, to minorities, to particular fields of human service—and to investigate the extent to which that commitment may, or may not, parallel the commitment and operation of available federated campaign options.

If the corporate commitment is to all areas of human need within the entire community, it most probably will plan to retain substantial responsibility for its local contributions within the discretion of its own staff. This will ensure maximum flexibility of response to changing needs and conditions.

The responsibility for local contributions that is delegated to the dedicated volunteers and staff of federated fund drives will be monitored by corporate employees who are well informed as to community needs and services. Hidden costs of in-plant campaigns will be reviewed as a basis for informed response to the pressures for increased availability and use of corporate procedures, staff, and facilities.

PART TWO

11

Aid to Education: A Solemn Duty

The contribution here in question is towards a cause which is intimately tied into the preservation of American business and the American way of life. Such giving may be called incidental power, but when it is considered in its essential character, it may well be regarded as a major, though unwritten, corporate power. It is even more than that. In the Court's view of the case, it amounts to a solemn duty.[1]

Twenty-five years ago, the Chancery Division of the Superior Court of New Jersey upheld the legality of a corporate contribution to Princeton University in the case of *A. P. Smith Manufacturing Company* v. *Barlow.* That landmark decision, appealed to the Supreme Court of the United States but upheld, established the legitimacy of corporate giving. Since 1953, support of education, and particularly of higher education, has been a notable aspect of corporate philanthropy.

The reasons for such support are not difficult to understand. The Council for Financial Aid to Education (CFAE) expresses it this way:

> The case for corporate support of higher education is simply that such support serves the interests of the company and its stockholders. There is a vital interdependence between the corporation and the campus which implies that there are important benefits to business which stem from its support of the academic community. The existence of such benefits means that corporate grants to education represent an investment of the business dollar, not merely an act of philanthropy.[2]

CFAE explains that these benefits to business are people, knowledge, public service, and the social environment. Educated workers are

[1]Report of the Chancery Division of the Superior Court of New Jersey, *A.P. Smith Company* v. *Barlow, 1953.*

[2]*Aid-to-Education Programs of Leading Business Concerns and Guidelines for Corporate Support of Higher Education* (New York: Council for Financial Aid to Education, 1974), p. vii.

clearly a vital element in all corporations, particularly in today's technological society. College and university graduates are, in just about all cases, the principal sources of the newly educated workers that business requires.

Business organizations also depend upon knowledge—almost as heavily as on educated workers. A major portion of basic research is conducted in our leading universities. Out of this effort comes the basis for new ideas that can be developed, produced, and marketed by commercial firms to the tangible benefit of business and society. It is only natural for business to contribute to the wellsprings of knowledge that are the basis for the new and innovative products and services introduced by the commercial and industrial sectors.

There is also corporate benefit from many of the public service functions of our educational institutions. Some of these are well established and widely known, such as hospitals or the educational and cultural programs available to people in the community. Recently, educational institutions have entered new areas of community involvement such as day-care centers, urban planning and rehabilitation, advisory services for minority businesses, and special programs for the foreign-born, the elderly, and the handicapped.

The final benefit that CFAE points out is the social environment. Education is a substantial factor in the economy, in the standard of living, and in the determination of the structure and character of our political systems and social organizations.

Level of Corporate Support to Education

In 1976, 36.5% of the corporate contributions dollar went to education. The only area receiving a larger percentage was health and welfare, with 39.1%. Programs for matching employee gifts increased from 2.8% in 1974 to 3.3% in 1976 because of the growing number of gift-matching companies and the adoption of multiple matching (2 to 1, 3 to 1, etc.) by some firms.[3]

Corporate support to education takes many forms. Here is a breakdown from 1976 statistics[4]:

Unrestricted operating grants	17.0%
Capital grants	15.9
Research grants	15.4

[3]Advance Report from the *Annual Survey of Corporate Contributions, 1976,* based on selected data from *Annual Survey of Corporate Contributions, 1976* (Conference Board) and *Corporate Support of Higher Education, 1976* (Council for Financial Aid to Education).
[4]Ibid.

Employee-gift matching	9.1
Scholarships and fellowships	8.2
Education-related organizations	5.2
Student financial aid	5.0
State and national fund-raising organizations	5.0
Precollege institutions	3.3
Other	15.9
Total	100.0

There have been some significant changes in the areas that corporate contributions have supported in the past few years. Unrestricted operating grants, for example, represented 35% of the total amount of corporate support in 1970—almost double the 1976 percentage. Support for construction of new facilities also decreased from 19% in 1970 to 16% in 1976; scholarship and fellowship support declined from 13% to 8%, and contributions to education-related organizations decreased from 13% to 5%.

While these areas were receiving a declining percentage of corporate support, other areas were receiving more. Research grants almost doubled from 8% in 1970 to 15% in 1976, and student aid went from 4% to 5%. Matching gifts also accounted for a larger percentage of the corporate giving dollar in 1976 than five years earlier. Support of precollege institutions stayed at about 3%.

In dollars, corporate support to education has increased over 12 times in the past 26 years, from $43 million in 1950 to $550 million in 1976, according to CFAE. The 1976 amount represents an increase of more than 20% over the amount contributed by industry in 1975. According to Raymond C. Johnson, CFAE president in 1978:

> There is no doubt that part of this increase is a result of increased corporate profits. However, a great deal of credit goes to the growing number of corporate chief executives who are placing responsibility for corporate philanthropy at the highest levels of management, very often taking active leadership themselves.[5]

The 1975 amount, $450 million, represented an increase of 1% over 1974, when profits declined 10%. "This was the fifth time in the past 20 years," noted Mr. Johnson, "when a decrease in corporate earnings was accompanied by an increase in education support."[6] Business is often willing and able to give more to education when the corporation's own fortunes are at less than record levels. This attitude demonstrates a determined corporate commitment to educational support. It also reflects an awareness of the continuing and accelerating financial problems of higher education.

[5] *Corporate Support of Higher Education, 1975* (New York: Council for Financial Aid to Education, Inc., 1977), p. 4.
[6] Ibid., p. 2.

CFAE points out that "throughout the 1960's, the total expenditures of colleges and universities rose rapidly as a result of the upsurge in enrollment. Between 1959–60 and 1969–70 these expenditures rose at an average rate of 13.9% per year." When the enrollment declines of the early 1970s should have resulted in a leveling of expenditures, however,

> double-digit inflation resulted in significant increases in the costs of all the products and services consumed by educational institutions. . . . As a result of these influences, college and university expenditures increased 11.4% in 1973–74, 14.9% in 1974–75, and 11.4% in 1975–76. In the current academic year (1976–77), the total budgets of all institutions of higher education are estimated to be in excess of $49 billion, roughly double what they amounted to in 1969–70.[7]

Educational institutions are looking to corporations, alumni, foundations, and government funding to help narrow the gap between lower revenues due to decreasing enrollments and higher costs caused by inflationary price increases in salaries and other operating costs. Alumni are now providing about 25% of total voluntary support, and other individual givers and foundations give close to this percentage.

Educational institutions will require the full support of the business community since corporate gifts now represent only about one-sixth of the $2.4 billion of total voluntary support that colleges and universities receive from all sources.[8] There is need to initiate corporate support for a large number of educational institutions that currently receive no meaningful assistance from business. CFAE has reported, for example, that of some 1,700 colleges that had participated in the annual *Survey of Voluntary Support of Education* over a recent seven-year period, only 1,154 had reported receiving *any* corporate support whatever, and many of those received very little. It's not surprising, therefore, that some business leaders have long felt that corporate support must definitely be increased.

About 10 years ago, a group of business leaders in Cleveland pledged to work toward contributing 1% of net domestic income to higher education. This is more than twice the average corporate support given to education. The Ohio Corporate One Percent Program merged with CFAE in 1974, making the 1% goal one of the criteria recommended for corporate giving by the council. The One Percent Plan is beginning to take hold. Thirty-five companies in the Ohio group have increased their contributions to an average of 0.94% of taxable income, according to CFAE, and "more than 100 companies in the U.S. now subscribe to the one percent goal."[9]

One of the most active proponents of setting higher goals for giving is John T. Connor, chairman of Allied Chemical Corporation, who

[7]Ibid., p. 6.
[8]*Annual Report 1976–77,* CFAE, p. 3.
[9]*Annual Report 1975–76,* CFAE, p. 10.

recently served as chairman of CFAE. These are his remarks in the council's *Annual Report 1974–75:*

> This is no time for corporations to be doing anything less than the most they can for higher education. The corporate world has too much at stake in education's continuing quality, diversity and independence to fall short in support now.

Mr. Connor was not just urging *others* to act. He convinced his own board of directors that their company should do more. Early in 1976, the Allied Chemical board adopted a goal of increasing the company's total aid to education by 7% annually, plus the inflation rate used by the corporation for planning purposes. By the way, 7% was the average annual rate of growth of corporate support for higher education in the period from 1949 to 1969—a period of substantial and sustained growth in corporate support. Mr. Connor said that:

> this new goal represents a realistic and practical way for Allied Chemical to increase its aid to education by scheduling a steady rise in the real value of our contributions, regardless of the decline in the value of the dollar.[10]

Business leaders are beginning to respond to this kind of message and example. Arthur M. Wood, then chairman of the board of Sears, Roebuck & Company, and Gaylord Donnelly, chairman of the Executive Committee of R. R. Donnelley & Sons, sponsored a meeting of chief executive officers of leading Chicago firms in 1976. The goal of the meeting was to encourage these corporations to increase their contributions to education and to move Chicago into a position of leadership in this regard.

In the same year, an effort was started under the leadership of Robert O. Anderson, chairman of Atlantic Richfield, to increase corporate support of California educational institutions by California companies. About 12 companies in the group, by the way, subscribe to the 1% concept.

An approach to increased *total* corporate giving in the Minneapolis–St. Paul area will also have an impact on educational support. About 30 companies there have formed the Twin Cities Five Percent Club—pledging to allocate 5% of pretax net income for contributions to all charitable causes. As J. Moreau Brown, former vice-president of CFAE, has indicated, "Even if the percentage going to education remains constant at about forty percent, the increase in the total dollars will mean more dollars for all charitable causes." Brown explained this phenomenon in charitable giving by repeating the old expression, "A rising tide lifts all the ships."[11]

It will be interesting to observe how the efforts of John Connor and

[10]John T. Connor, address at Lehigh University, Bethlehem, Pennsylvania, June 4, 1976.
[11]J. Moreau Brown, "Corporate Support of Education: The Last Frontier," *Grants Magazine* (September 1978): 230.

the former champions of corporate support such as Frank Abrams of Standard Oil of New Jersey (Exxon), Alfred Sloan of General Motors, Irving S. Olds of United States Steel, Walter P. Paepcke of Container Corporation, and others will affect business philanthropy to education in the future.

Corporations that decide to begin or to revitalize their support of education should not have a difficult time finding out how to do it. The Council for Financial Aid to Education, with over 400 supporting corporations and company foundations, has as its primary purpose the encouragement of corporate giving. In carrying out this objective, it has established many activities, including statistical research and surveys to gather information; goal setting; and the preparation of "how to" information explaining the scope and mechanics of various types of educational support.

CFAE communicates this information in a variety of ways, including personal visits to corporations (about 900 a year), conferences for business leaders, media coverage, publicity, and publications. The CFAE "bookshelf" contains all the information a corporation needs to establish an effective educational giving effort. Because of this wealth of information, it is not necessary to get into the details of such activity in this book. The following CFAE publications, however, are particularly helpful in my view. These publications can be obtained from CFAE at 680 Fifth Avenue, New York, NY 10019. The costs shown are 1979 prices.

Interface—Growing Initiatives by the Corporation and the Campus toward Greater Understanding. Outlines more than 100 initiatives by corporations, colleges and universities, and others that have brought together the corporate and academic worlds, including new courses, faculty-loan programs, visiting fellows, dialogues and meetings, student internships in business, career counseling, enlistment of executive talent for better campus administration, and joint ventures to solve national and local problems. (68 pages; 1977; $10.00.)

The CFAE Casebook. Aid-to-education programs of over 200 leading business companies, listing administrators, total budgets, and allocations by program. (10th edition, 1978; $12.00.)

Voluntary Support of Education, 1976–77. Contains a college-by-college listing of voluntary support by sources as well as a tabular and historical profile of voluntary support by source and purpose. Data from leading independent secondary and elementary schools are also included. (Published annually; $9.00.)

Corporate Support of Higher Education, 1976. Based on an annual survey of corporate contributions jointly undertaken by

CFAE and the Conference Board, this study reports on national trends in corporate giving to colleges and universities by industry groups, by marketing areas, and by purpose. ($3.00.)

Guidelines for Corporate Support of Higher Education. The rationale for corporate support of higher education, how to establish a program, and a suggested checklist for processing requests for support. (12 pages; 1975; $2.00.)

How Corporations Can Aid Colleges and Universities. A quick look at the ways in which the average company can offer higher education a helping hand and at the same time benefit itself. (28 pages; 2nd printing, 1974; $2.00.)

How to Develop and Administer a Corporate Gift-Matching Program. The essentials that the corporate contributions executive will need to know in order to set up an efficient and rewarding employee-gift–matching program. (22 pages; 1977; $2.00.)

How to Develop and Administer a Corporate Scholarship Program. The rationale for corporations' having an interest in funding scholarships for children of their employees and other young people and the best ways to set up a program are discussed in detail. (44 pages; 1975; $2.00.)

Guidelines for a Corporate Fellowship Program. Corporations wishing to stimulate the growth of knowledge in their own or any other field of specialization, and those interested in preserving the research facilities and faculties of the major universities, will find many useful suggestions in this booklet. (52 pages; 1976; $2.00.)

"The Welcome Mat Is Out." Highlights of the survey conducted by Louis Harris and Associates, Inc., for CFAE, which uncovered the enthusiastic interest of academia in closer relationships with the corporate world. Includes 750 interviews with persons from 150 colleges and universities, both public and private. "A rare opportunity for corporate–campus interaction exists that should be grasped now, because it may not always be there." (20 pages; 1977; no charge.)

New Goals for Corporate Giving to Higher Education. A summary of the need for new approaches to corporate giving, with suggestions of a number of possible ways of formulating goals for educational support. (16 pages; 1975; no charge.)

The Contributions Executive. A quarterly newsletter with news, facts, and ideas for the executives in charge of company aid-to-education programs. (Available only to corporate executives.)

A perusal of these publications will disclose that there are many ways that corporations can assist colleges and universities. They include unrestricted operating grants, as well as restricted operating grants for research, departmental programs, faculty compensation, international education, library assistance, physical plant maintenance, and other needs. Capital grants can be made for new facilities or to endow important chairs of teaching. Aid can be channeled to individuals in the form of scholarships, fellowships, educational loan programs, and teacher recognition grants.

Corporate Matching Gifts

Programs of matching employee charitable gifts have been in existence for several decades. The Corporate Alumnus Program started by the General Electric Company in 1955 was the forerunner of this effort. J. Moreau Brown, who served as vice-president of the Council for Financial Aid to Education (CFAE), put this first program together when he was at General Electric. More than 700 corporations now match employee gifts to educational institutions—generally at the range of $25 – $500 per gift.

The Council for Advancement and Support of Education (CASE) serves as a clearing house for information on corporate educational matching-gift programs. It publishes annual reports on gift matching, including "Matching Gift Details," containing the names of participating firms and major provisions of all known corporate educational gift-matching programs. These materials can be obtained by writing to CASE, Suite 530, One DuPont Circle, Washington, DC 20036.

Because information about matching educational gifts is readily available from CASE and CFAE, it is not necessary to go into all the details of this program. It might be helpful, however, to summarize the important aspects of the matching-gift concept:

> The matching idea itself is simple. The sponsoring company or foundation anounces to employees that it will match their contributions to colleges, universities, technical institutes, and sometimes precollege institutions. As a rule, the matching will be on a dollar-for-dollar basis up to a prescribed ceiling. Each company establishes its own ground rules covering such matters as (1) employee eligibility, (2) institutional eligibility, (3) minimum and maximum amounts per gift which will be matched, (4) maximum amounts per employee, (5) maximum amounts per institution, (6) the kinds of gifts, (7) the frequency of payment, and (8) the administrative procedures to be followed.[12]

---

[12] *Handbook of Aid to Higher Education* (New York: Council for Financial Aid to Education, 1974), p. A-42.

Employers who are not comfortable with an open-ended commitment may be concerned about instituting a matching-gifts program. A reasonable forecast of expenditures can be estimated, however, by the following formula (annual cost = .02 × number of employees × $100). After the first year, the company will have actual experience as a guide to future budgets.

There are three basic benefits of gift matching:

1. It is an appropriate way for the company to support the institutions that have educated its employees.
2. It provides a strong incentive for employees to support the schools they have attended.
3. It allows the employee to share in the decision as to where the company and its educational support should go.

Matching-gifts programs have generated a significant level of support for educational institutions in the United States. In 1976, according to CASE, about 700 companies contributed $15 million to 1,200 colleges, universities, and independent schools through matching-gift programs.

There is plenty of room for expansion of the gift-matching concept, since only a small percentage of the 4.5 million eligible individuals nationally actually participate! There has been some disappointment at the relatively low participation, although the dollars generated are recognized and appreciated.

Some companies are attempting to make up for the relatively low participation by matching on a two-for-one or even a three-for-one basis. The two-for-one firms are Carrier Corporation, Gulf & Western Industries, International Paper, Jewel Companies, Johnson & Johnson, Montgomery Ward, Pennwalt, Polaroid, SCM Corporation, Teledyne, and several dozen other major companies. The elite three-for-one companies among major firms are CertainTeed Corporation, Exxon, and Quaker Oats.

A matching-gifts program results in a dispersion of company funds to a number of institutions even for a corporation with several thousand U.S. employees such as Syntex. We began our program in 1969, and matching gifts have gone to over 50 college and universities:

University of Arizona
University of Arkansas
Brigham Young University
Brown University
Bryn Mawr College
University of California
University of Colorado
Colorado College
Dartmouth College
Dominican College
Douglas University
Drew University
Gallaudet College
Georgetown University
Golden Gate University
Harvard University
Holy Cross College
Johns Hopkins University
Kenyon College
Lakeland College
Lawrence University
Lehigh University
Lincoln College
Menlo College
Mills College
University of New Mexico
New Rochelle College
New York University
Northeastern University
University of Oregon
Oregon State University
University of the Pacific
Pomona College
Pratt Institute
Princeton University

Ripon College
Simmons College
University of Southern California
Stanford University
Valparaiso University
Valley Forge Military Junior College
Virginia Military Institute
Washington and Lee University
Washington University
Wheelock College
Whittier College
University of Wisconsin
Worcester-Polytechnic Institute
Yale University

I would like to emphasize the importance of matching gifts by one example: Dartmouth College. For this information, I am grateful to J. Moreau Brown, class of 1939, and Robert J. Finney, Jr., Director of Development at Dartmouth.

In the 1976–1977 year, Dartmouth received $1.3 million in corporate support, from 543 companies. Over one-third of the funds were matching gifts from 458 firms. The matching gifts ranged from $10 contributed by several companies to $31,511 from Exxon—and averaged $1,043 from each of the 458 matching-gift firms.

Eight firms gave $10,000 or more in matching gifts. These included Aetna, American Express, Arthur Andersen, Citicorp, Exxon, Ford, Gulf Oil, and IBM. Their combined matching gifts accounted for 25% of the total gift-matched dollars.

I would like to mention that Dartmouth has always been one of the leading institutions in terms of its ability to encourage a large percentage of its alumni body to contribute annually: 60%. This is an important factor in its achievement of a high level of gift matching from business firms. Obviously, if the percentage of alumni who give is small, this seriously limits the potential of gift matching and vice versa.

I am pleased that my own *alma mater,* Holy Cross College in Worcester, Massachusetts, has also achieved a high percentage of alumni support. Digressing from matching gifts for a moment, I actually became interested in aid to education while I was still attending Holy Cross. Another member of the class of 1952 and myself were asked in our senior year to serve as co-chairmen of our Silver Jubilee Gift Committee.

Although it was difficult to be thinking 25 years into the future, we felt it was important to take some steps to ensure that our return to the college in 1977 would be not only enjoyable to us but meaningful to the college in terms of a substantial class gift.

Another alumnus of the college was in the insurance business and suggested a plan for our class to get a head start on its fund raising for the Silver Jubilee Gift. It was a simple plan but an effective one as it worked out. We encouraged 105 members of our class each to purchase prior to graduation a $1,000 life insurance policy with premiums payable for 25 years. Each purchaser agreed to have the accumulated dividends from the policy flow into the Silver Jubilee Gift fund, where they gained further interest. Fifty-six members of the class paid their premiums for the full 25 years, accumulating $32,660.91 of dividends and interest for the class's 25th anniversary gift fund. With this auspicious start to the campaign, our class donated $156,419 in 1977—the highest amount given by any Silver Jubilee class in the college's history.

As an added fillip, several members who maintained the original insurance policies for the quarter century were encouraged to name Holy Cross as the beneficiary of the policy so that the college will ultimately share not only in the interest but in the proceeds as well.

Matching gifts do not require much promotion to maintain the stream of dollars from the companies. All that needs to happen is for a graduate or friend of the university to write a check to obtain the company gift. That's a nice way to raise money. It's also an excellent way for institutions to receive broad-based unrestricted support from the private sector.

There is need, however, for better communication and encouragement of employee gifts by the companies that have such programs. There is also need for educational institutions to encourage matching gifts among their alumni and friends. Some companies will provide lists of employees who are graduates of a specific school so that the institution can contact these individuals to request a personal gift that will trigger a matching company gift.

Scholarships for Children of Employees

Another way of providing company educational support and increasing employee involvement in contributions programs is to set up college scholarships for the children of employees. It is possible to do this with a tax-deductible contribution, provided certain IRS conditions are met.

One effective way of doing this is through the National Merit Scholarship Corporation. The company and NMSC agree on a minimum and a maximum scholarship award. This provision is necessary since the awards, after being made on academic ability, are related to financial need.

The company announces the scholarship competition, including test dates, and distributes applications to all employees. The forms are returned to the company, then sent to NMSC, which administers the competition. Based on the outcome, NMSC notifies the sponsoring company of the names of the winners and the recommended amount of the awards.

Using NMSC has several advantages. The company does not have to do any testing or financial evaluations. This procedure ensures all that the scholarship award will be based solely on merit. For information about an employee scholarship program, contact National Merit Scholarship Corporation, 990 Grove Street, Evanston, IL 60201.

Another organization that administers a corporate scholarship program is the Citizens' Scholarships Foundation of America, Inc. In 1978, it was conducting 13 programs at a low administrative cost of 5% or less of the awards distributed. The foundation is located at One South Street, Concord, NH 03301.

Most corporate support of education has been given to private institutions of higher learning. This is necessary and understandable. Our company's support has been given principally to privately supported colleges and universities. This support has gone to institutions that have educated our employees; to those that are performing scientific research in areas of particular interest to the company; and to those with which we share a close relationship because they are near our major facilities.

This is particularly true of Stanford University—one of the world's leading educational institutions. Our company offices, our international research center, and the headquarters for our operations in the United States are located on land leased from the university in the Stanford Industrial Park. This proximity and the sharing of many educational and scientific interests with Stanford has resulted in a considerable amount of company support going to Stanford programs and projects.

There is an interesting story about the beginnings of the relationship between Stanford and Syntex that illustrates how corporate support of education can have a dramatic impact.

In 1957, Proctor and Gamble selected Stanford University as one of 10 universities scheduled to receive a gift of $20,000 annually for at least five years. Stanford decided to use this money to strengthen its chemistry department and reported to Proctor and Gamble a year later that it had hired two chemists with exceptional scientific credentials in the field of the synthesis of steroid compounds. One was Dr. Carl Djerassi, who had joined Syntex in Mexico City in 1949 to help Dr. George Rosenkranz, the present chairman of Syntex, to perform some exciting scientific work that *Fortune* in 1951 said was "probably the most remarkable technological contribution ever to come from south of the border."

It was Djerassi who was instrumental about a decade later in recommending to the Syntex board of directors that Syntex should establish in the Stanford Industrial Park of Palo Alto, California, its first United States-based research institute (molecular biology) in 1961 and, a few years later, its international research center on a 105-acre site in the park. It did so in the early 1960s. By 1975, Syntex had developed this site into a major complex of research buildings, offices, and a pharmaceutical manufacturing facility.

Syntex prospered in its new location and expanded worldwide as a producer of pharmaceuticals, animal health products, and fine chemicals. Its commercial success enabled the company to establish a contributions program. Meanwhile Stanford's chemistry department continued to expand and needed a new building in the mid-1970s. Syntex was asked for support and pledged a major contribution. The $20,000 grant of Proctor and Gamble had indeed developed unforseen but fantastic leverage!

Support of Stanford University is consistent with our belief that we should concentrate our giving in those locations where we have facilities and people and where there is a potential for involvement on many levels and in many areas between the institution and our company and its employees.

This involvement is also based on our belief that corporations do indeed have *a solemn duty* to support those colleges and universities that are doing an effective job of teaching the business and other leaders of the future. It is my belief that our institutions of higher learning are doing a good job in this regard, and I believe that most business leaders would agree with this assessment.

Need for Corporate Attention to Primary and Secondary Schools

There is another level of education, however, that is moving into a deep performance crisis: our elementary and secondary schools. This problem was highlighted recently in a *Business Week* article, "Costly Schools That Do Not Educate," by Theodore H. Martland, deputy superintendent of Schools in Waterbury, Connecticut.[13] Martland states that there were 49 million children enrolled in elementary and secondary schools in the 1977–1978 school year—about 90% of them in public schools—where they were taught by 3.5 million adults. Expenditures for education *at all levels* are expected to reach $144 billion in 1978, or $12. billion more than 1976–1977, he said. Since CFAE estimates the total budgets of all institutions of higher education in the academic year 1976–1977 to be in excess of $49 billion, this would leave about $83 billion as the cost of other educational programs in 1976–1977. This means that about 63% of the educational dollar goes to institutions other than colleges and universities and that the bulk of this amount is spent by public elementary and secondary schools.

Given the rapidly rising rate of school expenditures, Martland said that they "would absorb the entire gross national product by the year 2000." He pointed out that "since 1940, salary costs have increased tenfold—far in excess of the rate of inflation in the rest of the economy" and that "cost per teacher has risen at the same time that the average number of pupils per teacher has been reduced." He mentioned the following factors as the reasons for the growing cost-effectiveness crisis in public school systems across the country:

[13]Theodore H. Martland, "Costly Schools That Do Not Educate," *Business Week* (January 30, 1978): 9.

- Decreasing teacher-pupil ratios that are not proven to have any direct effect on student achievement and rates of learning. He reports that a Rand Corporation study in 1972 stated the "reduction in class size, a favorite high-priority reform in the eyes of many schools systems, seems not be related to student outcome."
- There is no correlation between pupil or teacher performance and the salaries and other benefits awarded to teachers in public school systems. "Contrary to what most educators say publicly," he said, "few teachers are observed, assessed, guided or managed."
- The traditional weak management of public schools is getting worse: "Until school administrators are assigned management prerogatives, responsibilities, and authority, schools will continue to be mismanaged and unaccountable."

Martland ended his fine article by saying, "It is time to rethink the whole education question and to demand that the educational establishment produce an effective system that truly focuses on the individual student and the needs of contemporary American society."

I also believe that most businessmen will appreciate Superintendent Martland's analogy:

> Imagine, if you can, a corporation where the workers with the most demanding tasks are at the low end of the pay scale, where the supervisors have no control over personnel, operations, or funds, where the board of directors negotiates directly with the union to set pay scales and working conditions. You have just described a typical American school system, and in doing so, you have identified some of the things that have produced a shocking increase in educational costs with no demonstrable improvement in the product.

Martland points out that "If the educational system continues on the path it has been following, it will soon face taxpayer revolts." In California, this has already happened.

Residents and businesses are much less willing to approve higher local school budgets because of the escalating tax burdens they impose. In California and many other states, the property tax is the principal method of raising funds for local public schools. There have been enormous increases in such taxes in recent years in most California communities. California's Proposition 13 has shifted more of the educational funding burden from the local community (property tax) to the state (income and sales tax). Whether this will alleviate the increasing gap between school costs and school revenues remains to be seen.

This is a situation that has important consequences for businesses that pay property taxes—and most do. Prior to the passage of Proposition 13, the amount of property taxes our company paid that were allocated to local public school education in the Palo Alto area was about one-half million dollars! And this figure is only for our principal location in the United States. It doesn't include property-tax allocations by our subsidiaries in other parts of the country. Corporate support of public school districts through property and other taxes represents the major "contribution" of business to education. It is not a voluntary one, of course, but the dollars are real and significant. It is important for corporations, therefore, to monitor how these corporate tax dollars are being spent and to become involved with organizations that are working for effective education at an affordable price.

Our company has always felt that there is need to focus some attention and resources on education at lower levels. Primary and secondary schools are eligible recipients of our gift-matching program. That is why we have given support to several organizations and institutions that are doing some innovative things in terms of improving the quality of public education at the elementary and secondary levels and in terms of providing special programs to certain types of students. There are three examples that I would like to describe: the Palo Alto Learners Association, the Children's Health Council, and the Charles Armstrong School.

Palo Alto Learners Association

Many professionals and some parents are concerned with the ability of the public schools to cope with special educational problems and to provide alternative methods for those students who can profit from them. There are three reasons that I say this. First, most school districts have grown rather large over the last 20 years and now suffer from many of the problems that most large institutions seem to have acquired. They contain a large number of established programs, but when special needs arise, they are simply not able to move quickly or at all.

Second, in many school districts enrollments are now beginning to decline, and this, combined with inflation, means that budget cuts or tax increases are necessary. Of course, there is something positive about this situation in that school districts are being forced to redefine their priorities, but it also means that some established and proven programs will be cut and that new programs will have very little chance of being implemented, regardless of their importance.

Third, in California and many other states, teachers have won the right to collective bargaining. This is by no means improper and may even be necessary, but it does mean that school boards and teachers tend to view themselves as adversaries and to spend much of their time negotiating contracts. My fear is that the students will be the losers at the bargaining table.

Given my concern about the future of public school programs, I was interested in the creation in 1974 of a new organization, the Palo Alto

Learners Association (PALA), whose purpose is to represent the *learner* and the learner's *educational interests.* Such an organization may strike some as unnecessary, since traditionally both school boards and teachers have argued that they represent the students (I prefer this term to *learners*) and that students are their prime concern. I am sure that most school boards and teachers feel this way, but given their developing adversary relationship, the necessity of budget cuts, and the fact that school boards represent business and residential taxpayers, administrators, and teachers as well as the students, I am not sure that the decisions being made are always the best ones for the students. Also I would argue that an organization like PALA can represent parents more effectively than they have been represented in the past. (Generally they have had to rely on petitions to or attendance at board meetings, and the PTA has been more a service organization than an aggressive lobby.) In any case, I can see no harm from such an organization—whose voting, dues-paying membership of 100 consists primarily of parents, plus a few older students (all employees and residents of the school district are eligible to join)—and I see much possible good.

Thus far, PALA has proven to be an energetic group and has had some positive effect. For instance, two years ago it argued for an alternative budget preparation that would identify the costs of various instructional programs, for example, math, English, and even physical education. It also argued for the appointment of a trained negotiator from outside the regular employees of the school district to represent the board of education in negotiations with the teachers. In both cases the board agreed. It is not entirely clear precisely how much influence PALA had in these decisions (they may have been ideas whose time had come), but clearly PALA had some influence.

Primarily, PALA spends its time studying the proposed contracts between the school board and the teachers and then recommends changes, always arguing from the point of view of the possible effects on the students. For example, it does not currently favor a reduction in class size. At least, it does not in Palo Alto, where the student–teacher ratio is one of the lowest in the state. Reduced class sizes are beneficial (although they are not the answer to all problems, as we naively assumed in the 1960s), but such reductions, PALA argues, should not take place at the expense of special programs that the students sorely need. In another district, of course, a group like PALA might very well argue differently.

PALA has successfully argued against the teachers' organization's being able to negotiate procedures for program evaluation and for setting district priorities. PALA felt that these are the prerogatives of the school board and that if they were negotiable, the public would be, in effect, excluded from participating in the determination of these procedures. At present, PALA continues to argue against the existing inclusion of instructional supervisors, who perform both supervisory and evaluative functions, in the bargaining unit of the employees whom they supervise and evaluate. Such inclusion, PALA feels, will compromise the evaluation process and will ultimately affect the quality of programs and instruction. As a manager, I couldn't agree more. The division of supervisors and those supervised is one that most labor unions readily recognize, and I am amazed that the inclusion of these two groups in the same bargaining unit ever came about.

PALA's ultimate goal is to be seated at the bargaining table as a recognized representative of the students. This is not a proposition that school boards or teachers' organizations are likely to accept at present, and PALA does not expect such inclusion to happen soon. They have hopes, however, and in the meantime will continue to promote what they feel is best for the students.

The company's support of PALA began with only a modest contribution. But this is a case in which a little support may go a long way. The organization is a small one and just beginning to become effective, but to my mind it is important for more than its local influence. I would hope that it can become a model for similar organizations throughout the country so that parents, students, and even teachers can have an alternative voice in the important educational decisions that will be made in the next decade. PALA's address is 570 Alvarado Row, Stanford, CA 94305.

Children's Health Council

Perhaps the least understood but fortunately the fastest-growing area of education deals with the mental, physical, emotional, or other handicaps that make it difficult for children to live a normal life.

The Children's Health Council in Palo Alto, California, is one of the first organizations founded in this country to deal with these serious problems in a multidisciplined way. Dr. Esther B. Clark, a pediatrician at the Palo Alto Medical Clinic, started the organization in 1953. At that time, it was primarily concerned with children who were mentally retarded or physically handicapped.

As the years passed, however, the State of California opened facilities for such children, and the Children's Health Council changed its focus, somewhere in the mid-1960s, from mental retardation to other disabilities. At present, even though many local school districts have programs for the educationally handicapped or learning disabled, the council still operates in this area and is one of the few organizations that can deal with the more severe cases.

The council, in fact, works closely with the local schools, and many of the children it works with are referred by them. The schools in turn deeply appreciate the council's services because their psychologists are unable to deal adequately with all the children they should. In some cases, they lack the diagnostic resources to do so, and in some cases, they are simply understaffed. On the elementary level in Palo Alto, for example, there is one psychologist for every two schools, or some 600--700 children. The council also takes children referred by physicians or brought in by parents who feel that they have nowhere else to go.

The council handles as many cases as it can, and in 1976, it handled more than 700, accounting for 20,000 visits to the institution. Once it accepts a referral, it then administers a large number of tests for intelligence, neurological abnormalities, physical coordination, learning disabilities, and mental health. The testing program involves many professionals who then meet to talk about and diagnose the child's problems. The diagnosis may result in the council's accepting the child into its own programs or in referral to another organization or back to the schools. A child suffering from schizoprenia (this is rare), for example, will be referred to a psychiatrist. Or perhaps the child, once his problem and an individualized program have been defined, can in fact be accommodated by the public schools.

One of the unique features of the council is its day school for children up to 8 years of age. The school's capacity is 40 children, and the council hopes that after age 8 these children can return to the public schools. Typically, there are eight children in a classroom with two teachers and a volunteer, and such a ratio of staff to children is absolutely necessary. These children, who may suffer from emotional problems, language and other learning disabilities, hyperactivity, or coordination problems, need a great deal of special care and individual attention in order to overcome their difficulties, gain an appropriate achievement level, and rebuild their confidence in themselves. Their days must be planned almost to the minute; left alone for five minutes, many will become physically aggressive and or go out of control.

The council also offers counseling for parents, which is almost as important as the programs for the children. Children with handicaps are often difficult, and many parents are unable to cope with them. The council's hope is that if the parents can understand the kind of problems their children experience, they can better cope with and even help the children. Small changes in family routines, for example, or changes in parents' expectations of their children often make an enormous difference.

The council's budget for 1977 was about $750,000. Of this, approximately 40%, or $300,000, came from revenue for services rendered. This amount included only about $100,000 from patient fees, which are on a sliding scale based on ability to pay. The balance in this category consisted of state and county funds. The remaining 60% of the budget, or $450,000, resulted from individual gifts and donations; from corporate gifts; from foundation grants; from remembrances and bequests; and from its ongoing fund-raising events.

Obviously the council has attracted much local support, in terms of both corporate and individual giving and volunteer labor. It has, for example, an auxiliary that operates several local shops for the council's benefit and that organizes fund-raising activities, such as the annual summer concerts conducted for a number of years by Arthur Fiedler. At the same time, the council's administrative expenses were less than 15% of its budget, which, I should note, is quite low.

Some 10 years ago, I joined the council's board of directors for a year to help the council with its fund-raising program, which even then was quite good. The Children's Health Council is at 700 Willow Road, Palo Alto, CA 94304.

The Charles Armstrong School

Another exceptional institution is located in our area: the Charles Armstrong School, which teaches children with specific learning disabilities. Learning disabilities have many manifestations, including delay in learning to talk; difficulty in learning and remembering printed words, reversal of some letters (such as *b–d, p–g*) or the order of letters in words *(was–saw, quiet–quite);* persistent and bizarre spelling errors; delay in establishing right- or left-handedness; confusion about directions (right and left, up and down); cramped or illegible handwriting; and defective skills in the mechanics and organization of written composition.

These specific learning disabilities have been given the name *dyslexia.* It is believed to be hereditary; and most of its victims are male—75 to 85%. It was first identified during the 1920s by Dr. Samuel Orton, a neurologist and professor at Columbia University. The 6,000-member Orton Society is a national organization that disseminates information on the considerable amount of research that is being done to understand and treat dyslexia.

There have been some well-known dyslexics who have coped with their learning handicaps, including Albert Einstein, Thomas Edison, and Nelson A. Rockefeller. J. William Adams, headmaster of the Caroll School in Lincoln, Massachusetts, which specializes in teaching dyslexics, believes that there are millions of adults who still may not know the source of their reading difficulties. In a *Wall Street Journal* article, he related

> the case of a middle-aged dyslexic business executive who never learned to read and guards against his family discovering his secret. Nightly he pretends to skim the newspaper. In restaurants he orders "whatever you're

having" because he can't decipher the menus. Road signs are made into a game so his family won't guess he can't read them. Only a swift intelligence and a fine secretary carry him through the day.[14]

It is estimated that about 8 million students in the United States suffer with some form of learning disability, many undiagnosed and thinking themselves stupid or incapable. One significant finding emerged several years ago in a study of delinquent youth, conducted by Dr. Allan Berman of the University of Rhode Island. He reported that 56 to 70% of a sizable group of delinquents tested *had never learned to read or write.* Many failed to learn because of learning disabilities even though some were highly intelligent.

When our company first heard about the Armstrong School, the director was Scott Donahey. Donahey, who graduated from Stanford and obtained a master's degree from Johns Hopkins, was drawn into the subject of dyslexia while he was an English teacher at St. Joseph's School in Menlo Park, California. He was contacted by Dr. Wilbur Mattison, chairman of the Armstrong Foundation, which was created to honor the late Charles Armstrong, founder of the Menlo Medical Clinic. Armstrong was the author or co-author of 22 scientific publications, including the *Physician's Handbook,* widely used among medical practitioners. The foundation developed an interest in dyslexia in 1965 and held three public symposiums on it and several teacher-training workshops before opening the school in 1968. Donahey was offered a teaching position at Armstrong and joined it in 1970 after getting special training.

The Charles Armstrong School was started in a converted house and garage. In its first year, it had 18 students in grades 7 through 11. It later expanded into Sunday school classrooms at the adjacent Presbyterian church. In 1974, it relocated to a vacant public school under a lease with the Ravenswood school district. In the 1977–1978 school year, it had 86 students, ages 7 to 17, coming from nearby and outlying areas.

It has a high teacher-to-student ratio: about 10 students in the lower grades and about 4 in the high school. The school uses a multisensory approach to the teaching of letters and numbers. That means that the students, often in unison, recite the sounds and draw the letter in the air or on the palms of their hands or on their legs. They are taught with as many senses as possible, to compensate for the problem with their visual perception—which is the dominant learning faculty for most children and the one most used in the regular classroom.

Working together is an important element of the learning process because many dyslexic children have high levels of distractability and have great difficulty working on their own. The carefully structured program of teaching encourages the development of self-discipline and good work habits, so that many of the inherent impediments to learning

[14]Debbie Simon, "The Battle to Read," *Wall Street Journal,* October 13, 1977, p. 1.

may be overcome. It is intended that the children will return to regular school classrooms when they can do so with a high degree of confidence that they will not fail. This expectation has been realized, since virtually all of the school's 250 "graduates" have successfully returned to regular schools.

Funds for the Charles Armstrong School come from several sources. The school charges fees ranging from $3,000 annually for the lower grades and $3,400 for the high school. There are scholarships for some children, and the fees of others are sometimes paid by neighboring public school districts that do not have adequate programs for students with these serious learning disabilities. Foundations, corporations, and individuals also provide financial support. Grants have been made by the Morris Stulsaft and Gamble Foundations of San Francisco; the Hewlett, the Packard, and the San Mateo Foundations in our area; and the Educational Foundation of America in Westport, Connecticut.

Our company began annual scholarship support in 1976, which was awarded to the son of a reporter at the *Palo Alto Times,* Jay Thorwaldson. Thorwaldson wrote a nice letter to us after he had been informed that our company had provided the scholarship funds that enabled his son to attend:

> Perry was at Armstrong last year, after three increasingly frustrating years in public schools. He has gone from nearly two years below grade level and thinking of himself as "the dumbest kid in my class" to above grade level and grandly self-confident—something we never dreamed possible during three years of struggling to find out what was blocking him. Syntex, through Armstrong, is helping to salvage a bright young mind—something which I feel is beyond monetary value.

It does take many dollars to keep programs going at Armstrong and at the dozen other schools in the country that are doing important work in understanding and dealing with the widespread and serious problems of children with learning disabilities. Corporations should support these innovative educational institutions and also find out what the local public and private schools are doing to provide special educational programs for children with learning disabilities. In California, there are state-funded programs, but they reach only 2% of the student population, and the percentage requiring assistance is possibly 10 to 20% of all students.

The private institutions, like the Charles Armstrong School and the Children's Health Council, are developing the knowledge and techniques that enable students with learning disabilities to be educated. But regular public and private schools and other institutions in the community must implement these programs if a large number of talented youngsters with learning disabilities are to be allowed to reach their full potential.

12

Free Enterprise: Should Business Support Those Who Don't Support the System?

Hostile groups of scholars are, to a large degree, responsible for the antibusiness bias of many of our young people today. And I do not believe it is in the corporate interest to support them–which is what we do to a greater or a lesser degree with unrestricted funds.[1]

David Packard's remarks to the Committee for Corporate Support of American Universities on October 17, 1973, was the opening gun in a dispute and dialogue that has been going on for the past five years between business and the academic community. Needless to say, it provoked an immediate response from some members of the academic establishment. The idea that business had an obligation—or even more dangerously, a right—to be discriminating in its support of higher education was taken in some quarters to be a violation of "academic freedom" at least or the U.S. Constitution at most.

Packard was certainly not acting as a corporate vigilante determined to shape the policies and activities of our institutions of higher learning to his own purposes. In beginning his talk, he said that

> I am still strongly devoted to the cause of the private university because I believe it to be an institution of tremendous importance in our society. It is an institution not only with a distinguished tradition, but one that has a vital role for the future welfare and progress of our country.

It is important to understand that Packard was a member of the Committee for Corporate Support of American Universities from 1958, a group that included business figures such as Jim Black, John Collyer,

[1]David Packard, "Corporate Support of the Private Universities," remarks to the Committee for Corporate Support of American Universities, New York, October 1973, p. 11.

Donald David, Charles Dickey, Devereux Josephs, Neil McElroy, Tex Moore, Juan Trippe, and Sidney Weinberg. The purpose of the committee was to identify a select group of universities deserving special support over and above what each corporation was already doing for education. The committee's guidelines for selection included four factors.

First, the universities to be supported were to be private universities—not tax-supported schools. Although it was recognized that many state universities met the same standards of excellence as the leading private universities, it was felt that corporations were already providing substantial support to public institutions through the payment of income, property, and other taxes.

The second guideline was that the university receiving this extra support should have a graduate school of distinction covering a broad range of studies. The justification was that such institutions were a major source of professional people needed by the corporation; that they were centers of important research; that they were a major source of the Ph.D.'s and professors for all levels of higher education; and that these major private universities gave important leadership to all of higher education in America.

The next guideline set down by the committee was that "the amount given to any of the universities should be substantial and that it should be continued over a period of years."

The final guideline was that these additional corporate gifts to these special universities should have *no restrictions* on the use of the funds.

What David Packard was saying in 1973 was that the guidelines established in earlier years were still in effect and satisfactory—*with one exception:* "The only exception I would make is the guideline stating that corporate funds given to private universities should be unrestricted in their use by the university." Here is what he said to justify this position:

> I recognize that for the university, unrestricted money is most valuable. It allows the trustees, or the administration, or the faculty to undertake programs which might otherwise not attract financial support from the outside. It does not necessarily follow, however, that unrestricted money, used as it has been used, is always in the interest of the corporation. That, however, is precisely what the corporate officer considering a contribution to a university should be thinking about. Should our corporation make an unrestricted contribution and leave it to the trustees or the administration or the faculty to decide how the money should be used, or do we have a responsibility to our stockholders to be sure the money contributed will, in some defensible way, benefit our corporation?

Packard's response to this question was unequivocal: "The case for a corporation giving unrestricted funds to a private university can no longer be supported."

Packard went back to the guidelines and pointed out that an unrestricted gift was not likely to be used to help a professional school that would be training students that business would employ. He commented that the Graduate School of Business at Stanford University, where he served as a trustee, received no funds from unrestricted gifts. He concluded that

> to the extent a corporate contribution is to be justified on the basis that it helps assure a continuing supply of professional people, the funds must be designated specifically for the professional schools the corporation wants to support.

In respect to the second guideline, Packard stated that very little unrestricted money was directed to support the many excellent research programs at private universities: "Most of the research at these institutions is supported by the government or by large foundations." He added that he felt "these universities would be better off if more of their research was supported by business and less by the government," and he encouraged his corporate colleagues to do just that.

Commenting on the third guideline, Packard said that because these major private universities were an important source of professors for all of higher education, this placed "a double responsibility (on the corporate donor) to make sure his dollars are constructive rather than destructive—and there is no way to do this with unrestricted money."

Summing up his position, Packard asked a few rhetorical questions:

- Is kicking ROTC programs off the campus the kind of leadership we need?
- Is prohibiting business from recruiting on the campus the kind of leadership we need?
- Should these universities serve as havens for radicals who want to destroy the free enterprise system?
- Should students be taught that American corporations are evil and deserve to be brought under government control?
- Should a board of trustees sit as sole judge of the social responsibility of each American corporation—and use this as a basis for deciding whether its stock should be held in the university portfolio?

Packard's response to these questions was summed up in this advice to his corporate colleagues on the Committee:

> In the future, let's focus our money and our energy on those schools and departments which are strong and which also contribute in some specific way to our individual companies, or to the general welfare of our free enterprise system.

As I said earlier, Packard's comments caused a spontaneous if not altogether rational response from some segments of the academic community and the world of philanthropy. Several years later, the debate was still going on. When William E. Simon was secretary of the treasury in 1976, he also made some remarks on the subject, which were challenged by Roger W. Heyns, then president of the American Council on Education. In a letter responding to Heyns's criticisms, Simon made this statement:

> I do not suggest that gift giving be conditioned on the institutions' presenting only the views I believe in. But should they be supported if they present only the views I do not believe in especially when I perceive such views to be a direct threat to our economic and personal freedoms? . . . I have no objection to the presentation of other economic views so long as the principles of the market mechanism are also presented and the subject is taught fairly. Teachers are given a rare privilege in having access to the instruction of students. They should not violate that trust by concentrating on only one approach or by consciously attempting to bias their students. Diversity of opinion and dissent are both necessary and desirable for a democratic system such as ours to function properly.[2]

The next great salvo was fired by Henry Ford II, chairman of Ford Motor Company, when he resigned as a trustee of the Ford Foundation early in 1977. The move left the foundation's board without a representative of the family that founded it. In his resignation from the board, Henry Ford offered some thoughts that he felt were appropriate:

> The Foundation exists and thrives on the fruits of our economic system. The dividends of a competitive enterprise make it all possible. A significant portion of the abundance created by U.S. business enables the Foundation and like institutions to carry on their work. In effect, the Foundation is a creature of capitalism—a statement that, I'm sure, would be shocking to many professional staff people in the field of philanthropy. It is hard to discern recognition of this fact in anything the Foundation does. It is even more difficult to find an understanding of this in many of the institutions, particularly the universities, that are the beneficiaries of the Foundation's grant programs.[3]

Henry Ford commented that he was "not playing the role of the hard-headed tycoon who thinks all philanthropoids are socialists and all university professors are communists." He was just suggesting to the trustees and staff of the Ford Foundation "that the system that makes the Foundation possible very probably is worth preserving." He concluded his remarks by encouraging them "to examine the question of our obligations to our economic system and to consider how the Foundation, as one of the system's most prominent offspring, might act most wisely to strengthen and improve its progenitor."

Henry Ford's comments, unlike Packard's, got a great deal of attention in the public media. One of the more thoughtful responses was

[2]Personal communication from William E. Simon to Roger W. Heyns, March 22, 1976.
[3]Personal communication from Henry Ford II to the Board of Trustees of the Ford Foundation, January 1977.

contained in an article by Irving Kristol that appeared in the *Wall Street Journal* on March 21, 1977.[4] Kristol said that Ford's comments "created reverberations within the academic and business communities, exciting latent and powerful anxieties about the relations between the two realms." Because of this, he said, "there already has been a great deal of hypocritical nonsense uttered about this matter." Kristol started by saying that "it is a fact that the majority of the large foundations in this country, like most of our major universities, exude a climate of opinion wherein an antibusiness bent becomes a perfectly natural inclination." He did allow that these foundations and universities "are not homogeneous or totalitarian institutions" but nevertheless agreed with Henry Ford that the Ford Foundation "seems more interested in supporting people and activities that display a habitual animus to the business community" and that Henry Ford "was not suffering from delusions of persecution."

Kristol, resident scholar at the American Enterprise Institute and co-editor of the quarterly *The Public Interest,* was not puzzled, nor did he see any paradox in this state of affairs.

> Foundations and universities are for the most part—not exclusively I would emphasize, but for the most part—populated by those members of the "New Class" who sincerely believe that the larger portion of human virtue is to be found in the public sector, and the larger portion of human vice in the private. . . . Since foundations and universities are the ideal-germinating and idea-legitimizing institutions of our society, this bias—and that word may here be used descriptively rather than polemically—is a serious problem for those of us who are concerned for the preservation of a liberal society under limited government.

Kristol went on to say that "expressions of concern are quickly countered by accusations that, should such concern become more widespread, 'academic freedom' would be endangered." He labeled this attitude a "red herring," while allowing that it would be dangerous if angry citizens thought they had the right to prescribe foundation policies or the content of a university curriculum or the composition of the faculty. He said that there was even danger in businessmen's trying to endow chairs of "free enterprise" on a university campus: "Economists in a university, after all, are supposed to teach economics, not free enterprise or socialism."

Then Kristol outlined his firm belief that corporations had not only the right but the obligation to be discriminating in things they supported:

> It does not follow that businessmen or corporations have any obligation to give money to institutions whose views or attitudes they disapprove of. It is absurd to insist otherwise yet this absurdity is consistently set forth by college presidents, and in the name of "academic freedom" no less. When David

[4]Irving Kristol, "On Corporate Philanthropy," *The Wall Street Journal,* March 21, 1977.

Packard and William Simon made the perfectly reasonable suggestion that corporations look before they give, and discriminate among friend, neutral and foe in their philanthropy, they were denounced in the most vehement terms by universities which seemed to think they had some kind of *right* to that money. They have no such right. If they want money from any particular segment of the population, it is their job to earn the good opinion of that segment. If they are indifferent to that good opinion, they will just have to learn to be indifferent to the money too. That's the way it is, and that's the way it's supposed to be in a free society where philanthropy is just as free as speech.

Kristol went on to criticize business leaders for their naive approach to corporate philanthropy—not just aid to education. "For the sad truth is," he said, "that the business community has never thought seriously about its philanthropy, and doesn't know how." In many respects I agree with this view, although it may be an overly harsh assessment. Kristol continued:

Some corporate executives seem to think that their corporate philanthropy is a form of benevolent charity. It is not. . . . Charity involves dispensing your own money, not your stockholders. When you give away your own money, you can be as foolish, as arbitrary, as whimsical as you like. But when you give away your stockholders' money, your philanthropy must serve the longer-term interest of the corporation. Corporate philanthropy should not be, cannot be disinterested.

Kristol said that corporate philanthropy should

include as one of its goals the survival of the corporation itself as a relatively autonomous institution in the private sector. And this, inevitably, involves efforts to shape or reshape the climate of public opinion, a climate that is created by our schools, our teachers, our intellectuals, our publications, in short by the New Class.

He said that the first step in reorienting corporate giving would be to stop giving money to support those activities of the New Class that are inimical to corporate survival. He also suggested a more positive step "for corporations to give support to those elements of the New Class—and they exist, if not in large numbers—which do believe in the preservation of a strong private sector." These include, he added, "those not necessarily 'pro-business' or even much interested in business but individuals who *are* interested in individual liberty and limited government." Here are his concluding comments:

This is a melancholy situation, for in any naked contest with the New Class, business is a certain loser. Businessmen, who cannot even persuade their own children that business is a morally legitimate activity are not going to succeed, on their own, in persuading the world of it. You can only beat an idea with another idea, and the war of ideas and ideologies will be won or lost *within* the New Class, not against it. Business certainly has a stake in this war—but for the most part seems blithely unaware of it.

Kristol's pessimistic conclusion is correct to some degree, but I think that business leaders are awakening from their dreams. One such dramatic awakening involved Dow Chemical, Central Michigan University, and Hollywood's Jane Fonda, champion of the oppressed. Fonda was a paid speaker at Central Michigan University in the fall of 1977. While discussing the political climate, the state of the economy, and legal justice, Fonda announced that Dow Chemical USA, a corporation based in central Michigan, is part of a "new group of rulers and tyrants." She said that Dow and other tyrants "have learned to manipulate the tax laws to get away from paying their fair share." She forgot to mention, as George Will stated, that Dow had paid taxes of $430 million in 1976![5] She also seemed to be unaware that Dow had contributed $73,000 to Central Michigan in 1976 and that the university was one of about 450 schools receiving money from the company.

Fonda's remarks, which were covered in the media, evoked a response from Dow's president, Paul Oreffice, in a letter directed to Central Michigan University president, Harold Abel. Oreffice wanted to know if any of the company's contributions were used to pay campus speakers. The letter questioned the $3,500 fee paid to Fonda so she could "spread her venom against free enterprise" to university students and then went on to say that Central Michigan University would receive no further aid of any kind from the company until Dow and university officials could meet to discuss where the company's support was going.

It seems clear that Dow and other corporations are going to spend more time to find out where their support of higher education is going. My own guess is that unrestricted giving will become less attractive, but this is no reason for corporate aid to higher education to decline. In fact, the manifold possibilities of restricted giving are such that most corporate objectives and guidelines can easily be achieved.

Universities are diverse institutions—probably the most diverse in our society. They are by their very nature made up of individuals from different backgrounds, professions, ethnic stock, and religious and social upbringing. The curriculum also includes a great diversity of subject matter, from poetry to mathematics, engineering to fine arts, accounting to language studies. Also there is a great diversity among our colleges and universities in terms of religious and social philosophy.

This diversity presents many options for the corporation wishing to meet its responsibilities in the area of aid to higher education. In the case of our company, we have provided unrestricted support to education in only one way: through matching gifts. All other support has been restricted, or to use a better and more meaningful word, *designated* for a specific program or project. I believe this is the proper way for corporations to distribute support to higher education. It is consistent

[5]George F. Will, "Money Talks," *San Francisco Chronicle,* November 3, 1977.

with the strategy for corporate giving that I have described throughout this book.

I also feel that the issue is not limited to the area of higher education. It is a point of view that should be kept in mind when considering grants to many different types of nonprofit organizations and causes.

Corporations have no obligation to provide funds to organizations or individuals that are devoted to the replacement of our economic, political, and social system by some other system. This would be foolhardy.

Looking at it from another viewpoint, it is appropriate for corporations to provide support to worthwhile organizations that are proponents of the free enterprise system. I also believe it is desirable for corporations to support organizations that believe in the system but want to make the system work more democratically and productively. This view implies that the nonprofit organization seeking support is not only well motivated but can formulate changes that are capable of practical implementation.

On the other hand, it is unwise for corporations to fund those who, while well motivated, would damage or destroy the system they nominally support with reforms that are unworkable or unnecessary.

For many years, there have not been many nonprofit organizations that were capable of defending or reforming the system in a manner that would gain much support outside the business community—in the media, in the professions, or in the academic community. This is changing. Some organizations have emerged that are worthy of corporate support. I would like to describe several of them briefly. These organizations operate in different areas: public interest law (Pacific Legal Foundation); public interest accountancy (Accountants for the Public Interest); economic research (Council on Economic Priorities); and public policy rssearch (American Enterprise Institute). Finally, I would like to discuss one of the oldest and still an extremely viable program: Junior Achievement.

Pacific Legal Foundation

The Pacific Legal Foundation is the first in a new line of "anti-Nader's-raiders" programs defending the "other side" on a host of environmental, social, and economic issues. It supports the free enterprise system and the concept of individual liberties, limited government, and the reasonable use of one's property. PLF believes that welfare is a privilege and not a right. It believes in balance and common sense in the determination of public issues.

Ronald Zumbrun, the foundation's president, attributed the organization's success to the fact that it "is in the mainstream of public thinking on most issues." In the environmental area, for example, PLF believes that there has to be some balance between the social and economic ramifications of what is being proposed and the environmental aspects. PLF also feels that the purpose of welfare is to help the poor, not to serve as a means of redistributing wealth. PLF has litigated to remove unneedy people from the welfare rolls so that those who are truly in need receive more help.

PLF was organized largely through the efforts of the late J. Simon Fluor, retired chairman of Fluor Corporation, headquartered in Southern California. Fluor, along with other businessmen, raised over $100,000 in corporate contributions to launch PLF in California in 1973.

An article in *Barron's* in 1977 said that the foundation has been involved in over 100 cases since its inception, of which 50 have been concluded; the PLF was victorious in four out of every five.[6]

According to *Barron's:*

> PLF has prevented environmentalist groups from halting construction of a strategic base for the Trident Missile, the nation's top nuclear deterrent system . . . it has fought restrictive zoning laws and compelled the federal government to re-introduce DDT to save the forests of the Northwest from the ravages of the tussock moth.

Some of the foundation's most notable actions have been in the area of welfare spending. PLF won a lengthy fight in California for the right of the state to introduce a computer system that matched the Social Security number of welfare recipients to detect fraud. According to *Barron's,* this effort was so successful in cutting welfare costs that "the PLF crew subsequently was called in as consultants in Illinois and other states to set up similar programs."

Approximately one-third of the foundation's funding comes from individuals and the rest from charitable foundations, corporations (over 500), and even labor unions. In its first three and a half years, the PLF grew from a California venture with a staff of 5 to a national organization of 40, including 15 lawyers, and a Washington, D.C. office that monitors regulatory agencies and litigates in the federal court in the District of Columbia.

There have been charges that the PLF is a tool of big business. Zumbrun resents and denies this allegation. He points out that the foundation meets the Internal Revenue Service test for a tax exemption as a public interest firm. Beyond that, Zumbrun states that "we are the only public interest law firm that is oriented to the *total* public interest, not just a portion of it." Zumbrun says that the PLF "will

[6]Dana L. Thomas, "More Freedom Fighters: Some Public Interest Law Firms Oppose Big Government," *Barron's* (August 15, 1977): 5.

continue to seek to give balance before the courts in major public interest issues. When the system is functioning well we will stand up and back it when it is taking heat." I think that most corporate executives will agree that this is an objective worthy of corporate support.

The headquarters office of the Pacific Legal Foundation is 455 Capital Mall, Suite 465, Sacramento, CA 95814.

Accountants for the Public Interest

The accounting profession has lagged behind the legal profession in the area of public interest services. Legal aid services were available in the 19th century in the United States. But even legal aid remained for many years a charitable rather than a professional responsibility. Public interest laws came along in the middle of this century with the advent of civil rights legislation and protest. Environmental problems also became a subject of serious concern to public interest lawyers. Few would dispute the assertion that the legal profession has shown a commitment to public interest activities that has surpassed that of most other professions.

The concept of public and community service grew less quickly in the field of accounting—in large part because of the conservative attitudes of the profession. Morton Levy, in his book *Accounting Goes Public,* has documented the development of the public service and public interest activities of the profession. Levy points out that the first Certified Public Accountants licensed in New York in 1896 assisted those who were unable to pay. But again, as was the case with lawyers, this was seen as charity rather than the acceptance of professional responsibility.

One of the first efforts to assume that professional responsibility was the assistance given to support the black capitalism efforts of the 1950s and 1960s. The effort was not successful. Levy says that "in a massive misuse of talent, tens of thousands of hours have been spent by well-meaning and highly trained professionals to little effect."[7] The profession had made a commitment but, unfortunately, in an effort that had unattainable objectives. Neverthless, it raised the consciousness of many talented accounting professionals and established the concept of a community role for the profession.

This effort was followed by programs to assist individual taxpayers—an idea that started with Professor Bernard Goodman at the University of Hartford in Connecticut. Again, the motivation was good but the results were disappointing. As one state society respondent put it, "We were there but the low-income taxpayer didn't take advantage."

[7]Morton Levy, *Accounting Goes Public* (Philadelphia: University of Pennsylvania Press, 1977), p. 15.

Another initiative of the profession was the establishment of accounting aid societies, first in Des Moines, Iowa, in 1969 and later in Charlotte (North Carolina), Detroit, Hartford, and Minneapolis. The program organized accounting professionals and students to provide services to small businesses, nonprofit organizations, and low-income individuals.

Out of this background, Accountants for the Public Interest emerged in San Francisco, California. Levy said that it was "born of strong parentage—frustration and inspiration": frustration because the founding group had trouble finding the right outlet for its talents and experience; inspiration because of the success of other public interest groups that were making their mark on society.

But the founders had some solid concepts on which to build their new organization. They knew that public policy questions were getting more complex—whether they related to the delivery of health services, the cost-effectiveness of various government programs, the equity of taxation, the mediation of labor disputes, or the effectiveness of new regulations affecting political campaigns. They also knew that accountants had a unique talent for the investigation, analysis, and evaluation of data.

The 11 founders of API established the criteria for selecting those they would help, which continue to be the criteria today: the client (1) must be an organization involved in a charitable or an educational endeavor; (2) must be unable to pay for the services needed; (3) must accept that the work will be performed in an objective and independent manner; (4) must agree not to edit or excerpt from the report without prior permission; and (5) must evidence a serious commitment to the project or issue involved.

Before accepting an assignment, API also determines that the issue is a reasonably broad one—and not one that affects only a small group. API also reserves the right to release the report it has prepared if the client fails to do so because the findings are not consistent with the client's position. Finally, API requires the client to evaluate API's work after it is completed.

API uses a team approach consisting of the executive director, the API staff supervisor, the volunteer-in-charge, and a member of the API executive committee. In the first five years of API, about 200 professional accountants volunteered to participate in the program.

During 1974, four API-affiliated organizations were established in other cities and 40 additional ones in the following two years supported by a national association incorporated in 1975. These organizations have been involved in a number of projects:

1. A year-long study of skilled nursing facilities funded by the San Francisco Foundation and supported by 22 volunteers.

2. A project to examine the fee structure of the Title 10 Day Care Service in Denver, Colorado.
3. A project for Rhode Island Health Associates, Inc., to provide information on start-up and operating costs of running an average-sized school breakfast program and the identification of the resources available to pay for these costs.
4. A review of the accounting policies, financial reporting requirements, and forms required by the Federal Housing and Urban Development agency in their low- and middle-income housing projects to facilitate better fiscal management of such projects and to lessen the loss of taxpayers' dollars.
5. In conjunction with San Francisco Mental Health Association, studying the fiscal aspects of citywide mental health programs and training 20 mental health volunteers to interpret the city budget and related fiscal information.
6. A series of fiscal workshops for nonprofit organizations in the San Francisco Bay Area to assist them to become more fiscally accountable, including assistance on record keeping, taxes, cash flow, budgeting, and regulations governing nonprofit groups.

API's initial funding came from the Stern Fund in New York, which provided the entire $26,000 budget for the first year of operation. Subsequently, funding for the San Francisco organization and the APIs in other cities came from a variety of sources, including foundations, individual accountants, and a few accounting firms. Support from the "Big Eight" national CPA firms and their corporate clients has been limited, partly because of the feeling that API might be taking an advocacy position despite the fact that it has never done so. Also some accountants, as Levy mentions, felt apprehensive that APIs would offer them competition and for this reason withheld their support. Far from competing, the work of API has actually created some business for a CPA firm. Levy said that when the San Francisco Parent-Teacher Association enlisted API in its attempt to understand the financial affairs of the San Francisco Unified School District, certain of the findings prompted the board of education to strengthen its management control system and resulted in a $50,000 fee to a national CPA firm.

Corporate support would be extremely helpful to API organizations across the country. The larger CPA firms are reluctant to support API because of an exaggerated concern that one of their corporate clients might not feel in complete harmony with API's efforts. If corporations would support API, therefore, accounting firms, large and small, would feel more comfortable in providing financial assistance, and this is where the major funding for API should be generated—from within the profession. A few corporate dollars could substantially open up this funding source within the profession.

Corporations should feel comfortable with the approach and the efforts of API. It is independent and objective. Corporations are familiar with the methods and character of the accounting profession. The objective of API is to bring facts and professional judgment into the deliberations surrounding important public policy issues. The value of this effort should be readily apparent to most enlightened businessmen and businesswomen.

Accountants for the Public Interest has affiliates in Atlanta, Austin (Texas), Boston, Chicago, Denver, Los Angeles, Miami, northern New Jersey, New York City, Philadelphia, Portland (Oregon), Providence, (Rhode Island), Toledo, San Francisco, and Washington, D.C.

Council on Economic Priorities

In November 1970, a new organization presented a paper before the New York Society of Security Analysts. The unique aspect of the presentation is that it discussed what companies in the pulp and paper industry had achieved and had not achieved in their efforts to combat pollution. The paper and other reports were widely covered in the business and public press.

The report ranked the efforts of a number of companies. Some were surprised by the good marks they received; others were disappointed at the detailed disclosure of their lackluster efforts.

This report was the first major study of the Council on Economic Priorities, founded in 1969 by Alice Tepper Marlin, formerly a securities analyst for Burnham & Co.

She never considered herself a militant or an activist and countered this suggestion with the remark that most militant groups would consider the CEP reactionary for proposing that capitalism can become more responsible. As Flora Lewis reported in the *Charlotte* (North Carolina) *News*, "Far from blowing up the citadel of capitalism, her approach is to make it the vanguard of the drive for change. The arsenal she is collecting is simply information."[8]

The purpose of this information is to provide the public with facts and figures that will permit them to evaluate the social performance of corporations. The CEP analyzes and reports on what individual companies are doing and provides information upon which informed judgments and decisions can be based. The credibility, and therefore the success, of the CEP is largely dependent upon objectivity in both its research and its presentation.

Like all research operations, the CEP collects available source material, including company reports, trade journals, and governmental

[8]Flora Lewis, "Social Concern Comes to Wall Street," *Charlotte News*, April 11, 1970.

and private reports. It also relies heavily on firsthand data provided through questionnaires and personal interviews. In the beginning, companies were not very responsive to the CEP's requests for information. For the study on pollution in the pulp and paper industry, only one or two responses were initially returned out of questionnaires sent to 25 companies and 132 mill locations. Personal interviews of management provided much more helpful information, and eventually most of the firms provided the information requested. When it was time to update the first report, the companies were much more anxious to cooperate, since most felt that the original study had been objective and they now wanted to present the best picture of their efforts.

One interesting aspect of the study was the disclosure that some of the most financially successful companies in the pulp and paper industries had done the best job installing pollution control equipment before being legally required to do so. This finding upset the previously accepted notion that any such expenditure for pollution control would have an adverse competitive effect on the firms making such investments.

Following this report, the CEP conducted a number of other studies, including those on power plant economics, the employment of women and minorities in major retail-chain organizations, competition in the pharmaceutical antibiotic market, public and Indian coal leasing in the West, the interchange of personnel between defense contractors and the Department of Defense, and pollution control in the steel industry.

Support for the CEP has come from several dozen foundations, individual contributors, and a number of corporations, banks, and investment firms that have been institutional subscribers at $1,000 per year.

When Alice Tepper Marlin founded the CEP, she wanted it to be the "Dun & Bradstreet for the socially concerned." The business community today may not be totally in favor of another Dun & Bradstreet in the social area, but the public has certainly shown an interest in the idea. It would appear, therefore, to be in the best interests of business not only to cooperate with the efforts of the CEP but to support them.

The Council on Economic Priorities is located at 84 Fifth Avenue, New York, NY 10011.

Junior Achievement

Early in this century, two businessmen organized the first Junior Achievement company in Springfield, Massachusetts. They were Horace Moses, then president of Strathmore Paper Company, and Theodore Vail, who later became chairman of American Telephone & Telegraph

Company. During the first 10 years, the program spread slowly to four other New England cities and reached New York City in 1929. In the 1930s, Junior Achievement companies were formed in about a dozen additional cities.

Junior Achievement got a big boost in 1941, when Charles R. Hook, then president of Armco Steel, arranged for some of the JA students to make a presentation to the National Association of Manufacturers convention in New York. The message was delivered to 750 top business people from around the country and was enthusiastically received. World War II temporarily slowed the growth of Junior Achievement, but in the five years following the war, the program expanded dramatically.

The scope of Junior Achievement today is remarkable. Almost 300,000 high school students are involved in a significant way in Junior Achievement programs in about 1,100 communities throughout the country. Over 90,000 individuals and firms contribute dollars and other resources to JA activities, including people power—over 33,000 adult volunteers participate.

Although the programs of JA have expanded, the initial concept is still the cornerstone of the organization's philosophy; that is, by *experiencing their place* in the free enterprise system, young people will understand and support that system. Junior Achievement, then, is in a sense the nation's oldest youth economic education program—and one of the most successful. The main difference between JA and other economic education approaches is significant: the student is able to participate in a model free-enterprise-situation "company" rather than merely being a passive recipient of information or propaganda about the economic system. I think this is a very important distinction.

Two-thirds of the young people in JA programs are involved in setting up and running their own JA small businesses. The recruiting for JA participants is conducted entirely through the schools, and over 110 school districts around the country have been sufficiently impressed by JA's academic value to offer high school academic or activity credit to students who join the program.

Dr. Sidney Marland, president of the College Entrance Examination Board and one of the many educators who support JA, recently said:

> From the beginning, Junior Achievement has been concerned with the correctness and self-evident feasibility of blending education and the workplace. That, in brief, is what career education is all about, and that, I think, is what has been the genius of Junior Achievement.

How do JA companies operate? It's not a very complicated format. Groups of approximately 20 students under the guidance of adult volunteers, called *advisers,* organize and operate a small business, meeting one night a week for two hours for a period of time that roughly parallels the school year. The students are 10th-, 11th-, and 12th-grade students.

The students perform every basic activity of a real-world business including:

1. Selling stock to capitalize.
2. Electing company officers.
3. Selecting a product to manufacture or a service to offer.
4. Keeping books and mapping marketing plans.
5. Paying salaries, rent, and even taxes (as appropriate).
6. Producing, promoting, and selling their product or service.
7. Liquidating the company at the end of the school year by publishing an annual report and returning dividends to the stockholders.

It is interesting that about 85% of JA companies are manufacturing operations. Their product list is almost endless, including desk pen sets, automobile trouble lights, silk-screened T-shirts, smoke detectors, and marble nameplates. Service companies have published a newspaper, established a modeling agency, and organized a bank to handle the financial transactions of other JA companies.

Junior Achievement programs have benefits both for the students and for business. By helping them understand the free enterprise system, JA enables these young people to visualize a place for themselves in it. They learn what they enjoy most about being in business—planning, finance, selling, new product development, marketing, personnel work—and this knowledge helps them in their later choice of a career. And even those who don't make a career in business are better-educated citizens and consumers because of their JA experience.

Young people who have been in Junior Achievement have attitudes much more favorably inclined toward business than those of the general public, whose information about the business world often is scanty—leading to misconceptions about how our system functions. A survey of JA members, for example, disclosed that they understood that the average profit of all industry after taxes is about 5% rather than the "up to 45%" response that college students gave in a recent Gallup Poll.

JA fills a real niche because few high schools offer separate courses in economics, and of those that do offer them, only about half require such a course. Also career counseling for business employment often is not very helpful to the students in a practical way.

Some of the country's leading business executives and retired executives are involved in Junior Achievement. They include G. J. Tankersley, president of Consolidated Natural Gas Company; John D. deButts, chairman of American Telephone & Telegraph Company; Russell DeYoung, retired chairman of Goodyear Tire & Rubber Company; Charles

F. Myers, Jr., retired chairman of Burlington Industries, Inc.; Eugene A. Cafiero, president of Chrysler Corporation; James J. Ketelsen, president of Tenneco Inc.; J. Edwin Matz, president of John Hancock Mutual Life Insurance Company; Paul F. Oreffice, president of Dow Chemical USA; and Frank T. Cary, chairman of International Business Machines Corporation.

Cary, serving as chairman of the JA national board of directors, had this interesting comment about the organization:

> Not long ago, one of my associates came to see me to describe a remarkable growth situation. He told me he was representing the largest conglomerate in the world—an organization of 250,000 people working in 251 divisions, and every one of them profitable. But the real clincher came when he asked me what I thought the average age of their dynamic and energetic labor force was. I guessed 35 . . . but it turned out to be 16![9]

The national office of Junior Achievement is located at 550 Summer Street, Stamford, CT 06901, and regional offices are in West Hartford, Connecticut; Rocky River, Ohio; Earth City, Missouri; Seattle, Washington; and College Park, Georgia.

[9] *Junior Achievement Annual Report, 1976–77,* (Stamford, Conn.: Junior Achievement, 1977), p. 2.

13

Helping Minorities: Education, Jobs, and Housing

My own son graduated from high school. When he went to apply for a job, he could not read or write well enough to fill out the employment form.[1]

Minority education is one of this country's most pressing problems, because it is only through education that most of the problems of poverty will be overcome and that minority groups will be able to participate fully in (and thus alter) American society. How such education is to take place, however, is not obvious. After fifteen years of government programs and monies, attempts at desegregation, and much discussion, we still do not seem to be significantly closer to the dream of equality in education (and thus racial equality). Test scores in minority communities continue to remain significantly lower than those in white communities, crime and drug abuse in these communities is on the rise, and so on. Even the media seem tired of reporting such problems.

Many concerned people feel terribly frustrated. Sometimes, it seems that nothing can be done. This is not true, of course, but we are beginning to realize that there are definite limits to what can be done. In the end, answers cannot be imposed on minority communities; they must be generated from within. The best that those on the outside can do is to help them to help themselves.

I hope that the reader does not think that in saying this I am being unduly harsh or that I am speaking smugly out of a reactionary business ethic. I think that this is a realistic appraisal, one that is based, in part, on the remarkable success of the Nairobi Schools in neighboring East Palo Alto, which has an 80–90% black population. And I would hope that this

[1]Gertrude Wilks [Mayor, East Palo Alto, California] "Recipe for Building a School."

is the kind of school that those of us outside the minority communities would choose to support with money and resources.

In brief, the Nairobi Schools are a series of private, cooperative schools organized between 1966 and 1970 that range from preschool through high school and also include two day-care centers and a Saturday day-school tutorial program. They operate under the guidance of a parent organization, the Mothers for Equal Education (MEE), and are largely the result of the dedication of one woman, Gertrude Wilks.

At this point, I think it best to let her tell part of the story. There is anger, commitment, even humor in her voice. I quote from her pamphlet "Recipe for Building a School":

> In East Palo Alto during the early sixties, troubles were brewing. As the community turned from white to black, the schools changed from fine to deplorable. Many of us looked the other way and accepted the baby-sitting ways of our administrators and teachers, grade one through high school. After all, who ever heard of ordinary black folk complaining that educators didn't know what they were doing—or worse yet, they did know but wouldn't admit it even to themselves. But a few of us were disturbed. My own son graduated from high school. When he went to apply for job, he could not read or write well enough to fill out the application form.
>
> Well, we fought the high school district Board of Trustees. There was no change at all. We developed a Sneak-out and then a Transfer Plan, so that high school students could be educated in neighboring white districts. Although these transferred students gained academically, they were psychologically torn. The subtle rejection of institutional racism has a dagger's edge. Our students were demoralized. There seemed to be no way unless we were to build our own school. We did.
>
> I realize that all black communities have similar problems. That's why I'm giving you the recipe we used. If you aren't sure that you need it, hold onto it. You may soon change your minds.
>
> Why a recipe? Well, I could say formula. That would sound more professional. But we are not really professionals. More Black people are skilled in kitchen work than laboratory pursuits. We know how to work a recipe into our own specific individual pudding; but we really wouldn't feel comfortable altering a formula "just a little bit" to satisfy our needs.

If there is one thing wrong in taking this passage out of context, it is that Mrs. Wilks makes establishing Nairobi Schools sound easier than it was. It wasn't easy, and later in the pamphlet she delineates the kinds of problems she encountered. Most basic was the fact that at first only a few people were willing to get involved. She knew that many blacks were dissatisfied with the education their children were receiving, but she also knew that it is hard for blacks to voice criticism of the schools. "Treat people with care, because they may be frightened when they hear themselves talking about the system." I shudder when I think of the time she must have spent just talking to people.

Then there were problems such as where classes should be held. Her advice on this is as good-natured and to-the-point as ever:

> Now, school houses—old-fashioned or new—are lovely. However, learning is something that happens between teachers and students. It can happen any place at all. Use whatever is available to you: a home, a church, an empty store.

MEE began its classes in a church, and over the years, it gradually acquired a series of houses for its various schools. This method was found to have many advantages, so many that students, teachers, and administrators connected with Nairobi Schools would be reluctant to give up the intimacy of their houses even if they were unexpectedly offered an "appropriate" building.

The first school, the Saturday Day School, was intended to supplement the regular schools. It opened in October 1966 with 20–30 students. The program initially offered tutorial work only in reading and writing, but MEE knew immediately that it had a winner. People kept coming, and the program went so well that the next year the curriculum was expanded to include tutorial work in mathematics and in following years courses in African dance and black awareness. To this day, the Saturday Day School is well attended, often attracting families from other parts of the Bay Area. MEE will soon open a second Saturday center.

The Saturday Day School was important for more than its immediate results; it also provided MEE the confidence and experience it needed to plan for a full-time elementary school, which opened in 1969. The confidence was so great, in fact, that when several children had unexpected troubles with the local high school, MEE opened a high school even before its elementary school was under way. The need was there, and MEE went ahead. Both schools got going very quickly. At the present time, almost 60 students are enrolled in the elementary school, but the high school ceased operations a few years ago.

These enrollment figures are not large, but the students who attend do quite well. Their test scores are well above those in the public schools, and the Nairobi Schools are confident enough to guarantee that they can teach a child to read in one school year. The high school students also have had no problem in going on to college. In 1973, for example, the three who graduated went to Pomona, Chapman, and Humboldt State Colleges.

Test scores and admission to college are not, however, the only measures of success; they are simply the most tangible. What is just as important is the community spirit that the Nairobi Schools are creating. On the one hand, there is the sense of community that is felt by those involved in the schools; on the other, there is the value that the Nairobi Schools themselves place on involvement in the larger community.

The Nairobi Schools are cooperative, and they have always demanded a lot from the parents. (In fact, they even turn down families who do not seem ready to make the appropriate commitment.) In part, this has been necessary for the schools' survival. Tuition is based on ability to pay, and very few have been able to pay the maximum amount ($1,100). As a result, parents must do maintenance work and fund raising. These are time-consuming (and we should remember that many black families are single-parent families and that in most others both parents work). To help with fund raising, special benefit dinners and concerts are frequently given. The staff too makes sacrifices, and it is not unusual for them to work without pay.

However, this is not the only way in which the schools are cooperative. They also encourage parent participation in the classroom. The Nairobi Schools are not unique in such an emphasis, of course; several years ago, the State of California initiated the Early Childhood Education program, which provides funds for parent participation in grades 1–3 in school districts that request such aid. The Nairobi Schools carry such participation even further, however, and try to implement it in all grades. The psychological benefits, for both parents and children, are enormous—particularly in a black community. Unfortunately blacks, even more than whites, are likely to feel that they have nothing they can teach their children. Once they realize that this is not true, the children's learning accelerates and family ties become closer.

Thus far, what I have said about the Nairobi Schools could be said about most alternative schools, which, typically, are also concerned with the student as an individual. They want "to accept the student as he is" and to encourage him "in developing a positive self-image." The only unusual thing is that such a school should, in fact, be found in a black community.

There is one important way in which the Nairobi Schools differ from most alternative schools, however, and that is in the emphasis they place on the student's relationship with the community. They want to assist the student "in developing positive identification with the community," "in dedicating and gearing his academic life to the improvement of his community," and "in gathering the skills necessary" for such improvement. In short, as Mrs. Wilks writes, they want "to assist the student to stop talking and start doing." Many alternative schools in the white community, by comparison, seem self-indulgent.

Recently, Gertrude Wilks went to China, and she returned as convinced as ever that the cooperative and community-oriented goals of the Nairobi Schools are right. What she saw in China impressed her very much (ignoring for the moment the question of ideology and international politics). In China, children are integrated into community and family life. Factories are located close to the schools, and both schools and child-care centers are well supplied with basic materials. Nowhere did she see signs of regimentation or an unhappy child. This, in brief, was a society with a purpose, and that purpose was reflected in everything she saw.

Unfortunately, the Nairobi Schools have a continuing financial problem. At a minimum, it takes approximately $7,000 a month to operate them. They generally make the payroll, but not always. Fortunately, the faculty and administrators are so dedicated to the schools that they have accepted the fact that salary cuts are sometimes necessary; and when they have to be made, they are made from the top down.

The schools have received several grants from the San Francisco Foundation, the San Mateo Foundation, the New York-based National Commission on Resources for Youth, and the Rosenberg Foundation—the latter to enable the high school to conduct a history project of the local community. Although some of these grants have been large, none of them has provided the kind of major assistance that would ensure a sound financial position for the schools.

In addition, corporate support has been spotty. There have been donations of unrestricted funds from Xerox, educational materials and supplies from Xerox and Woolworth's, released time by Lockheed for an employee, and two temporary buildings donated by the Bank of America.

Syntex made its first contribution to the Nairobi Schools in 1968 and then began annual contributions for unrestricted use in 1971. For the first several years, Syntex's support provided a teaching intern through the STEP program at Stanford. Later our annual contribution was used to build a fence around the high school, thus greatly reducing its vandalism problem. Since that time, our funds have helped to support several members of the teaching staff. The company has also bought tickets to special benefits and has contributed to conferences that MEE has sponsored. The address of the Mothers for Equal Education is P.O. Box 10777, Palo Alto, CA 94303.

United Negro College Fund

In 1944, Dr. Frederick Patterson and a group of college presidents formed the United Negro College Fund to help meet the operating expenses of 27 historically black colleges and universities. The present number of participating institutions is 41. Most of the schools belonging to the United Negro College Fund Federation were founded in the 1870s. While most of them were hardly more than high schools and trade schools in their early years, they have developed into established colleges and universities today. All except one in Ohio are located in the South; seven in Georgia, six each in North Carolina and Texas; five in Alabama; four in Tennessee; three in South Carolina; two each in

Mississippi, Louisiana, Florida, and Virginia; and one in Arkansas.

Christopher Edley, executive director of UNCF, points out that "Many of the blacks going to college today are still going to the public and private predominantly black institutions because they simply cannot afford to go to the more expensive predominately white colleges." Although students at UNCF institutions pay a yearly average of $1,500 for tuition (two-thirds of the national average for private colleges), more than 30% of UNCF students still require scholarships or other types of financial aid because their parents earn less than $10,000 per year. Even so, many parents work at two jobs to contribute something to their child's education. It is vital, therefore, for UNCF schools to provide financial assistance and they do: $50 million a year for scholarships, work aid, and other assistance programs.

Why do 50,000 students go to these predominantly black schools —coming from every one of the 50 states and 62 foreign countries? In an age when the word *integration* has become a symbol and goal of minority advancement, what is the role of the predominately black school? There is clearly a valid and critical role:

- UNCF schools provide higher education for thousands of students who are economically deprived. Many of these young people could not get an education if these schools did not exist.
- These schools also help students overcome inadequate high school preparation so that they can reach standard college level.
- UNCF colleges and universities provide the special understanding and programs that are needed by many of their students—many predominantly white schools' commmitment to the black students, while sincere, is limited by their own financial problems.
- UNCF schools can provide the leadership, talent, and skills that will not only train the black student but also strengthen the black community and the nation.
- Finally, these schools can analyze and interpret the culture, the experience, and the aspirations of black Americans. Christopher Edley says that "many young blacks want to go to a black school. . . . These schools enable black culture to remain vital and alive and are the repositories for it, ever deepening and developing this special existence."

All of the black colleges and universities in the United States (including UNCF schools) have educated 75% of black Americans with Ph.D.'s, 85% of black physicians, 80% of black federal judges, 75% of black officers in the armed forces, and most of the elected black officials and business men and women. The black community, which appreciates the value of these schools better than anyone else, provides over $5 million a year to UNCF schools in addition to their support of the annual fund campaign. Many of the more than 200,000 living alumni of UNCF colleges and universities are a vital part of this effort of the black community to support its own institutions. According to the Council for Financial Aid to Education, alumni support for black private colleges rose to a record level of 23.8% in 1976. CFAE also reported that six years ago, alumni support of the schools constituted only 2.9% of total support but that alumni giving has doubled—to 6% of the overall total.

The corporate community has also recognized the value of these schools and has vigorously applied its dollars and other resources to the cause. The 1976 UNCF national fund drive realized $13.5 million, of which $5.1 million, or 38%, came from 6,753 corporate contributors. Three corporations gave over $100,000: UPS Foundation, General Motors, and IBM. Twelve other corporations gave over $50,000, including Johnson Publishing Company, Equitable Life, U.S. Steel, Exxon, Ford Motor Company, Texaco, Celanese, ITT, Monsanto, Burlington Industries, Proctor & Gamble, and Xerox.

The extent of corporate support to UNCF is directly related to the outstanding corporate leadership that the organization has experienced. The national campaign chairman of the 1976 drive was Thomas A. Murphy, chairman of the board of General Motors—the third consecutive year he served in that capacity. John R. Opel, president of IBM, served that year as chairman of the National Corporations Committee. A. Dean Swift, president of Sears, Roebuck and Company, served as the national campaign chairman in 1977.

Corporations have helped in many other ways in addition to making cash contributions. Booz, Allen & Hamilton helped UNCF operate more efficiently by providing detailed management studies without cost. Touche Ross & Company donated accounting services. AMF Inc. underwrote the Arthur Ashe Tennis Benefit. Equitable Life contributed staff to update contributors' lists and other projects. Hilton Hotel Corporation donated rooms and dinners in connection with the Sammy Davis, Jr., birthday benefit for UNCF. American Can lent an executive for a year to organize a nationwide fund-raising effort directed at unions.

The Morgan Guaranty Trust Company recognized in the early 1970s that there were not enough black bankers and middle-management executives. It sent its own experts to Atlanta University to work with UNCF school officials in organizing a scholastic banking and middle-management training program. It provided key faculty people from its own staff. It established a sound student loan program so that young people could afford to take the course, and then it helped these graduates get jobs, some of them with Morgan. Finally, Morgan Guaranty put $300,000 into the program to make sure it worked. Atlanta University now has the only fully accredited school for banking among the black colleges. Its enrollments are up 50% over the start of the program, and its graduates are obtaining starting salaries from $15,000 to $20,000.

For years, IBM has been sending expert teachers from its staff to teach at black colleges for a full year. At Xavier Univerty in New Orleans, three such teachers turned around the school's computer program and made it a valuable productive asset to the school. The school now uses its computer both as a teaching tool and as an administrative resource.

Olin Corporation began a program in 1969 to enlarge the tiny trickle of black engineers entering the job market each year. Its program involved four UNCF undergraduate schools in Atlanta—Clark, Morris Brown, Morehouse, and Spelman—and Georgia Tech. The program enables black students to take three years of instruction at their own colleges, then the last two at Georgia Tech. Olin put $350,000 into the program and encouraged other companies to add hundreds of thousands more.

Since only 750 of the *Fortune* 1,300 companies are now contributing to UNCF, there is still more support that can be forthcoming from the business community. The money raised has to be divided 41 ways, so added dollars are very important. I wonder how many companies employing skilled black UNCF graduates fail to contribute to the education that made these graduates possible. If these companies would shoulder their fair share of aid to black colleges and universities, the vital work of UNCF institutions could be considerably expanded and enhanced. The United Negro College Fund, Inc., is located at 500 East 62 Street, New York, NY 10021.

Council for Opportunity in Graduate Management Education

A college education is the expected goal of most talented high school students today. Minority students anxious to fulfill their aspirations know that it will be hard to make it without an undergraduate degree. But in many parts of our society, even an undergraduate degree is not enough. If minorities are to achieve important positions in society commensurate with their numbers in the population, they will also have to experience and benefit from specialized education on the graduate level. This is particularly true in the areas of law, medicine, engineering, and business, and several organizations have been established in recent years to respond to the financial and other needs of minority students seeking graduate education in these professional areas.

One of the first programs was the Consortium for Graduate Study in Management (CGSM) founded in 1966 with a Ford Foundation grant. Dr. Sterling Schoen, a Washington University professor with a missionary commitment to getting minorities into the power structure, was the chief force in starting the program. In addition to Washington University's school of business, five other business schools were involved: the universities of Southern California, Indiana, Wisconsin, Rochester, and North Carolina. In 1974, these six schools graduated more minority MBAs than all United States graduate business schools combined in 1967. CGSM's budget in that year was $750,000, with $475,000 coming from 134 companies, including IBM and General Motors.

Four years after the start of CGSM, 10 of the more prestigious business schools set up their program. The group includes Harvard, the Massachusetts Institute of Technology, the Wharton School at the University of Pennsylvania, Stanford, Columbia, Chicago, Carnegie-Mellon, Cornell, the University of California at Berkeley, and Dartmouth's Amos Tuck School of Business Administration. The Alfred P. Sloan Foundation made a founding grant and continued to provide funds through 1977.

This program is called the Council for Opportunity in Graduate Management Education (COGME), and I first heard about it in 1972 when the then president of the organization, Norman P. Clement, Jr., visited my office in Palo Alto. Clement, who is an executive with one of the country's leading management recruiting firms, knew firsthand that the need for minority management expertise far exceeded the availability of such talent. He also stated that minority communities greatly need skilled business leadership and that the country needs increased minority involvement in its economic processes. It was COGME's role, he said, to increase substantially the number of minority students graduating from the master's degree programs in management at the 10 member schools. This increase would be achieved by an active program of recruitment and financial assistance. Our company contributions committee agreed with Clement, and we began providing annual support in 1972. Over 100 corporations now provide support each year.

The figures in Table 5 show how minority student enrollment in COGME schools and minority student interest in COGME support have grown since the program was initiated.

Table 5. COGME Enrollment and Applications for Support[a]

Academic Year	COGME Support Applications	Minority Enrollment in COGME Schools
1969–1970		257
1970–1971	404	435
1971–1972	600	606
1972–1973	608	580
1973–1974	650	575
1974–1975	725	520
1975–1976	813	505
1976–1977	775	494
1977–1978	730	506

[a] Source: Council for Opportunity in Graduate Management Education.

About 175 students are helped annually now through COGME financial assistance, and a total of 1,150 students have received support since the program begain in 1970. More than 95% of COGME-sponsored students have successfully completed the two-year course of study leading to an MBA degree, and many have graduated with honors.

COGME and CGSM MBA graduates are moving into responsible positions in American business and industry. That's a plus for the individuals involved, for the minority communities that are finding important leadership, and for the corporations that are finding skilled young people with the capacity to become productive and socially concerned executives. COGME is located at 675 Massachusetts Avenue, Cambridge, MA 02139.

Mexican-American Legal Defense and Educational Fund

When Syntex was organizing its program of minority support in the early 1970s, we decided that a portion of our support should be directed at efforts to assist Mexican-Americans. Although Hispanic-Americans are the second largest minority in the United States, they had the reputation of being the "forgotten minority." Our company was more sensitive to this situation than other firms, since Syntex began as a small research organization in Mexico City. Many of the executives of the company spoke Spanish, and even today, the company has pharmaceutical and chemical operations in Mexico. Also, in Santa Clara County in California, where Syntex has a major facility, there is a large Mexican-American population.

In searching for constructive ways to support Mexican-Americans, we heard about a San Francisco-based organization called the Mexican American Legal Defense and Educational Fund, or MALDEF. I contacted MALDEF for more information and found out that it was started in 1968 because of the realization in the Mexican-American community that if its members were to participate fully in a democratic society, they must seek and demand justice through available legal means. But it was painfully obvious that the most serious obstacle to equal justice was the lack of lawyers attuned to the problems and needs of the barrio communities. In California, for example, there was only one Mexican-American lawyer for every 9,500 Mexican-Americans, while there was one Anglo lawyer for every 530 citizens.

I was also told that there were only 414 Mexican-American law students among the more than 50,000 law students in universities across the nation in 1971. Of the 58 federal district judges serving in that year, only 2 were Spanish-surnamed. Of the 961 judges serving the state courts in the Southwest, only 32 had Spanish surnames. In the same region, there were 590 state district attorneys and public prosecutors, and only 3% of them were Spanish-surnamed.

The objectives of MALDEF were twofold: to provide effective legal services to Mexican-Americans and to encourage the development of Mexican-American lawyers. The latter program was the one we began supporting in 1971 because we felt it would provide solid long-range benefits for the Mexican-American community.

In the 1969–1970 school year, 118 students in law schools were provided with $90,000 of financial assistance by MALDEF, and according to the organization, 53% would not have been able to attend law school without the assistance. These funds were further leveraged because law schools participating in the program provided matching assistance to MALDEF grantees. In the first five years of the program, 772 grants were made, providing $477,500 in assistance to Mexican-American students in 45 participating law schools.

MALDEF was founded with a $2.2 million five-year grant from the Ford Foundation. The organization has sought and obtained support from other foundations such as Abelard, New World, Jefferson E. Peyser, San Francisco, Trull, and John Jay Whitney.

Corporations were also attracted by the substantial social benefits of the MALDEF program, and by 1977 about 100 companies were providing contributions. They included American Airlines, AT & T, Avon Products, Bank of America, Castle & Cooke, CBS, Clorox, Cummins Engine, Eli Lilly, Equitable Life, Foremost-McKesson, General Electric, General Mills, General Telephone, Hewlet-Packard, Kaiser Aluminum, Levi Strauss, McGraw-Hill, Norton Simon, Occidental Life Insurance, Pacific Telephone, Pet Milk, Prudential Insurance, Safeway, Singer, TRW, Inc., Varian Associates, Wells Fargo, and World Airways. MALDEF is located at 28 Geary Street, San Francisco, CA 94108, and has regional offices in Denver, Los Angeles, San Antonio, and Washington, D.C.

One of the reasons for the success of MALDEF has been the distinguished leadership that organization has had since its inception. Its first general counsel, Mario Obledo, was appointed by Governor Edmund Brown to be head of California's Department of Health and Welfare. Vilma Martinez, President and General Counsel for MALDEF since 1973, became the first Mexican-American to be appointed a regent of the University of California in 1977.

Cooperative Chicano Student Residence

One of the easiest requests for a contributions executive to deal with is the written appeal that is not addressed to a specific individual but begins with the salutation "Dear Sir" or "Gentlemen." These appeals are generally unsucessful because of the feeling that someone who really is serious about asking for support will take the time to direct the proposal letter in a less generic fashion.

I received such a letter around Thanksgiving in 1969. It came from a group calling itself Frente de Liberacion del Pueblo, and this name provoked my interest so I decided to read it. I am glad that I did. It was from John C. Gamboa, treasurer of the organization, which was located on the campus of the University of California in Berkeley. Gamboa pointed out that the number of Chicano students had doubled on the campus but that there was little financial aid for books and personal expenses. He went on to describe how the Chicano students were going to change this condition:

> Rather than complain and ask [the university] for more money, when we know that there is none available, we have developed a scheme to help ourselves. There is an unoccupied fraternity house which can house thirty students. We feel that we could live in and operate this house on a student co-operative basis. This would greatly decrease our housing expenses and at the same time provide the atmosphere and kinds of meals we had at home, which we all dearly miss. To implement our plan we need the initial $3,000.00 required for security deposit and the last months' rent. We are appealing to your concern in the problem faced by the Chicano students at U.C. Berkeley, and hope you can provide some financial assistance in our efforts to help ourselves.

The ingenuity and self-help aspects of the plan appealed to me. They also made an impression on a friend of mine, Ray Schneyer, manager of human resources programs at Lockheed Missiles & Space Company in Sunnyvale, California. Ray and I were involved in several Mexican-American organizations, and I called him shortly after receiving the letter from Gamboa. Schneyer had received the same appeal. He knew most of the young people who were involved and was impressed with their enthusiasm and dedication. He told me that the group was operating a counseling program for high school seniors aimed at bringing more Mexican-American students into Berkeley. They were responsible, in part, for increasing from 22 to about 200 the Chicano membership in the educational opportunity program at the university. He said that by establishing the co-op, it would allow the students to live on expenses of about $95 monthly, rather than the $135 they were then spending. The $40 they would save would go for books, clothing, and other needs. Schneyer convinced Lockheed's management to provide $1,250 and asked me to request our management to do the same. Syntex did agree to participate on an equal basis with Lockheed.

On a Saturday evening early in 1970, my wife, Ann, and I went to Berkeley to see the newly opened La Raza Student Co-op at 2732 Durant Avenue. Ray Schneyer and his wife attended too. It was a joyful occasion. There was a good Mexican dinner and music. We had an opportunity to meet the fine young people who would rather do something "than complain"—and they did something special and lasting. Today the Chicano Co-op is called Casa Joaquin Murrieta. It is located at 2336 Piedmont Avenue, Berkeley, California. Ron Chavez is the current manager, and he says that the Casa provides meals and housing for 36 students.

Chicano Film Institute

Also in 1970 I had an opportunity to become acquainted with another Chicano student group at San Jose State University that displayed an equal amount of initiative and perseverence. The Chicano Film Institute was organized in 1969 and received early funding from the federal Economic Opportunity Commission, the antipoverty agency. The objectives of the Institute were to:

- Encourage Mexican-Americans to use multimedia as a creative form of art.
- Provide the Mexican-American community with a professional cadre of photographers and cinematographers who would be capable of training other Mexican-Americans in these fields.
- Provide the commercial and educational media with videotapes, films, and other audiovisual material dealing with Mexican-American activities.
- Create a center to produce and become the repository for films and other audiovisual material dealing with Mexican-Americans and Mexican-American themes.

In November 1979, we had a meeting at Syntex with two of the leaders of the Chicano Film Institute, Benjamin Ybarra and Tello Morales. They explained their plans and showed us a film that they had produced. About one month later, the company agreed to provide funds for the printing equipment that was required for work in color photography. The following year we provided funds for several other pieces of color photographic equipment and a synchronous tape recorder used to incorporate sound in films.

In 1972, I received a letter from Ybarra in which he mentioned that in a two-month period, the institute was working on three sound films with the equipment the company had donated. In addition, the institute was offered $1,000 to go to New Mexico to complete a documentary film on the land-grant movement. Ybarra ended his letter with this comment:

> The tremendous amount of cooperation and understanding that we have received . . . has left us with a profound understanding of how much power we (the business and community sectors alike) have in perfecting the quality of our society.

In 1973, we donated a final piece of equipment—a professional 16-mm motion picture camera—and later in that year, we hired the institute for a filming assignment at Syntex. Self-sufficiency had grown out of self-reliance.

Opportunities Industralization Center West

Opportunities Industrialization Center West is a nonprofit corporation established in 1965 to provide work-orientation and job-training classes and to assist in the employment of unemployed and underemployed members of minority groups in San Mateo County, southern Alameda County, and parts of Santa Clara County. In its first 10 years of existence, OICW trained and placed more than 5,500 individuals. OICW graduates earn on an average about $5,500 per year more than they did before training. Courses provided include job readiness, auto body repair, food services, clerical skills, electronics assembly, health occupations, metal trades, retail sales, keypunch, janitorial maintenance, and English as a second language. OICW also offers intensive counseling in attitudinal and motivational development. Although OICW is a local and locally funded organization, it is one of 130 affiliates of a national organization started in Philadelphia by the Reverend Leon H. Sullivan. Its headquarters are located at 3224 Sixteenth Street, N.W., Washington, DC 20010.

Stanford Mid-Peninsula Urban Coalition

The National Urban Coalition was formed in 1967 to encourage action on urban problems by bringing together leaders from all elements of the community: business, labor, local government, and minority groups, as well as the traditional organizations of concerned citizens. At its most active point, there were local coalitions in 46 cities in the United States. The headquarters of the organization are at 2100 M Street, N.W., Washington, DC 20037.

Ira Hall, who was the young black executive director of the Stanford Mid-Peninsula Urban Coalition in 1967, said, "If we can't put it together here, then I don't see much hope for any place else in America." By "it," Hall meant the solution to the increasingly familiar complex of problems that came to be almost synonymous with urban areas: poverty, bad housing, unemployment, haphazard growth, and inadequate education.

It is easy *not* to see the trouble on the San Francisco Peninsula. The part of it that most people see still seems one of the loveliest places on earth. What aren't easily seen are the poverty pockets, the suburban ghettos that have become appendages to the larger peninsula communities during the last two decades as the numbers of blacks and Mexican-

Americans grew dramatically in this once almost exclusively white, Anglo-Saxon suburbia. In communities like East Palo Alto, the welfare rolls are heavy, unemployment is high, and housing is substandard and overcrowded. The Stanford Mid-Peninsula Urban Coalition was formed in 1968 to cope with these problems. Dolly Sachs has been the executive director since 1975.

Two business leaders played the principal roles in getting the organization under way: David Packard of Hewlett-Packard and Dr. Edward Ginzton, chairman of Varian Associates. Packard said:

> Intelligence, reason, understanding, and conviction are the ingredients needed to solve the problems of a combined society, which we hope to build on a foundation of better communication and better understanding among the responsible people in our community.

And so the Urban Coalition initially was simply a forum that brought together the diverse elements of the peninsula community: business, labor, government, education, religion, blacks, browns, whites. But discussion led to action.

Coalition members launched the first two Minority Enterprise Small Business Investment Companies (MESBICs) in the country: the Arcata Investment Company (a subsidiary of Arcata National Corporation) and the Palo Alto Capitol Corporation (a Varian Associates subsidiary).

The coalition helped to establish a Housing Development Corporation to respond to the need for moderate-income housing in the area. The corporation has created over 400 decent, well-designed low-income housing units in the peninsula area.

A food co-op was started in neighboring Redwood City in a district with a large Mexican-American population.

A health task force was established under the leadership of Dr. Russel V. Lee, founder of the Palo Alto Medical Clinic. The task force worked closely with the Charles L. Drew neighborhood health center in East Palo Alto, which is funded by the federal Office of Economic Opportunity. The task force proposed to the OEO that the project be allowed to become a self-supporting community health center with co-op membership and a medical staff under subcontract to the OEO. In 1977, Dr. James Strand, medical director of Syntex Laboratories, joined the coalition board of directors and became involved with the work of the health task force.

Another task force on Juvenile Delinquency Prevention organized Sun Porch, a residential treatment center for young girls ranging from 12 to 15 years of age. Individual, group, and family counseling are provided by a qualified and experienced staff.

Impressive as these programs are, they don't begin to meet the real needs of the peninsula area. But that came as no surprise to Ira Hall and Dolly Sachs, who knew that the coalition could not do the job by itself.

The coalition's purpose was to try to get people to recognize common problems and to care enough to work together to do something about them. It did not intend to become a big bureaucratic operator of a lot of programs. It wants to stimulate them, to get them off the ground, to marshal the resources, to show what can be done. In that kind of role I think it can really make a difference. But there is still an enormous stretch of ground to cover in the peninsula area and in other communities across the country, and no final verdict on the outcome is possible yet.

National Consortium for Black Professional Development

The National Consortium is a nonprofit organization of 30 industrial corporations and institutions of higher education committed to the development and implementation of a national program to increase substantially the pool of black professionals in the critical areas of employment demand, including the applied and natural sciences, business administration, communications, engineering, and law. The organization is located at 1816 Morris Place, Louisville, KY 40205.

For its members, one of which is Syntex, the consortium identifies, recruits, and places qualified black professionals. It also provides personnel and management research studies geared to identifying regional and or geographical areas for black professionals; consults with its member firms on establishing developmental programs to increase the number of black professionals in their work forces; arranges shared-costs professional training programs between its member firms and neighboring colleges and corporations; recruits undergraduate or graduate students for cooperative education programs; administers and coordinates any fellowship scholarship programs financed by its member firms; assists in the development of science-demonstration competition projects in cooperation with neighboring school districts in which its members have an interest; and develops academic-strengthening programs for students in areas near its members' divisions or subsidiaries, either unilaterally or cooperatively with school officials.

In addition to its membership in the Consortium, Syntex has contributed toward the publication of *Project Abstract: Quarterly Science and Engineering Newsletter for Science-Gifted Black Students,* intended for grades 4 through 8.

In providing assistance to minority organizations, Syntex has been guided by principles expressed in Morgan J. Doughton's book *People Power: An Alternative to 1984:*

> People react and participate to the degree that they sense in an action some potentiality to their own lives. This sense of potentiality is an attitude and feeling no outside influence can instill very easily. It is a sense that depends

upon awareness—upon perceived relevance to one's own intentions and purposes, and upon confidence in one's own ability to bring the goal about. Nothing less will work very well. These are not things successfully programmed. Nurturing and reinforcing these qualities requires that people have responsibility and that they be involved in linking systems—that people *do* instead of being passive, and that their doing be through organizational forms bringing mutual respect and aid.[2]

[2]Morgan J. Doughton, *People Power: An Alternative to 1984* (Bethlehem, Pa.: Media America, 1976), pp. 149, 150.

14

Support for Women's Causes

Women holding executive-level positions are about as hard to find as chicken-poxed children.[1]

At a 1977 luncheon meeting of top company executives, one of them happened to mention that his wife had returned to college. As the conversation continued, it was discovered that not one of the wives of these fifteen executives was devoting herself exclusively to the traditional role of wife–mother–community volunteer. Every one of them, even a mother of nine, was working toward a bachelor's or an advanced degree or else was gainfully employed.

The larger half of the population (51%) is clearly at work bringing about a substantially different society from that we have known. Women are changing themselves, their families, their employers, their institutions, their world.

One of the dramatic ways that they are changing our society is by entering the work force. In the years 1975–1977, according to the Bureau of Labor Statistics, over 5 million jobs were created in this country and 3 million were filled by women. The large number of women entering the job market is a factor in the high rate of unemployment. The economy is creating new jobs—every year since 1970 except for 1975—and we now have about 94 million people employed, the highest number in our country's history. *Forbes* magazine, in its January 19, 1978 issue, said, "Over half of all women in the prime childbearing age group of 25 to 34 years are already in the labor force" and 60% of job seekers are women.

Despite the growth in the number of employed women, they lag behind men in earning power. The median salary for a woman in 1974 was $6,772, while a man's was $11,835. Influence too is unequal in

[1]Gail Sheehy, *Passages* (New York: Dutton, 1974), p. 223.

corporations as it is in almost all other institutions. Only 1% of top corporate management is female, only 5% of middle management is female, and only 15% of entry-level management is female.

Business and Society Review has kept a tally of the number of women serving on boards of major corporations.[2] In 1972, there was a "mere handful" of such women; by 1975–1976, about 100 major corporations had added women to their boards; and in 1977, the publication identified 340 companies and said the number "is still growing."

I feel that this trend is encouraging and hopefully will produce some important and measurable benefits. It should encourage companies to offer more and better opportunities to women employees. It should make these corporations more sensitive to the role of women in society—apart from their contributions to the work place. I also believe that it will have an effect on corporate giving policies and practices in respect to women's causes.

Corporate and foundation support has, of course, long benefited women—through agencies that help families and children and provide other important services that women need.

Several years ago, our company decided to review those organizations that we were supporting that did not serve women exclusively but that might have a high proportion of women beneficiaries. We found that women were benefiting from many of the programs and projects that the company supported:

- About 200 of the 600 public affairs internships of the Coro Foundation have been filled by women.
- A college scholarship program to benefit Mexican-Americans awarded one-fourth of its scholarships to women.
- The Council for Opportunity in Graduate Management Education provides financial support to minority students attending leading graduate schools of business. About 20% of the recipients of COGME grants have been women.
- Over 50% of the recipients of support from the United Negro College Fund are women.
- Women have received 40% of the scholarship supports at the San Francisco Conservatory of Music—a group we have supported since 1974.
- Two minority job-training and placement agencies that we were supporting reported that a substantial portion of the individuals they helped were women—40% in one organization and 65% in the other.

[2]Leonard H. Orr, "Out of the Typing Pool and onto the Board: A List of Women Directors," *Business and Society Review* (Summer 1977): 27.

Women have clearly benefited from many organizations that corporations and foundations have supported over the years. What has changed in the past 10 years, however, is the emergence of a women's movement and the founding of many organizations with the *primary* purpose of directly and exclusively furthering women's causes. These efforts have not received significant support to date from either foundations or corporations. Mary Jean Tully in a Filer Commission study said that a review of foundation grants designed to improve the status of women could identify "only something in the neighborhood of $12 million in foundation grants from the beginning of 1972 through the end of 1974."[3] During this period, total foundation grants were $7 billion. Corporate support was even less, according to Tully, showing "only 12 corporations that have contributed to feminist organizations." I have not seen any figures on current foundation or corporate support, but it is undoubtedly higher than the levels of 1972–1974.

One of the reasons I anticipate more support in this area is that women are organizing to encourage and facilitate it. In the mid-1970s a new organization was formed: Women and Foundations. In 1977, it changed its name and enlarged its mission: Women and Foundations/ Corporate Philanthropy (WAF/CP), 211 W. 56 Street, New York, NY 10019.

Jing Lyman, a board member of the Rosenberg Foundation in San Francisco, heads the board of WAF/CP. She told me that the organization has three objectives: (1) to increase the number of women in policy-making positions as senior staff and trustees in organized philanthropy; (2) to promote grantmaking and other foundation and corporate policy on behalf of women; and (3) to establish regional networks of women and men concerned with these issues and in expanding communication with each other.

According to *The Grantsmanship Center News,* the group will be involved in several activities to accomplish these goals: education communication, monitoring, and advocacy.[4] It is understandable that women would like to change the underrepresentation of women in the philanthropic world. GCN pointed out that "a 1976 study by Leeda Marting showed that only 19 percent of foundation trustees and 29 percent of foundation professional staff were women." No such statistics are available for corporate philanthropy. It is not uncommon, however, for women to administer corporate contributions programs, including those at Boise Cascade, Borden, Columbia Broadcasting System, Douglas Aircraft, Maytag, Merck, Olin, PPG Industries, Schering-Plough, Scott Paper, Time, Inc., and Western Electric.

[3]Mary Jean Tully, "Who's Funding the Women's Movement," *Research Papers,* The Commission Private on Philanthropy and Public Needs (Washington, D.C.: Department of the Treasury 1977) p. 1383.

[4]"Group Promotes Women's Issues in Philanthropy," *The Grantsmanship Center News* (July–September 1977): 65.

In the field of education, corporations have for some time responded to the needs of women, according to the Council for Financial Aid to Education Inc.[5] A section of CFAE's *Handbook of Aid to Higher Education by Corporations* devoted to "Women's Education" included these examples:

- The Procter & Gamble Fund has included annual unrestricted grants to 15 colleges for women.
- CBS Foundation has since 1956 made unrestricted grants to private institutions from which women employees meeting criteria of executive responsibility and length of service were graduated.
- Sperry and Hutchinson, Xerox, and IBM have made contributions to the Radcliffe Institute, which is designed to expand the choices open to women in scholarship, the creative arts, and the professions.
- Mobil awards scholarship funds to women through the Business and Professional Women's Foundation, which administers the grant and makes the selections.

As a director of public relations in two corporations, I have employed and supervised a number of women. Over the years, I was able to encourage and train three women who moved from clerical positions to staff positions with managerial responsibilities. This was a rewarding experience. It is also encouraging to see this happening in other parts of the company, as well as to see qualified women hired directly from schools and universities or from other companies into managerial positions. Although progress is being made, it will be necessary to continue these efforts for some time before the inequalities will be removed at all levels of corporate employment.

The highest ranking woman in our organization is the brilliant and charming Dr. Miriam Stoppard—a physician who is managing director of Syntex Pharmaceuticals in England—who is married to the playwright Tom Stoppard and is the mother of two children. She also finds enough time to write interesting newspaper articles and to appear on television.

I need not go into the reasons for our almost exclusively male top echelons; they are the same reasons that exist everywhere and have been documented in endless books and articles. But changes are coming and we welcome them. Indeed, we hope in some ways to help bring them about.

For our women employees, we have established a strong affirmative action program with a full-time director. A career advisory board has been created consisting entirely of women employees. The board is

[5]*Handbook of Aid to Higher Education by Corporations* (New York: Council for Financial Aid to Education, Inc., 1974), p. A-17.

assisted by an outside consultant who has already established a formidable record in helping women advance in their careers.

Several programs suggested by the career advisory board have been implemented. There is an ongoing series of one-day career-planning workshops. A career-planning workbook that was developed at the company elicits a great deal of preparatory work from the people attending these workshops. Because of the prework and the Strong-Campbell Interest Inventory test, which is taken and scored in advance, the brief but well-planned workshops are very effective in helping employees understand how to take charge of their careers.

Another program is a two-day workshop for secretaries and clerical employees conducted by another experienced consultant. Those who have attended have said that one result has been to lift the "just a secretary" limitation from people's minds.

Another in-house program that we found successful also demonstrates, I believe, a sensitivity to the feelings and needs of women. In fact, the American Cancer Society selected the program as "an outstanding example of public education in the fight against the number one cancer killer of the nation's women." In its public education programs, ACS points out that 1 in 14 women develop breast cancer but that by learning and using self-examination techniques, women could nearly eliminate breast cancer as a leading cause of death. Of the women who are treated for breast cancer 90% have detected the cancer themselves, and when caught in its early stages, the rate cure is 86%.

In 1975, the company decided to conduct an employee educational program on self-examination for breast cancer, under the direction of the firm's health services nurse, Deane Appleby. Of the company's 550 female employees in Palo Alto, 350 attended the program, with 183 receiving individual counseling on the techniques of self-examination from the company's nurses and volunteer nurses from the American Cancer Society. Four of the women discovered suspicious lumps and were sent to their personal physicians for further evaluation. Two of the women were found to have malignant tumors and were treated.

Although the activities I have mentioned here have not been directly connected with our community relations or corporate giving programs, I have related them because I think they exemplify what, in my mind, is the finest kind of public relations—that is, not just saying what good things you do, but *doing* the right thing (the fair thing, for instance, or the humanitarian thing, or the ecologically sound thing). It also fits the old homily about charity beginning at home, except that increasing opportunities for women is not charity—just sound moral behavior and good business practice. But the company has also contributed funds and services to an interesting list of agencies oriented toward women.

Resource Center for Women

In the San Francisco Bay area, as in other urban areas, the women's movement has fostered a wide variety of new organizations. They range from health centers through child care, athletics, arts, education, women's studies and research, centers to help the victims of rape and other physical abuse, legal aid, and employment counseling.

In the early 1970s, when we were thinking about increasing our involvement in women's programs, a group of women visited with me and Dr. Jack Zenger who was then vice-president of human resource development. They showed us their plans for opening a Resource Center for Women in Palo Alto.

They demonstrated to us that this community, while outwardly affluent, presents special problems for women. In Santa Clara and San Mateo counties, the divorce rate is higher than the national average; indeed, in some years, there are more divorces than marriages. It frequently happens that a woman's circumstances change dramatically, almost overnight. Moreover the highly technical nature of most nearby employment offers few if any entrees for people trained in liberal arts or education, as most women are.

Ellie Shelling, one of the women who spoke to us, pointed out that women in transition (caused by divorce, reentering the job market, changing careers, facing unemployment of husbands, or other changes) need special help to make decisions. The Resource Center was planning to offer counseling, employment information, and other tools to help these women. The women planning the center also hoped to encourage local employers to be more receptive to local women looking for reentry into employment.

There were no comparable existing centers to use as models in evaluating plans for the Resource Center for Women. Yet, in our view, Shelling, who was to become president of the organization, and the others had a good grasp of the tough problems facing women and a realistic picture of the business world. They were also spending a year researching actual community conditions before opening their center. The Resource Center for Women sounded like the kind of place that would provide good services for women employed at Syntex and for families of male employees. The women who would be opening the center appeared to have not only commitment but the talents necessary to carry out their plans.

In August 1973, the company made a cash contribution toward start-up funds for the center. As the center grew and expanded over the next few years, we continued to award annual grants and also to offer support in other ways.

Our company's personnel office maintains a liaison with the center and regularly sends our list of job openings to be displayed there. Hundreds of other employers do the same. Women who are seeking employment constitute a large percentage of the clients who come to the Resource Center. Thus, there is a very active and constantly changing library of local opportunities being used by at least 20 women every weekday.

Our conference facilities have been used several times by the staff and volunteers from the center. In 1975, the center requested space to hold a conference of local affirmative action officers. During this training session, the participants agreed that they needed a more regular forum for sharing ideas about employer affirmative-action programs. As a result, the Resource Center began to publish a monthly newsletter on the subject and to distribute it to San Francisco Bay Area employers.

One strong appeal for us in the Resource Center has been its local emphasis. Not only does it serve clients (about 1,500 per month) mainly from the peninsula area, which stretches from San Jose to San Francisco, but it also derives its financial support from local sources: corporate gifts, foundations, and member-donors. It retains an identity as a community-based agency and has never been supported by government agencies or large federated campaigns.

In 1976, the center sought and gained help from prominent local business leaders who agreed to serve as advisers, helping especially to broaden corporate contacts for funding and for marketing the consulting services that were developed by center personnel for businesses and their employees. In contrast to a board of directors, which provides overall leadership to the center, this Business Advisory Committee meets only once or twice a year and also responds to specific requests for help.

The first Business Advisory Committee clearly indicates the widespread commitment being made by corporations to women's organizations and services. Members include Vernon Anderson, a business consultant; John Boreta, president of Buttes Gas and Oil Company; Albert Bowers, president of Syntex Corporation; Robert L. Chambers, chairman and chief executive of Envirotech Corporation; Carl Djerassi, president of Zoecon Corporation; Herbert M. Dwight, president and chairman of Spectra-Physics, Inc.; Noel Fenton, president of Acurex Corporation; Thomas Ford, president of Ford Land Company; Mary Lanigar, retired partner of Arthur Young and Company; William Laughlin, then chairman of Saga Corporation; Frank Leach, president and chief executive of Arcata National Corporation; John M. Lillie, president of Leslie Salt Company; Richard Lyman, president of Stanford University; and Alejandro Zaffaroni, president and chairman of Alza Corporation.

In its first four years, the Resource Center had a number of accomplishments:

- Signed up more than 1,000 individual supporting members.
- Designed and implemented "Training for Finding a Job," a pilot project for single, unemployed heads of households under grants from the San Francisco, San Mateo, and James Irvine Foundations.
- Established in-house training in management, research, public relations, and publishing for its volunteers, 70% of whom have left for paid employment.
- Ran a 10-week course, "How to Succeed in Business by Creating your Own," to train entrepreneurs in business development.
- Published the *Directory of Bay Area Colleges and Universities,* containing information on degree programs, testing, financial aid, and bibliographic resources.
- Published the booklets "Financial Planning: Pre- and Post-widowhood," "Seeking, Finding, and Enjoying Your Career," and "The Résumé and Other Aids for the Re-Entry Woman."

The address of the Resource Center for Women is 445 Sherman Avenue, Palo Alto, CA 94306.

Stanford University Center for Research on Women

We have also participated in programs generated by the academic community in relation to women. These projects tend to be centered on research and education, the traditional activities of universities and colleges.

One project came to our attention through Cynthia Davis, daughter of a former Syntex vice-president. She was named as coordinator of research for the newly formed Center for Research on Women (CROW) at Stanford University. She visited me to learn about fund-raising methods for this nonprofit center devoted to the study of changing roles for women and men in society.

Later, after we received a proposal from them, the company made a cash donation to help set up the center's programs in research and education. The research was to be done by Stanford faculty and students in an interdisciplinary approach where investigators from the university's seven schools could come together.

The first research topics that developed show the range of topics possible in such a center: "Women and Small Group Interaction on the Job," "Women in the Labor Force," "Women and Mass Media," "Health Care Standards for Women," and "Women and History."

In addition to research, CROW planned to provide education through seminars, workshops, and lectures. Educational programs for the Stanford community were to focus on women in academic work and the changing roles of men and women for purposes of personal, career, and life-style planning.

Even after Cynthia Davis moved on to another position, our contact continued with CROW, mostly in an advisory capacity. Corporations are often in a position to help a program such as this more through consulting and referrals than through cash contributions—a reality that is sometimes overlooked both by the grant maker and by the organization seeking funds. An exchange with CROW illustrates this point.

CROW sought our financial support for a series of workshops on women and health, a topic on which we have expertise, since the company develops and markets health-care products. I asked Dr. Audrey Wells, a Syntex product manager for oral contraceptives, to help me assess the program. Because of Wells's expertise, she not only recognized everyone on the list of proposed speakers for the workshops but also suggested other speakers to cover the spectrum of professional opinion on the topics that were planned: childbirth, birth control, informed consent, and occupational health hazards, among others.

Educating Women for Science

A similar situation occurred in 1976, when we were asked for support of a conference called "Educating Women for Science" at Mills College in Oakland. When we looked at the agenda for this conference, we saw that there was only *one* speaker from an industrial research organization. We suggested that the program include commercial career descriptions in order to present a realistic picture of local employment opportunities to undergraduate and graduate women in science.

The planning committee followed our suggestions and invited another woman scientist from industry: Dr. Ruth Havemeyer, a product development manager at Syntex. As a further contribution, the company printed a transcript of the proceedings of this conference, which saved considerable expense for the conference planners.

The well-attended conference covered a variety of interesting topics, including minority women in science; problems for the female premed and medical student; why and when young women get deflected from science; science career reentry; and jobs for women in science. The program was developed by Dr. Jean Fetter, assistant director at the Center for Teaching and Learning at Stanford University.

Ruth Havemeyer is now a member of the Mills Advisory Council for Natural Sciences and Mathematics. This group of scientists from industry and universities aid in establishing contact between the college's students and the "real world" through industrial internships, field trips, seminars, and job recruitment.

The interactions with Mills College and CROW are not, in my view, attempts on the part of a donor to dictate or unfairly influence the programs funded. Instead, they show that corporate involvement can contribute more than a check, especially when a business has considerable experience in the areas where nonprofit organizations are working.

There is an interesting sidelight to the Mills College project. It highlights the "multiplier" effect of certain types of projects that are first conceived and implemented on a local level and then repeated in other localities or carried out on a regional or national scale. The Mills College conference was, as far as we could determine, the first one held in the country on the subject of educating women for scientific careers. That is one of the reasons we were attracted to it. It seemed to us that, if successful, it could lead to related efforts in other localities, or the subject could become attractive to a national organization. The latter actually happened in 1978.

We were alerted in 1977 that the New York Academy of Sciences was planning a "Conference on Expanding the Role of Women in the Sciences" in March of the following year. It would be co-sponsored by the Association for Women in Science Education Foundation. We were asked to provide some support and did so, joining a number of other firms, including American Can, Amaco, Burroughs Wellcome, Campbell, Corning Glass, Exxon, General Mills, Gulf & Western, Hoffman-LaRoche, Merck, Mobil, Sandoz, SmithKline, and Warner-Lambert.

The three-day meeting discussed the current status and future of women in the sciences; the opportunities for professional advancement; the need for altering attitudes toward women scientists and changing some government and academic policies; and the experiences of several women scientists in attaining substantial achievements in their careers.

Public Affairs Training for Women

Earlier in this chapter, I mentioned the public affairs internship program of the Coro Foundation and said that one-third of the participants were women. In recent years, Coro initiated a new program which provides excellent public affairs training exclusively for women.

Coro was started in 1942 in San Francisco by Van Duyn Dodge, an attorney, and W. Donald Fletcher, an investment company founder, to provide a training ground for young men and women in municipal affairs:

> Dodge and Fletcher reasoned that, if a young physician could fully understand illness only after seeing and treating living patients, that principle must apply equally to public servants. With the analogy of the diagnostician in mind, they pioneered the concept of internships in public affairs with the Coro Fellowship.[6]

---

[6]Kaye Moore, *Curriculum Guide to the Coro Public Affairs Leadership Training Program for Women* (San Francisco: Coro Foundation, 1978), p. 4.

From the founders' pioneering work during 1942 to 1947, Coro developed its best known program: The Coro Foundation Fellowship in Public Affairs, which produced its first 12 graduates in 1948. It has provided more than 900 outstanding young people with the basis for a lifetime career of effective public service.

Most of the nine months of training is done in the field. This includes opportunities to observe the activities of a number of government agencies; to participate in political campaigns; and to become acquainted with the operations, problems, and viewpoints of business firms, labor unions, communications media, and community service organizations. The interns also participate in personal exchanges with members of local and state legislative bodies, meet with stimulating guest speakers, and perform research projects in a variety of public and private sector areas.

The track record of Coro graduates has been exceptional. Donald Livingston graduated from Coro in the early 1960s and became the youngest director of consumer affairs for the state of California. Later, he was named director of programs and policy for the Governor's Office. In recent years, he has served as corporate secretary and director of public affairs for Carter Hawley Hale Stores in Los Angeles. He has demonstrated his commitment to the program by taking an active role in the Coro Foundation, serving for several years as president and chairman of the organization's national executive committee, and is presently on the board of trustees.

Sydney Nickerson, a 1973 Coro graduate, began her career in the public affairs department of Pacific Telephone & Telegraph. She is now director of editorial and public affairs for San Francisco's largest radio station, KCBS, and acts as an advisor to the Women's Program.

At a meeting held by the Conference Board in 1977, Richard M. Butrick, executive director of Coro, said that "billions of dollars are spent attempting to solve public problems, and it is curious that only a fraction of that amount is invested in examining and understanding how individuals in that system go about thinking, communicating, and dealing with their responsibilities."

It is fortunate that we have a few organizations that are trying to meet this objective. We need others, as Dr. Richard Lyman, president of Stanford University, pointed out in his remarks at the *Time* magazine's Leadership Conference in Washington, D.C. in 1976. He called for the expansion of public affairs leadership programs, saying that "100 Coro Foundations around the country wouldn't be too many!"

Over 200 corporations contribute to the Coro Foundation, including Allstate, Atlantic Richfield, Bank of America, Carter Hawley Hale Stores, CBS, Chevron USA, Clorox, Del Monte Corporation, Dow Chemical, Exxon, Fireman's Fund, Foremost-McKesson, Garrett, General Electric, General Telephone, IBM, Levi Strauss, Monsanto, PG

& E, PT & T, Potlatch Corporation, Ralston Purina, Rockwell International, Sears Roebuck, Southern California Edison, Teledyne, Transamerica, TRW, Union Carbide, United States Steel, Wells Fargo Bank and Western Electric. Syntex has also been an annual contributor since 1969.

In 1977, a Coro intern, Nancy Freedman, spent four weeks at Syntex in our public relations department. As a project, I had her organize the material which is included in Chapter 20 of this book, "Better Transit Systems for Work Trips." It was a productive experience for Nancy, for me, and for Syntex. Nancy wrote that she "very much enjoyed learning about area public-transit problems, corporate responsibility with regard to transportation, and Syntex's particular role in the community." Nancy is now working toward a master's degree in business administration at Columbia University, and I know that she will be playing an important role someday in government, business, or the nonprofit private sector.

In the 1970s, Dick Butrick felt that the same principles of leadership education in the Coro Fellowship Program could be adapted to a more intensive program designed specifically for women. But first, how important is the need for public affairs training for women?

> It is now 1978, and of 100 members of the United States Senate, Muriel Humphrey (who will soon step down) is the only woman. Of the 435 members of the House, only 18 are women. Never has a woman served as a Supreme Court Justice. After 200 years of our nation's history, 507 men and only 5 women have served in the Cabinet. Look at the composition of city, county and state commissions—those high status volunteer positions—and the pattern repeats itself.[7]

An advisory group was formed by Coro to design a new program for women. It included Jan McLaury of Foremost-McKesson, Jing Lyman of Women and Foundations/Corporate Philanthropy. Leslie Luttgens, trustee of the Rosenberg Foundation, Sara Fernandez of the San Francisco Junior League, Carol Marchik at the Stanford Graduate School of Business, Frances Gendlin of the Sierra Club, Sydney Nickerson of KCBS Radio, and 23 other women prominent in government, business, and public service organizations.

It was decided that the program would be an intensive, ten-week examination of the forces that combine to create public leadership, using the San Francisco Bay Area communities as a laboratory. The curriculum would be modeled on the tested format of the Coro Fellowship, including field work, seminars, and special week-long sessions in communications, group processes, and state government.

The goals of the program would be (1) to expose the participants to the major sectors influencing public affairs (government, politics, labor, business, media, and community organizations); (2) to provide an

[7]Ibid., p. 4.

opportunity to learn the skills necessary for leadership responsibilities; (3) to supply a link between the participants and those active in the public decision process; and (4) to prepare the participants to become effective leaders in public service.

It was decided to limit the program to women over 30, because they would bring a substantial base of knowledge and experience to the program and, even more important, an appetite for accomplishment.

An individual gift of $12,500 funded a pilot program. Then the Junior League of San Francisco funded one-half the cost of a two-year program. Matching funds were obtained from individuals, several local foundations, and businesses including Hewlett-Packard, Potlatch Corporation, Southern Pacific, and U.S. Leasing International.

The Junior League not only provided financial support but also 12 capable volunteers over the first two years of the program. Several corporations donated equipment, printing, and other services, and these in-kind services approximately equalled the dollars that were spent.

The pilot program was held in the fall of 1975. Joan Lewis, a participant in the pilot program, spent three days at Syntex as her business assignment.

Joyce Ream became full-time director of the women's program and served in that capacity until she left Coro in 1978 to be the president of Women and Foundations/Corporate Philanthropy. She was replaced by Kaye Moore, writer and editor of the *Curriculum Guide to the Coro Public Affairs Leadership Training Program for Women* which was published in 1978. (Single copies at $25.00 can be obtained from Coro Foundation, 149 Ninth Street, San Francisco, CA 94103.)

In the first three years, the program trained over 100 women. A survey showed that 46% of the graduates are paid employees; the remainder are engaged in public service activities as volunteers. A little more than half of the graduates are involved in government and politics; about one-third in service organizations; the remainder in education and other areas.

The connection between later achievement and the Coro training is often clear and direct:

> the two women who were hired as administrative assistants by their own legislators through their work in the program; the nurse who wrote a successful grant proposal for a comprehensive health care experiment; the Spanish-speaking political activist who finally found her niche in a nutrition program for migrant children; the school teacher who provided her mettle in a labor internship and was later hired by a large union to design and maintain their resource library.[8]

The important conclusions that can be drawn from the successful experience of the Coro Women's Program is "that women are seeking an

[8]Ibid., p. 97.

increased level of involvement in public affairs, that the talent pool exists, and that the training makes real and significant changes possible."

Other Contributions

In 1974, we received a letter from the AAU Women's Long Distance Running Committee inviting Syntex to be a patron of the upcoming Marathon Championships for the cross-country team.

Their request pointed out how many top international qualifiers live in the Bay Area and how events such as this one focus attention on women athletes and their achievements. Our modest cash contribution, along with others, supported the 26-mile competitive event on February 10, 1974, where two world age records were broken.

At the time, the idea of a women's race seemed a bit far out. Now many women are running—competitively and to keep in good physical condition. My wife, Ann, has become very active in this sport—running almost daily. One New Year's Eve, she quietly excused herself from a party we were attending (I remained) and ran a special five-mile race to welcome 1978!

The programs and projects covered in this chapter should be sufficient to suggest the range of possibilities open to corporations. There are many aspects to the women's movement and a variety of agencies concentrating on different goals. No corporation should have difficulty finding worthwhile projects with which it is in sympathy and to which it is capable of contributing expertise as well as funds. It is clear that the needs and opportunities are present. Corporations should go further on both internal and external fronts, increasing job and training opportunities for women and also supporting worthwhile efforts in their communities to provide women with the confidence and skills to reach their full potential in society.

15

Family Planning: Parenthood by Choice—Not by Chance

Population change touches all areas of our national life and intensifies our problems. . . . Stabilization of our population will contribute to the nation's ability to solve its other problems.[1]

The highest population growth rate in history is now building from the largest population base in history. There are some 200,000 more people in the world every day. And even the most successful population planning we might optimistically envision—that 25 years from now human beings would no more than reproduce themselves—even this success would still mean that within another 50 years world population would reach 8 billion, or twice what it is today.

Obviously, growth of this magnitude will strain all our resources. Nevertheless, a world of 8 billion people who may conceivably be able to manage their problems will be infinitely preferable to a world in which growth such as we are now experiencing can be checked only by disaster.

However we look at it, population growth is a mass problem that becomes more massive every year, every month, every day. We have at our disposal today mass media that can reach mass markets, techniques and channels that make it possible to send products to great numbers of human beings, and science, technology, and knowledge that have created ways and means that can effectively meet this profound and critical social need.

Looking at it another way—whether we like it or not, "Population is everybody's business." That has been the cry from population groups for years.

Fact: In the United States, illegitimate births in major cities comprise over 40% of total births.

[1]President's 1972 Commission on Population Growth and the American Future.

Fact: Over 1 million abortions will be performed in the United States this year.

Fact: Less than 1% of total foundation grants go to any activity in the population field—domestically or overseas.

I would suspect that the corporate track record is no better than that of the foundations. In terms of dollars and cents, population just hasn't been everybody's business. It's been of limited concern to firms and foundations.

In 1951, a Syntex research team synthesized a progestational agent destined to be a key ingredient in many of the world's oral contraceptives. Since the introduction in the early 1960s of these fertility control agents, they have been used by some 50 million women in developed and developing countries around the world. Research is continuing to explore how these and other contraceptive methods can make significant contributions to the alleviation of the serious worldwide problem of overpopulation.

In addition to research and developing new contraceptive methods, Syntex has also tried to do its part by assisting nonprofit organizations active in population and family planning.

Population Reference Bureau

One of the first organizations that we worked with is the Population Reference Bureau. The year was 1965, before anyone had heard much about the population explosion or read Paul Ehrlich's *Population Bomb.* But, remarkably, the PRB had been telling the world about its expanding population since 1929. It is the oldest private nonprofit group in the United States devoted to public education on demographic issues. It publishes the bimonthly *Population Bulletin* and other regular publications, operates an information service and a library; operates a population education program to assist teachers to introduce population concepts into the classroom; and consults with private and public organizations in the United States and abroad. With a philosophy that "will is more important than the pill," this group has continued to publish reports covering "The Impact of International and Internal Migrations," "Fertility Change in Small Cities in the Developing World," "Problems of Aging in the United States," "Catholic Perspectives on Population Issues," and "Black America and Birth Control." A comprehensive international newsletter, *Intercom,* is also published.

The PRB has slowly developed the characteristics that make it credible and respected as an organization concerned with the facts of population dynamics and their implications for human welfare. The Population Reference Bureau is located at 1337 Connecticut Avenue, N.W., Washington, DC 20036.

Population Crisis Committee

On April 25, 1974, a Declaration on Food and Population from 1,000 distinguished signers from 94 countries was presented to Secretary-General Waldheim at the United Nations in New York. We at Syntex had been asked by the late William H. Draper, Jr., to help gather signatures for this important document.

Our contact with Draper actually began some years earlier, and we began supporting the Population Crisis Committee, which he served as honorary chairman, in 1970. Draper was a crusader—tireless, courageous, and indomitable, a man of wisdom, driven by a single human desire: to alert the world to the threat of unlimited population growth and to generate support for programs in family planning directed at improving the social and economic well-being of all people.

The results of his efforts were to generate support for the U.N. Fund for Population Activities and the International Planned Parenthood Federation and to stimulate the World Population Year and the World Population Conference in Bucharest—all landmarks.

The PCC itself serves as a catalyst organization, supporting innovative family-planning projects and fund-raising programs in the population field throughout the world. A private organization staffed in part with volunteers, the PCC has no government contracts and depends entirely upon private contributions for its support. It is located at 1120 Nineteenth Street, N.W., Washington, DC 20036.

Planned Parenthood Federation of America

The Planned Parenthood Federation of America, also called Planned Parenthood/World Population, was founded in 1917 by Margaret Sanger to provide national leadership in the birth control movement. Today, it has 187 affiliates in the United States, operating about 700 clinics and serving a million patients a year in over 40 states.

Planned Parenthood's efforts in general are centered on the following activities:

1. Training programs for public health nurses.
2. Training for MDs and nurses in overseas programs.
3. Maintaining planned-parenthood clinics.
4. Providing family-planning services to more than 1.1 million clients.
5. Creating information and public awareness programs.

We have concerned ourselves at a corporate level with the national and international efforts of Planned Parenthood. Additionally, we elected to support the Santa Clara and San Mateo County Planned Parenthood Associations, because of their nearby location. We've provided meeting space for family-planning seminars and fund-raising activities; we've donated contraceptives and made cash contributions, and employees have volunteered a myriad of services to the organization. Planned Parenthood Federation of America is at 810 Seventh Avenue, New York, NY 10019.

The Alan Guttmacher Institute is the research and development division of PPFA. It monitors and analyzes laws, policies, regulations, and court decisions affecting the availability of family-planning services. The institute publishes a newsletter of federal government population policy and a bimonthly review of state laws and policies. AGI is located at 1220 Nineteenth Street, N.W., Suite 305, Washington, DC 20036.

Population Services International

A private, American-based, nonprofit organization, Population Services International, has made male contraceptives as common and accessible as soft drinks or bananas throughout the small Indian Ocean island republic of Sri Lanka, and both pills and condoms are sold through 30,000 shops in Bangladesh.

In a reverse of normal practice, PSI has given small grants to private pharmaceutical and condom manufacturers to promote their own contraceptives in new, high-risk markets. Additionally, PSI opened up work opportunities for women in Bangladesh and Sri Lanka, breaking through the strong barrier against the commercial employment of women, by providing them jobs as packers of contraceptive products.

Broadcast news of vasectomies: that's just what disc jockeys and radio announcers do in the Philippines in what is probably the only radio station vasectomy clinic on the air. This PSI-sponsored activity, through the local group formed for this purpose called MASSADS (Male Association for Surgical Sterilization for the Amelioration and Development of Society), conducts interviews before, during, and after the simple operation. It makes for popular radio listening, and at the same time it convinces many of the safety and simplicity of a vasectomy.

PSI uses a nonclinical approach to family planning and attempts to develop new "social-marketing" programs to provide contraceptives at low prices through retail shops so that people will not have to travel to distant clinics. The innovative aspects of this program have combined the most powerful forces of the marketplace to sell heretofore unknown products and philosophies in far corners of the world.

Population Services International is at 110 East 59 Street, New York, NY 10022.

The Pathfinder Fund

The late Dr. Clarence J. Gamble of Boston founded the Pathfinder Fund to introduce and promote improved methods of delivery of family-planning and population services and to influence the attitudes and values that determine pregnancy spacing and family size.

Dr. Gamble began his work in 1929 in the United States, helping establish the first public family-planning clinics in 40 cities in 14 states. His emphasis shifted overseas in the late 1940s. Pathfinder has assisted family planning in more than 83 countries of Africa, Asia, and Latin America.

Pathfinder encourages and helps fund a wide range of research, development, and demonstration projects: IUD research, oral contraceptive use, sterilization, paramedical training, training of administrators, communication, and publications.

Concentration is in developing countries, where the need for assistance is greatest. Work centers on developing local organizations that can aggressively carry on the family-planning work after Pathfinder assistance ends.

Pathfinder operates on gifts and grants from individuals, foundations, and corporations and with an annual grant from the U.S. Agency for International Development (AID). Pathfinder funds do what government dollars can't or won't do. Once Pathfinder money has led the way, often larger amounts of government dollars follow. The Pathfinder Fund is at 1330 Boylston Street, Chestnut Hill, Boston, MA 02167.

Zero Population Growth

ZPG is a grass-roots membership organization dedicated to achieving population stabilization in the United States through political action and public education. It is unique among population-oriented groups because it is the only one that directly lobbies at the federal and state levels, is primarily directed at ending United States population growth (although it does work to influence the United States foreign assistance program), and is the only one with an activist membership.

Zero Population Growth's efforts fall into four broad categories:

1. Development of and implementation of a *national population policy* that would, through voluntary means, end United States population growth in the near future.
2. Ensuring the availability of contraception and sterilization.
3. *Population education:* institutionalizing the study of population concepts, trends, causes, and effects at all levels of public education.

4. *Immigration reform:* urging reevaluation of United States immigration laws, policies, and practices to the end of integrating immigration policy within an overall United States population policy.

The California Federation of Zero Population Growth supports an office in Sacramento and has been active on a variety of issues, including family-planning services, sex education, population education, immigration policy, and others.

Syntex began contributing funds to ZPG in 1971, and Doug Graham, a Syntex executive, served as chairman of the California ZPG chapter for several years. ZPG is at 1346 Connecticut Avenue, N.W., Washington, DC 20036.

Planned Parenthood Affiliates of California

Locally, Syntex has supported another organization, the Planned Parenthood Affiliates of California. Originally founded as a coordinating body between the 17 Planned Parenthood affiliates in California to give and receive local and statewide information on family planning, it now attempts to make this highly specialized information available to community leaders and those in decision-making positions.

Legislative information (state and federal), studies, press reports, newsletters, and judicial information are available from PPAC. The group also publishes a monthly memorandum on bills pending in the legislatures.

PPAC develops data on the economic and social aspects of conception, abortion, VD, and adoption. The main use of this information is to encourage state agencies, legislators, public health groups, and local governments to pass legislation, write regulations, and organize programs that will ensure that public funds are being used to deal effectively with these social problems.

International Planned Parenthood Federation

If there is one generalization that can be made about these programs, it is that there is no one birth control technique, no one delivery system, no one single innovation that will be a panacea for the problems of population growth. The private sector still leads the way in taking risks—testing new methods and using new means to persuade governments to advance programs.

Countries and programs all need to experiment with different approaches to see what works best. A successful innovation in one country has to be adapted to fit different circumstances in some other country.

Working with villagers, women's groups, trade unions, and youth groups, private and governmental organizations are attempting to build new channels of communications and supplies to convey and implement the family-planning message. The International Planned Parenthood Federation is an important organization meeting this need. The projects it supports are examples of the way private funds can be used to assist governments to improve family-planning programs.

These projects include an industrial coverage program of education for men in Pakistan, since women cannot visit clinics or take pills without family consent; voluntary sterilization programs in Colombia; and health care and family-based distribution programs for contraceptives in almost 60 districts of Thailand.

The western hemisphere region of IPPF has its offices at 111 Fourth Avenue, New York, NY 10003.

Population Resource Center

Knowing which groups are most effective in this field and where to spend donation dollars may present problems for those companies not close to this particular cause. There are several very good resource groups, however, which can supply information, facts, and figures for the decision-making process.

An excellent resource for grant makers is the Population Resource Center. It was established in 1976 by retired investment banker, Henry McIntyre, to offer assistance in the population field and to help donors identify and fund meaningful programs compatible with other interests.

Since population is not a highly visible problem, the center presents donors with the details of the population situation existing today throughout the world, in the United States, and in the donor's own area. Projects fall into four general categories:

1. Biomedical—contraceptive development
2. Social science population policy
3. Delivery of family-planning services
4. Education, information, and communications

PRC advisers are also available for consultation in developing special projects for donors whose charters or fields of interest may be specialized. Once a field of interest has been identified, the center helps bring together the donor and the potential recipient for further discussion. The Population Resource Center is at 622 Third Avenue, New York, NY 10017.

There are other organizations operating on national and local levels to promote family planning and population control:

Association for Voluntary Sterilization was established in 1972 to promote voluntary sterilization as a method of fertility regulation. AVS, 708 Third Avenue, New York, NY 10017.

National Organization for Non-Parents promotes the child-free lifestyle as a realistic and socially accepted and respected option through educational and media programs. NON, 806 Reistertown Road, Baltimore, MD 21208.

National Right to Life Committee is an association of state right-to-life organizations working to overturn the 1973 Supreme Court decision on abortion by means of a constitutional amendment and other measures to protect human life before birth. NRLC, Suite 557, National Press Building, 529 Fourteenth Street, N.W., Washington, DC 20045.

The Population Council was started in 1952 to conduct in-house research in demography, reproductive biology, and new methods of fertility control. TPC, 245 Park Avenue, New York, NY 10017.

The Population Institute stimulates public awareness of population issues by working with other private organizations, the media, and with schools and universities. TPI, 110 Maryland Avenue, N.E., Washington, DC 20002.

We've just explored many options for companies to become involved in the solution of problems created by overpopulation and in combating overpopulation itself. Because this is a new and emerging area of corporate concern, I've tried to detail who's doing what in the field in order to point out that there are many ways for corporations to become involved in the population cause.

In a business sense, there is real economic value in averting the births of many unwanted and ultimately uncared for children. A world in which human fertility remains uncontrolled threatens to produce an overwhelming number of people whose numbers can be reduced only by steeply rising mortality.

Every unwanted birth entails unnecessary costs to the community in health services, education, and so on. Moreover, in countries where malnutrition, illness, unemployment, and short life-expectancies prevail, the social cost is extremely high in relation to any possible benefit.

And, in a situation where—by sheer weight of human numbers—forests are consumed for fuel, arable land is eroded, and the community is left helpless, it is not possible for long-run productivity ever to match the social cost. If we compare the cost of averting an unwanted birth with the cost of not averting it, the difference represents the eventual economic benefit to the community.

That's why population is everybody's business: whether we like it or not, we've already begun to feel the effects. It's now up to us to decide just what the quality of life will be. The decision has to be made very soon.

16

Addiction Research and Treatment

The best alternative to drugs lies simply in not turning off young people in the first place.[1]

There are probably half a million narcotics addicts in the United States today. Another 10 million Americans are alcoholics, and 53 million people use tobacco, despite staccato warnings concerning its ill effects. Millions of others abuse chemical substances including over-the-counter and prescription drugs—those who take a sedative to calm down in the evening or a stimulant to get going in the morning or other drugs to produce other subjectively desirable effects.

In a day when people mistakenly think that there is a tablet, a capsule, or a shot to relieve or cure every ailment, isn't it perhaps logical that a person lacking both knowledge and judgment would turn to drugs to cure what he or she perceives to be the ailments of modern society—or if not to cure them, at least to make it easier to live with them?

According to recent U.S. Army statistics, 10% of the garrison at Fort Hood, Texas—the Army's most populated base—abuse drugs and liquor so much that they require treatment. Other sources say abuse of drugs and alcohol is much more widespread, ranging up to 70% of the population of any military base. Of the 5,000 military security clearances canceled in 1977 servicewide, 1,500 were because of drug abuse.

Syva FRAT System for Detecting Drug Abuse

Drug abuse in the armed forces is not a recent phenomenon—it existed in near epidemic proportions in Vietnam. When the United

[1]George B. Leonard, *The Transformation* (New York: Delacorte Press, 1972), p. 195.

States finally decided to abandon the conflict in Southeast Asia, one of the most troubling problems for the Department of Defense was the potentially explosive effects of the return of hundreds of thousands of addicted servicemen to the United States.

I remember the situation well because a company that Syntex and Varian Associates founded in 1966 became involved in this situation. The Palo Alto company, called Syva, had developed a novel new system called FRAT to detect hard narcotics in human body fluids. The procedure consisted of mixing a drop of the subject's urine with an equal amount of a special Syva reagent and inserting it into an instrument where the results were immediately displayed. The Department of Defense used several of these Syva instrument systems in Vietnam to perform about 4,000 tests a day on servicemen leaving Vietnam. In 1971, the Department of Defense announced that the confirmed heroin addiction rate among these returning servicemen was running about 3.7%. The Veterans Administration responded to the crisis by expanding its network of five drug rehabilitation clinics to 27 so that it could handle 6,000 addicts a year.

The FRAT system evolved from basic research performed at Stanford University by Dr. Avram Goldstein, professor of pharmacology, and Dr. Harden M. McConnell, professor of chemistry. McConnell discovered a technique for imparting magnetic properties to biological molecules. Goldstein, for his part, introduced the concept of an immunological system using morphine-specific antibodies from the blood serum of rabbits for assaying opiates. Morphine is a breakdown product of heroin and is found in the urine of opiate users. Later in this chapter, I will describe some more recent research activities of Dr. Goldstein that may unlock the basic pharmacological mysteries of addiction.

The media have paid less attention to addictive diseases in the recent past not because the problem is getting any better but because public attention can be focused on an issue for just so long. In truth, the compulsive and excessive use of drugs, alcohol, and tobacco is as prevalent in our society as ever.

The social costs of these addictive diseases are devastating. They affect everyone, through the suffering of a friend or a family member as the victim of a drug-related crime, as a taxpayer supporting community or police programs, or as the carrier of insurance where rates are a reflection of social order.

Addiction Is Expensive for Business

Businesses suffer tremendous losses from absenteeism and other problems caused by addictive diseases.

Drunken employees, be they rank-and-file workers or top executives, not only have a high rate of absenteeism but generate safety problems on the job and create poor employee relations.

Despite millions spent to rehabilitate narcotics addicts, few are able to function successfully in society. Theft from employers becomes a serious problem when the addiction is to narcotics.

American cigarette smokers lose more days from work than nonsmokers. According to a federal survey released 10 years ago, each year there was an excess of 77 million workdays lost, 88 million workdays spent ill in bed, and 306 million workdays of restricted activity.

Addiction is a social disease in the sense that it grows out of economic, social and cultural conditions. But despite all the trouble it causes, surprisingly little is known about the scientific underpinnings of addictive diseases.

Just exactly how do narcotics and nicotine and alcohol act on the brain? How do they act upon "reward centers" of the brain? No one yet completely understands what changes in chemical balance or regulation are responsible for these dependent states—the states of craving more of the substance to which the person is addicted.

Narcotics addicts have been subjected to a plethora of treatments for well over half a century, yet relapse is still the rule after detoxification or incarceration. Methadone does not free addicts from drug use, it makes them dependent on a substitute opiate—most return to their habit once they go back to their old neighborhood and see their old friends.

"Cures" for alcohol and cigarette smoking involve "behavioral self-management techniques" but do not tackle the underlying physiological aspects of addiction.

Nevertheless, things are being done, and corporations have lent a hand in getting information about addicting substances into the public eye.

Addiction Education Program of Kemper Insurance

Kemper Insurance Companies has been one of the leading corporations in efforts to educate the public on the dangers of drug abuse and to help people deal with their addiction. When James S. Kemper, Jr., joined the company and was later named president of the company his father had founded, he already had a long-standing interest in the problems of alcoholism and drug dependency. As director during the 1950s of the Los Angeles Council on Alcoholism, he had acquired extensive knowledge of the role that industry could play in bringing its resources to bear on the illness of alcoholism. Also, long before the American public became concerned about the increase in drug abuse,

Jim Kemper had lent his assistance as a lawyer to the development of the Synanon drug-abuse recovery group, writing the by-laws and securing a State of California nonprofit charter for the organization.

In 1963, Kemper began its public information program with the publication of two pamphlets, written by Kenneth A. Rouse with editorial assistance from the National Council on Alcoholism. These pamphlets were "What to Do about an Employee with a Drinking Problem" and "Detour: Alcoholism Ahead." The former is an aid for employers in reducing costs and retaining valued employees; the latter helps supervisors and managers to identify the various work performance problems in developing alcoholism.

The objectives of this program were to stimulate and aid other companies, government, and other employers in the development of in-plant alcoholism-control programs along rehabilitative lines; to implement the corporate concerns of Kemper about alcoholism and alcohol abuse as community problems; and to provide the general public with knowledge about alcoholism and how to get help if affected by it.

By 1968, four more pamphlets had been published by the Kemper Insurance Companies:

> *Management Guide on Alcoholism and Other Behavioral Problems* (1963) serves as a resource for companies considering adopting controls for alcoholism, drug abuse, and emotional problems.
>
> *Guide for the Family of the Alcoholic* (1965) provides families with information that may lead to understanding and action in helping speed recovery for an alcoholic family member.
>
> *The Way to Go* (1966) is a factual summary for responsible people who drink, who drive, and who sometimes do both.
>
> *What about Drugs and Employees?* (1971) was written by Lewis F. Presnall, a nationally recognized authority on behavioral-problem controls in industry, who had been appointed by Kemper in 1969 to continue the direction of the corporation's programs. This booklet is a supplement to the "Management Guide." It outlines the formal policy of the Kemper companies regarding on-the-job instances of drug traffic and drug abuse.

The distribution of these booklets was launched in the early 1960s with advertisements in the *Wall Street Journal, Look,* and *U.S. News and World Report.*

The alcoholism booklet series has been promoted to business managers and personnel administrators, schools of alcoholism study, alcoholism rehabilitation centers, social service agencies, the general public, and youth clubs via periodic news releases in special-interest publications, trade publications, and the general news media. The series has enjoyed a total distribution of over 6 million copies in the past 14 years, averaging about 1 million copies in each of the past 3 years. Copies of these booklets are available, up to 50 copies free, from Kemper Insurance Companies, Long Grove, IL 60049.

Early in 1968, Kenneth A. Rouse conceived the idea that the National Industrial Conference Board (now called The Conference Board) might consider it worthwhile to do a 10-year follow-up study on its 1958 report, "Alcoholism in Industry." He discussed this with President Kemper, a board member of the NICB. Together they presented the idea for consideration to the board of directors. The suggestion was accepted, and subsequently the Kemper companies made a special $40,000 grant toward the cost of the study.

In May of 1971, Kemper produced a film on community action and drug abuse called "It Takes a Lot of Help." In coordination with this public service film, the National Coordination Council on Drug Education published a community action guide, "Common Sense Lives Here," which was offered with the film. The film's availability, at no cost to the general public, along with information about the booklet series and guidelines on in-plant controls for drug and alcohol problems, was published in a national advertising campaign. During the succeeding year and a half, the film was viewed by an estimated audience of 40 million people.

Kemper is also actively involved in supporting community groups who provide education, information, and counseling on alcoholism and drug abuse. The company has provided donations of funds and services in Illinois to such groups as the Lake County Council on Alcoholism, the Lake County Health Department, the Lake County Family Services Youth and Family Counseling Bureau, and Omni-House, a 24-hour crisis intervention service, youth and family counseling, and community referral service bureau.

Kemper has been a long-time supporter of the Boys Clubs of America. In 1977, the company specified that the firm's donations be used for the Boys Clubs' alcohol-abuse prevention program, "Project Teen." This is a national three-year program meant to instill in teenagers the importance of alcohol moderation. It provides a realistic approach to eliminating peer pressure to drink and educates on the physical, psychological, and cultural aspects of immoderate drinking.

A personal-assistance program at Kemper has aided employees and their family members with alcoholism, drug abuse, and other behavioral emotional problems for the past 16 years. This program is administered by two staff members, who are available via collect calls to employees companywide. The personal-assistance program is guided by the following policy statement:

1. We believe that alcoholism, drug addiction and emotional disturbance are illnesses and should be treated as such.

2. We believe the majority of employees who develop alcoholism, other drug addiction or emotional illness can be helped to recover and the company should offer appropriate assistance.
3. We believe the decision to seek diagnosis and accept treatment for any suspected illness is the responsibility of the employee. However, continued refusal of an employee to seek treatment when it appears that substandard performance may be caused by any illness is not tolerated. We believe that alcoholism, other drug addiction or emotional illness should not be made an exception to this commonly accepted principle.
4. We believe that it is in the best interest of employees and the company that when alcoholism, other drug addiction or emotional illness is present, it should be diagnosed and treated at the earliest possible date.
5. We believe that the company's concern for individual alcohol drinking, drug taking and behavioral habits begins only when they result in unsatisfactory job performance, poor attendance or behavior detrimental to the good reputation of the companies.
6. We believe that confidential handling of the diagnosis and treatment of alcoholism, other drug addiction or emotional illness is essential.

The objective of the policy is to retain employees who may develop any of these illnesses by helping them to arrest its further advance before the condition renders them unemployable.

For many years Kemper companies have hired recovered alcoholics. In 1971, Kemper became the first national employer to announce a nondiscriminatory policy of hiring recovered drug addicts. Guidelines were developed for personnel staff on interviewing and reference checking, bonding, job placement, and sensitizing of supervisory personnel. Unlike alcoholism and drug dependency controls in many companies, the Kemper program functions as well, if not better, among top-management personnel who develop these illnesses as it does at lower-paid occupational levels. The philosophy at Kemper is to strive for consistency in handling the stigmatized illnesses and their effects upon employees in a manner comparable to the way nonstigmatized illnesses are handled.

In the last three years, 350 Kemper employees were referred to the program or sought help voluntarily. Of those, 108 had problems with alcoholism and 116 had alcoholic family members. For the employees with alochol problems, Kemper had a 73% success rate. Everything is geared to help the employee keep his job. In 1976, out of 168 employees, Kemper lost only 33—most of whom were employees who left voluntarily for the same reasons that other people quit their jobs.

Efforts by Other Corporations

There are other examples of corporations that have made efforts in the area of drug and alcohol abuse education and treatment.

Abbott Laboratories, a pharmaceutical company with an obvious interest in the proper use of drugs, sponsored the writing of a pamphlet several years ago that answered common questions about drugs and drug abuse. It was distributed to the general public, schools, hospitals, pharmacies, and physicians, and it was syndicated in 147 daily newspapers.

Through the company's speakers bureau, Abbott scientists and physicians spoke to about 3,000 parents and students on the proper use of drugs each year. The company also donated $50,000 for the construction of a drug education classroom at the Robert Crown Health Education Center, serving 30,000 students in the Chicago area.

Union Carbide, working with the National Council on Alcoholism and Alcoholics Anonymous, commissioned a 12-minute film entitled "Need for Decision." It was designed to help supervisors in every industry to deal with performance problems that may be alcohol-related without diagnosing behavioral or medical problems. The film was requested by over 500 other companies.

Warner-Lambert Company loaned its auditorium to the Morris County (New Jersey) Drug and Alcohol Abuse Council for a series of seminars for industry and school personnel. The company also funded project "Breakthrough," which combined drug rehabilitation with a process of motivating young people to explore their own abilities.

Other drug companies that have funded drug educational or rehabilitation programs include SmithKline, Eli Lilly, Marion Laboratories, Ciba-Geigy, and Hoffman-LaRoche. Syntex lent its auditorium for meetings with low-income youngsters and drug project leaders. At other times, we've helped local organizations with the printing of brochures and stationery.

The Pharmaceutical Manufacturers Association, an industry group with which Syntex is affiliated, has made efforts to discourage the improper use of medicinal chemicals. The PMA's member companies account for about 95% of the prescription and over-the-counter drugs used in the United States. In 1970, the PMA, in cooperation with the American School Health Association, published a 216-page booklet, *Teaching about Drugs: A Curriculum Guide K–12*. By 1977, about 100,000 copies had been used in school systems not only in the United States but in countries abroad. As part of this project, the PMA also organized workshops at universities across the country to assist educators in implementing the use of the curriculum guide in elementary and high schools.

The PMA also developed several pamphlets for general distribution and a slide presentation on "The Problem of Drug Abuse." The national PMA speakers' service also makes company representatives available to community groups across the country to talk about the use of drugging substances. The association is located at 1155 Fifteenth Street, N.W., Washington, DC 20005.

Local Addiction Treatment Programs

In the San Francisco area, as in most other well-populated localities around the country, a wide variety of programs designed to combat addiction have been attempted. However, there is a growing determination to prevent addictive diseases and to provide the right kind of information early enough in a person's life so that he or she will be able to withstand the psychological pressures that commonly lead to addiction.

Other programs are trying to curtail drug use with the realization that forcing people to stop is unrealistic. Most local schools have drug education programs, outreach programs for parents, and teacher-training materials.

The "Drugs, Crime and Community" study at Stanford University has determined that the best grade levels for offering prevention programs are the sixth and seventh grades. By early high school, they found, it is too late to get a message across effectively.

Another local prevention program works with 12- to 18-year-old "predelinquents" or first offenders. The youngsters meet in groups of eight to rap about home problems, truancy, self-esteem—a whole constellation of factors that often predispose them to drug abuse. Working on all the problems at once in many instances helps the youngsters to level off on their drug use.

There are treament groups for the children of alcoholic parents. But social drinking among youth is on the rise. Figures for San Mateo County in California show that 10 years ago 65% of high school boys and girls had tried alcohol. In 1977, 88% had tried it.

Youngsters are smoking at a consistent rate. In 1968, 55.8% of San Mateo high school students had smoked. In 1977, the figure was 56.7%, having gone up to 59.1% five years ago. While there is a slight trend down in the figures, many adolescents are still getting hooked on tobacco today.

Community programs need sustained funding, one local expert said. Probably half the projects listed recently in California for combating addiction are now out of funding. Over the long run, this expert said, the problems will continue. There will be no solution, so we need to deal with it as best we can in order to keep as many people as possible from becoming dysfunctional.

But an intriguing question can be posed: Why does one person become addicted and not another? Some people seem able to smoke a few cigarettes a day, perhaps after a meal, but otherwise do not crave them. There are those who cannot stop drinking after the first sip of liquor. Others take it or leave it.

In the streets of Harlem, it is virtually a "rite of passage" for youngsters to try heroin. Most sample it, yet only a small fraction become addicted.

In Vietnam, thousands of soldiers used heroin under wartime stress. When they returned to this country, most were able to slough off the drug. A fraction of those using heroin remained hopelessly addicted.

Hospital patients given morphine for pain react to cessation of the drug differently. Some agonize, others find the withdrawal easier. Why?

Addiction Research Foundation

An effort to explain the underlying physiology of addiction is under way at the highly respected Addiction Research Foundation in Palo Alto. Founded five years ago on the premise that addiction is essentially a physiological problem compounded by sociopsychological influences, the foundation is pioneering both in new treatments and in new research.

Dr. Avram Goldstein, who was chairman of the pharmacology department at Stanford University for 15 years, created the foundation so that he could focus on addictive diseases without all the disruptions and distractions that come with university life. He now teaches a 20% load at Stanford and devotes most of his time to discovering the physiological cause of addiction. Goldstein has been widely acclaimed as one of the most brilliant and effective researchers in the United States today.

He is interested in narcotics and tobacco. The focus first has been on the opiates, since they are one of the most devastating of all addictive substances.

How does heroin act on the brain? All drugs, it seems, work by interacting with specific molecules in brain cells or cell membranes. This interaction triggers a chemical event called *drug action.* The specific brain molecules are called *receptors.* Receptors are known for a wide variety of substances in the brain, but Dr. Goldstein's group was among those who contributed to the discovery of a receptor for opiates.

The discovery was startling. The brain tissue of vertebrates (mice to men) contain specific molecules where heroin or morphine attach to nerve cells, like keys fitting into exactly the right lock. Once they are locked in place, a signal is passed on to another part of the brain to give the sensation of being high, to relieve pain, or, in the case of an overdose, to depress breathing. Receptor molecules are found almost exclusively in nervous system tissue (such as the brain and the spinal cord) and the nerve net of the intestine that controls intestinal contractions.

Since the first discovery, a whole family of opiate receptors has been found. One is located in the lower part of the brain stem where pain relief occurs. Another mediates feelings of reward and seems to be involved in the euphoric effect that opiates generate. From this line of research, there is the possibility of creating an opiumlike pain-killing drug that will not produce the euphoria and would thus be suitable for many medical uses in hospitals.

Once the receptors were discovered, a mystery remained. Opium and morphine are man-made substances. Why does brain tissue contain opiate receptors—unless there is an endogenous (inside) substance that behaves much as the opiates?

Soon another major discovery was made. The human body produces opiatelike substances that act on the brain just as morphine, heroin, and other opiates. They act like opiates, although their structure is quite different. These substances were named *endorphins* (for "endogenous morphinelike substances"). It would appear that endorphin is nature's natural defense mechanism against stress. Researchers today believe that endorphins have profound effects on human behavior, especially in the mediation of inner states. Endorphins affect the limbic system, where such feelings as tension, anxiety, aggression, and sexuality lie. Heroin addiction, in the light of this discovery, may well be a metabolic disease based on a natural endorphin deficiency in some individuals.

At this point, this theory is highly speculative. But it goes like this. Everybody produces endorphin for coping with stress and other upsetting influences. A few people do not produce enough endorphins naturally. When such a person received an opiate drug, his brain and body —suddenly for the first time—have enough of this substance to help him cope. He has always needed more of it. The craving sets in. Those with sufficient levels of endorphin who try heroin might better be able to fend off addiction. The drug is pleasant, to be sure, but their bodies do not react to the opiate in such a physically dependent manner.

Patients given a sufficient supply of thyroid hormone, Dr. Goldstein notes, will stop producing the hormones themselves. Their brains seem to release a signal that enough is being received, and the thyroid gland is put in a dormant state. Opiates may act in a similar way, reducing or wiping out the body's ability to produce natural levels of endorphin. The ability of a person to produce endorphin may become dormant or atrophy. Once the opiate is withheld, the brain may find itself totally without endorphins, and this lack may account for the incredible pain and severe discomfort of withdrawal. Withdrawal, Dr. Goldstein says, has been described as a bodywide toothache.

The foundation scientists are asking many questions: Is it possible to stimulate human cells to produce more endorphin? Is it possible to implant in the human system a time-release mechanism that would release nonaddictive, synthesized endorphins in order to maintain a balance and reduce the vulnerability of a prospective addict? It is possible that additional findings will lessen the time and suffering of withdrawal and maximize the release from addiction?

Many researchers around the world are fascinated by endorphins, which are providing clues to the nature of pain, pleasure, and the emotions. One area of research involves an explanation of how acupuncture works. A scientist in Toronto reported work with small animals in which he found that acupuncture prompts nerve cells to release endorphins, which then circulate as hormones to block pain pathways. Other research is focusing on severe mental illness and is seeking to find out if endorphins are involved in states of excessive anxiety, tension, or hostility.

At the Addiction Research Foundation, in the meantime, clinical work is proceeding around the new model of how opiates work. Testing of blood samples is just being done to compare levels of endorphins in addicts and nonaddicts.

Regular treatment is proceeding according to four steps. The first involves a chemical called LAAM, which is being tested at a number of other addiction centers around the country. LAAM produces a "flush" somewhat less than heroin, and the withdrawal is considerably reduced. Methadone, a similar drug, holds off withdrawal for 24 hours, but LAAM does this for up to 72 hours—giving the addict more time to free himself from the complications of his addiction.

While on LAAM, the addicts currently being treated are given intensive counseling. After several months, they go off LAAM. They experience withdrawal, but it is much less painful than the kind they would experience without the drug.

Finally, a dozen or so addicts have been given a new narcotic antagonist called *naltrexone.* It is a new approach being tested at about 12 other clinics in the country and seems to be effective. Naltrexone is a substance that seems to lock onto the opiate receptor (like opium), but it does not send forth any messages to produce euphoria or reduce pain. It simply acts as a plug, like a ball of wax or a wad of gum. If a former addict is tempted to shoot heroin, he can take naltrexone first. If he should succumb to the emotional or peer pressure to use the opiate, it will have no effect whatsoever on him for approximately 72 hours. Armed with naltrexone, a detoxified addict can reenter his old neighborhood and see his old friends, knowing that he has the backup support necessary to resist the old habit.

The Addiction Research Foundation receives most of its $1.25 million budget from the federal government. But, they say, government grants are tenuous. Each year, their funding requires Congressional approval. A 10% cut across the board could hurt badly. Moreover it takes up to a year after making an application to the government for the granting agency to reach a yes-or-no decision. Since it is important that there be a continuous and even an accelerated flow of scientific research activity, the foundation frequently seeks other funds.

One scientist, Dr. Sue Gentleman, who was staining some pituitary material with a chromatograph complained to a board member that she had been standing there for two months, separating and separating the material: "When I'm through I won't know what I've got. There will be 20 to 30 percent resolution. But with a $10,000 high pressure liquid chromatograph, I could do all the work in one and a half weeks. It would save all my time while you pay me and my assistant to do this. And we could get 80 to 90 percent resolution. We would know what we've discovered."

The problem was explained to a local businessman who had a friend at Altech, a company in Berkeley. Within a few months, the company donated the special machine to the foundation.

Another day Dr. Gene Baizman was also sighing in frustration. "If only I had a sterotaxic frame and generator," he said, "I could really move on the effects of endorphin on animal behavior."

The frame is a device that immobilizes animals so that researchers can probe any part of its brain in three dimensions. The frame cost $2,450. The problem was explained to Syva, and within one week the foundation had the funds to open up this whole new area.

The foundation now needs a gamma radiation counter, which will help them find out if their theories about natural levels of endorphin are true. It costs $10,000, and the foundation says it can't wait for a government decision. They need the instrument now.

Right now the Addiction Research Foundation is seeking $400,000 to set up a companion laboratory that would focus on nicotine addiction. Nicotine is what smokers crave, since nicotine-free cigarettes are not rewarding to habitual smokers. Next to nothing is known about the specific mechanisms by which nicotine affects the cells of the brain. There are nicotine receptors on the periphery of the spine, but no one knows if there are endogenous nicotinelike substances in the human body. One area of research should be to locate the specific area of the brain where a person is "rewarded" for using nicotine.

If there is a parallel mechanism of an internal substance, foundation scientists might be able to synthesize a nicotine inhibitor. A person would then be able to give up cigarettes without the sensation of craving the nicotine.

The foundation is also seeking a top-level scientist to head the nicotine research effort. However, they know that they will be looking for an established scientist with tenure. To bring such a man to the foundation, they will need to guarantee him a salary and a secure position. They are thinking how nice it would be to have $800,000 to establish an endowed chair for such a person at Stanford University—so that they could attract the very best person to tackle the problem.

The foundation may never have time to get to the problems of alcohol addiction, but the subject is in competent hands elsewhere. Dr. Dora Goldstein (Avram's wife) is one of the nation's leading researchers in this field. As a research associate in the department of pharmacology at Stanford, she is currently studying cell membranes to see how alcohol affects them physically (rather than chemically).

Alcohol seems to affect brain cells by disrupting membranes. Normal membranes have some rigidity as they pass sodium and potassium through their walls. But alcohol loosens up the membranes, literally making them mushy.

Another major area of research in alcohol today concerns to what extent the substance damages unborn babies. With large doses in animals, the effects are devastating. Scientists are working to establish what small amounts do, if anything, to human fetuses.

The question of what causes a craving for alcohol is unanswered. There is certainly a psychological basis for such addiction, and that is where most of the research is going on.

A new lead, related to this, is that scientists have just discovered a compound that, when injected in rats, makes them drink more. It could lead nowhere, but for the time being it looks very interesting to Dr. Dora Goldstein and her colleagues.

She, too, said that corporations can help this effort. Some companies provide travel grants for students or library funds to buy special books. All of these sorts of things are extremely helpful, she said.

The Swedish biochemist Theorell once told how he approached a foundation president seeking financial support for his basic research:

> *F.P.* If we give you the money, which disease do you intend to cure?
> *Theorell.* None at all. But do you have a watch?
> *F.P.* Yes.
> *Theorell.* What do you do in case it stops running?
> *F.P.* Well, I take it to the watchmaker.
> *Theorell.* Why do you take it to the watchmaker?
> *F.P.* What do you mean?
> *Theorell.* Well, you do it because the watchmaker knows how the watch is constructed and therefore how he can repair the watch. I try to find out how the living body is constructed and when we know that we shall be able to repair it.

Theorell received his grant, adding, "I sincerely hope governments, parliaments, research councils and private donors to science would come to the same conclusion. All applied research is founded upon basic research." I would add that while we are dealing in the best way we can with the enormous problems of addiction, we should support the efforts of those who might figure out a basic cause of the problem.

17

Employment: Looking for New Ways to Work

We believe that people deserve the opportunity to work in places where they can be creative, work cooperatively instead of competitively and take on responsibilities as their interests and capabilities merit.[1]

Early in the 1970s, the quality of a person's work life began to emerge as an issue central to many of our society's other concerns. Terms such as *job boredom, worker alienation,* and *the changing work ethic* became the focus for discussions, conferences, and a burgeoning new literature. Harold Robbins's *Where Have All the Robots Gone?,* Judson Gooding's *The Job Revolution,* and the massive report on *Work in America* published by the Department of Health, Education, and Welfare were some of the works that were influential in focusing attention on the problems of people who work—which is most of us.

Although much of the national interest highlighted the problems of the blue-collar worker, these same questions of work satisfaction in our home community of Palo Alto seemed to revolve around mid-career professionals (often engineers), college-educated entry-level workers, and women who were seeking to enter or reenter the job market. During this period, I began to have some conversations with my friend Sydney Brown about work. Our discussions covered questions like: "Is it only work if someone pays you for it?" and "How much unemployment *really* exists?" (I think Sydney was the first person I heard who used the term *hidden unemployment*) and "Can some kinds of work be destructive to people?" These discussions were eventually to lead into a relationship between several of us at Syntex and a new kind of community organization.

[1]Michael Closson, Sarah Johnson, and Debby Satten, *Work is for People: Innovative Workplaces of the San Francisco Bay Area* (San Francisco: New Ways to Work, 1978), p. 5.

Brown's interest in work followed a course that had started twenty years before when she had done a master's thesis on the employment problems of displaced persons after World War II. Her recent experience with people and jobs was more direct. She had worked for several years as a volunteer counselor for a nonprofit, grass-roots employment service in the adjacent black community of East Palo Alto. This was in addition to spending time counseling reentry women in a program sponsored by the YWCA and working with a Stanford University course for unemployed aerospace engineers.

Several years of talking with all kinds of people who were having trouble finding any kind of meaningful work had led her to the conclusion that our community as a whole badly needed a place that would support the individual's quest for constructive, fulfilling work and, at the same time, would strive to improve the quality of work in the wider community.

In our conversations, Brown envisioned an organization that would "wear two hats . . . one as a resource center and one as a social change agency." She felt that in this way people could be encouraged to think of how they can make changes in their own work lives and then would be provided with information, support, and job listings to help them do it. At the same time, this new organization would act as a force to encourage social change by endeavoring to implement new work patterns that would be more responsive to the needs expressed by the people who came for help to the resource center.

From time to time in the fall of 1972, I would see Brown, and she would tell me about the forays into the community that she and two friends were making. Their new organization was beginning to take shape in "think sessions" around various kitchen tables. These forays into the community to sample and survey existing employment resources were giving the three women an idea of what information and counseling existed already—and what kinds of help were lacking. After much thought, they had decided on a name for their new center; it was to be called New Ways to Work.

In December of 1972, I received an invitation to attend an open house celebrating the inauguration of the new community work-resource center. Although they still had no funding sources (having decided against charging fees because they felt it was inappropriate for a social change agency to depend on unemployed people for its major income), they had made arrangements to trade six months' free rent for the labor and materials necessary to renovate one room of an old residence, formerly used as a drug rehabilitation drop-in center and owned by the First Presbyterian Church.

When I arrived, the room had a cheery fire going and was furnished with comfortable overstuffed furniture. Shelves with information about training programs, job restructuring, affirmative action policies, and alternative work patterns lined the room, and a poster on the wall proclaimed "Caution: Human Beings Here, Handle with Care." I couldn't help mentally contrasting this setting with the sterile employment-agency offices I had seen, or the crowded, computer-oriented State Human Resources Development offices.

Several months after the opening of New Ways to Work, I was invited to a bag lunch there. In order to foster discussion of work-world issues, the staff had inaugurated a series of "brown-bag" talks. Some of the people coming to the center to talk in this informal manner with clients and NWW staff had been Jim Kuhn, a visiting professor of labor economics from Columbia University; Barbara Babcock, an expert on women's employment problems; Bill Gould, a leading authority on affirmative action from Stanford University's Law School faculty; and Myra Stroeber, then the only woman faculty member at Stanford's Graduate School of Business.

Arriving with my sandwich, I found about 15 people sitting around the room in a circle. Before we began to talk, Sydney Brown filled me in on the kinds of people that were coming to the center. About 80 men and women a month were coming to them for counseling. They included unemployed Ph.D.'s, reentry women, and people looking for alternative vocations.

In inviting me, the staff had wanted to talk about corporate social responsibility. To many of them, this was a new concept and they were not sure to what extent it had been accepted by major employers in the Bay Area. They felt it could be a motivating force that would encourage some of the changes in work patterns that they were trying to effect. The ensuing discussion was wide-ranging and touched on many issues relating to the quality of work and how employment patterns could be changed to allow for more flexibility and integration with the rest of a person's life.

After the lunch session ended, I stayed on to talk with Brown and another staff member, Barney Olmsted. I asked them if they had considered writing a newsletter that would pull together the kinds of information on alternative work situations and changing employment patterns that we had been discussing at lunch. I felt that employers would be interested in much of it and that it would be another way of projecting their ideas to a wider audience. I also asked how their funding was coming. They happily reported that they had been granted seed money for their first year's operation from the Luke B. Hancock Foundation. As they were about three months into the grant at the time, I suggested that they begin thinking about corporate contributions as one source of funds for their continued operation.

A happy postscript to my bag lunch arrived in the mail a month or so later: it was the first edition of the *New Ways to Work Newsletter* for employers.

Shortly after the center's first anniversary, I received a letter from Olmsted outlining a request for funding as part of a system of community support for the center. I passed the request on to some other members of the Syntex staff, among them Karl McCalla, who was then our affirmative action officer. McCalla decided to visit the organization and came back with a very positive report on the diligence and commitment of the NWW staff. Based upon his recommendation, the contributions committee decided to contribute to their support.

As time went on, I began to hear of special projects that New Ways to Work was initiating. Some of them follow.

Summer Youth Employment Service

Palo Alto is a suburban community. As in most areas today, jobs are hard to find for all age groups, but the younger, less-experienced job seeker has the hardest time of all. Because they felt that it was important to "help kids find something to do with themselves during the summer," NWW embarked on a special program of counseling and job development for young people. They had an emphasis not only on helping to find jobs but on encouraging the young people to *create* their own jobs. The center offered space in which they could pass on their own skills and talents by teaching classes. High school and college students could teach arts, crafts, music, backpacking—or anything else. The teachers arranged their own schedules and fees. A program of unpaid apprenticeships was also started—some in an architectural firm, a bakery, a bookstore, a bicycle shop—in which youngsters could learn various aspects of the business in which they worked. The first summer's program was such a success that when NWW asked us to help support the second year of operation, we not only contributed to the base funding but made an additional gift to the Summer Youth Desk.

In the summer of 1977, nearly 600 youths used the service—about 40 young people every day. Each was individually interviewed and counseled by one of the co-directors before being referred to jobs. These young people filled over 275 jobs listed with the Youth Employment Service and were given leads on over 400 other open positions.

An Affirmative Action Forum

In the fall of 1974, in cooperation with the City of Palo Alto's Human Relations Commission, New Ways to Work presented a one-day forum to diccuss and exchange information regarding ways that could lead to more effective methods of affirmative action implementation. We were pleased when Bob Dilks (now director of affirmative action affairs for the company) and Karl McCalla from Syntex were asked to lead a workshop on how to generate the support of managers and supervisors for affirmative action. In addition to their participation, the company sent three other staff people to the forum. The day's program started with a keynote address by Bill Hewlett, then president of Hewlett-Packard, calling for active participation by private industry in implementing affirmative action. Instead of rehashing compliance regulations or the need for such programs, the day's discussion moved on to focus on creative approaches to such areas as recruiting women for nontraditional jobs and keeping a balance between the affirmative action needs of women and those of minority men. The resource-people used on panels and in discussion groups were a combination of industry representatives and community-group people. Those of us who attended that day went away feeling that NWW had succeeded in giving us a broader perspective on one of our problem areas by involving some new voices in the dialogue.

Job Sharing

As New Ways to Work continued to expand its contacts with other people and groups exploring new work patterns, it began to develop an extensive file on job sharing. Even before the center opened, one of the major areas around which Sydney Brown and her friends had accumulated information was the restructuring of jobs, both in terms of content and in terms of time. On several occasions, staff members at the center commented to me about the growing numbers of people who came in looking for *permanent part-time* employment. They once estimated that 30% of the people they saw were seeking an alternative to the 40-hour work week. Therefore, a number of people at NWW had been interested in testing the feasibility of restructuring full-time jobs by having two people "share" them. On several occasions, they had helped one person who wanted career-oriented permanent part-time work to pair up with another person and interview for a full-time job as a team. A couple of these teams had been hired and were successfully sharing their jobs. NWW began to acquire a reputation as an authority on this new work arrangement, and more and more people started to come to them for help.

In the fall of 1975, I spent an evening with Sydney Brown at a friend's house. It had been some time since I had seen her, and I wondered how NWW and she were weathering the high rates of unemployment that had plagued our community for the past several months. She confirmed that the center had had a considerable increase in numbers of people coming to them for help. She also told me about a new project of the center that had recently been funded by the federal Comprehensive

Employment Training Act (CETA). NWW had been able to interest the state in testing the feasibility of teaching people how to share a job. The goal of their pilot project was to help those individuals who wanted permanent part-time employment to restructure full-time jobs by sharing them. In this way, they hoped to be able to employ more people and also to enhance the quality of work life for those who needed or preferred a part-time option. It was an interesting concept to me, and I asked her if she would send me some additional information on it. The next day, an "Employers Packet on Job Sharing" arrived in my mail.

I was not the only one interested in this new work arrangement. A few months later, Sylvia Porter wrote a column mentioning the NWW project, and it has now become known and discussed all over the country. It is probably the most "glamorous" of the "new ways to work" that the center has advocated. However, some of the other areas in which they have begun to build a special kind of expertise, hold a potential for influencing even larger numbers of people.

Constructive Work

An ongoing theme expressed by the people coming to NWW—and then articulated to the larger community through the organization's newsletter and contacts with employers—is the need that people feel for "constructive" work.

Attracted by the center's name, one of the first questions most men and women ask is "Have you really found a new way to work?" The job-sharing program is a help to those looking for new kinds of part-time positions, but by far the larger number need full-time employment. The Constructive Work project was begun in October 1976 as an effort to identify new models for these men and women.

Defining *constructive work* as work that is "compatible with the individual's needs and principles and, in addition, is ecologically sound in a humane environment," the project staff collected a series of detailed profiles of people and places of employment that are innovative in work process or product or service. The information already has been incorporated into a booklet, published in 1978, that serves as a model and an inspiration to those who feel as the worker quoted by Studs Terkel in *Working*, who said:

> Jobs are not big enough for people. It's not just the assembly line worker whose job is too small for his spirit, you know? A job like mine, if you really put your spirit into it, you would sabotage immediately. . . . My mind has been so divorced from my job, except as a source of income, it's really absurd.[2]

---

[2]Studs Terkel, *Working* (New York: Pantheon, 1974), p.521.

In watching NWW grow into a positive force in the Palo Alto, I had, on several occasions, encouraged Sydney Brown to put as much information as possible in written form—as a means both of helping spread the center's creative ideas and of developing a product that could provide an additional source of funding. (She, in turn, pushed at me to write this book.)

Consequently, when Sydney arrived in my office with a prospectus for a "how-to" book on creating a community work center, I was interested in exploring how we might help. I had known that she and her husband Robert McAfee Brown, the theologian, were moving to New York City and was glad that she wanted to write a blueprint for others out of her past few years' experience. With much encouragement by others and much hard work by herself, she completed the first draft of the manuscript before moving east. We contributed the services of Tom Lunde of our graphics group, who did the cover design, and Syntex printed the first edition in-house as an "in-kind" contribution. *The People's Guide to a Community Work Center* appeared early in 1977.

In the past four years, various members of the Syntex staff have related, in a number of different ways, to this unique organization. As we all explore and better understand the ramifications of men and women's desire for a better quality of work life, I hope that the corporate world and the wider community can continue to cooperate, and that, with the help of Brown's book, centers like New Ways to Work will proliferate.

In closing this subject, I would like to pass on some feelings that emerged in a discussion of this chapter with my friend and colleague Perry Leftwich. We agreed that the subject was compelling and of interest to many thoughtful people, especially those well-educated persons with whom the chapter is primarily concerned. It would be only natural for such individuals to seek satisfaction in the work they do, in contrast to the average worker who often has few options in what he or she can do. The chapter clearly differentiates one from the other and deals primarily with the professional.

Perry and I expressed positive feelings about what is being done with concerned professionals, but we had uneasy feelings about what is *not* being done with the work force as a whole. Perhaps our uneasiness stems from the belief that "job satisfaction" is not really the whole answer. We were reacting in a sense to Albert Camus's remark that with no work all life goes rotten; and when work is without soul, life suffocates and dies. We felt that Camus could have added: Without life all work goes rotten. But when life is soulless, work stifles and dies.

We decided that we cannot look to anything less than our whole lives—our families, our communities, our institutions, our beliefs, as well as our work—for feelings of completeness and self-esteem. Such a concept, we felt, embraces *all* of us—even the worker who repeats a dull chore hour after hour, year after year, and who has no real idea of intellectualizing satisfaction for his soul in the creative placement of an iron rivet.

18

Environment and Ecology

All things by immortal power
Near or far
Hiddenly
To each other, linked are
That thou canst not stir a flower
Without troubling a star.[1]

Just a few years ago, we woke up to the fact the world was a limited resource and that it and we were in the middle of an environmental crisis. We said good-bye to pelicans and wondered how long Bengal tigers and humpback whales would survive. We realized that the convenience of the automobile was giving way to the inconvenience of traffic, noise, and smog. The increased use of air conditioners, clothes dryers, and time-saving home appliances meant building more and more power plants to avoid blackouts and brownouts.

Worse yet, we were told that starvation was in store for the underdeveloped countries and that more respiratory diseases were in store for the affluent. If mankind continued on the present course, the demographers said, in 900 years there would be about 100 persons for each square yard of the earth's surface—land and sea. Meanwhile, the United States was running out of room for the 7 million junked cars, 30 million tons of paper, 28 billion bottles, and 48 billion cans we discarded each year.

In a few short years, we've all taken a good, hard look at the ecology problem. It's probably safe to say that some people have tried to do something about it. But awareness and trying haven't been limited to concerned individuals. Corporations, universities, governments, and

[1]Francis Thompson, "The Mistress of Vision." In *Complete Poetical Works of Francis Thompson* (New York: Boni & Liveright, 1918), p. 184.

private groups have begun to work at finding solutions. For, in the end, it will require the collective efforts of individuals and institutions if a healthy and productive environment is to be preserved.

In the past, the problem has been looked at in small units—what was done by this factory, what was done in this city, what was done by this country. Today we have the knowledge and the tools to look at the whole earth, to look at everybody on it, to look at its resources, to look at the state of technology, and to begin to deal with the *whole* problem. Commenting about our spectacular efforts in space flight, the late Margaret Mead said that one of the most important concerns we now have is the *tenderness* that we experience in seeing the earth as small, lonely, and blue.

The 17th-century poet Francis Thompson expressed in a spiritual way what we now know to be true for our physical universe. We truly live in a "holocoenotic" world, where all life and the physical processes within life are interconnected and interacting.

In college, I read Francis Thompson and admired his works, but it wasn't until one summer day in 1970 in Aspen, Colorado, that I grasped the reality of a physically and biologically integrated universe. Dick Beidleman, a Colorado College professor and environmentalist, was taking a small group of people into an aspen grove to emphasize an important ecological principle: "carrying capacity."

He brought us to the edge of the grove and asked us to listen. We soon heard a birdsong that he identified as a vireo, one of the birds that made its nest in the trees of the grove. He then asked us to move further into the grove, counting our steps to pace off a measured distance; then we stopped and listened. We now heard the same song. Was the bird following us? "No," Dick said, "it is *another* vireo." We repeated the procedure of pacing, stopping, and listening. The result was the same —right to the end of the grove! We discovered exactly how many vireos made their home in that aspen grove.

It was an interesting way to learn that creatures were instinctively aware of the principle of carrying capacity. That they knew exactly how much space they required for survival. They knew how much area would provide them with the food and necessities for their existence. They also had a way of informing other competitive creatures that this space was theirs and that trespassers would not be greeted in a friendly fashion.

I was so moved by this lesson in the woods that I sat down that evening and wrote a poem about it that I called "Aspen Grove":

> The warbling vireo puts out a fence of song
> So well hidden
> Not afraid to proclaim his rangeland·
> Even from his nest
> Where soundless chimes
> Little breezes make of Aspen leaves

And unrespecting gnats
Become day-long snacks
For the flycatcher in the grove

In a many ringed conifer
Spared many rings ago
By flame, wind and slide
That wasted wide
All but this solitary sky notched spruce
The siskin darts from high set limb
To chase airy seeds of native dandelion
Yellow bloomed weedy occupant
Of a weedy grove

Two young deer move among the middle
Distant trees and bush

The wild parsley and lupine pay no mind
Except to their own quiet beauty color

Thorne Ecological Institute

My experience with Dick Beidleman was shared by a diverse group of individuals who were spending five days in the Rocky Mountains at an environmental seminar presented by the Thorne Ecological Institute.

The seminar had been brought to my attention by Dr. Richard Waugh, then president of the company's chemical subsidiary in Boulder, Colorado. Waugh had attended the seminar the previous year and was so enthusiastic that he became a member of the steering committee to plan future seminars. Later I was to become a member of Thorne's national advisory committee.

Waugh said that the 1969 seminar was a stimulating and worthwhile experience from start to finish. The participants and staff, he said, represented an excellent mix of technical experts, laymen, and people from industry and government. They included a stonemason, a housewife, several college professors and deans, staff officers in the U.S. Corps of Engineers, representatives of the chemical and petroleum industries, officials from the U.S. Bureau of Reclamation, a state senator, a justice of the supreme court of New York State, the editor of the *Christian Science Monitor,* and a U.S. Congressman from Wisconsin.

The seminar in 1970 was attended by an equally diverse group, including Charles F. Luce, chairman of Consolidated Edison Corporation, and General Frederick J. Clarke, chief of the Army Corps of Engineers.

These seminars were organized by Dr. Beatrice Willard, executive vice-president of the TEI. In 1972, Willard was appointed by President

Nixon to the Council on Environmental Quality. She is currently professor of environmental sciences at the Colorado School of Mines in Golden.

In planning the sessions, Bettie Willard had several objectives. She wanted to develop an appreciation of basic ecological principles; to enhance the quality and extent of citizen leadership in environmental matters; and to offer a field exploration of ecology for leaders in business, government, politics, education, the arts, and communications.

The key to the success of the seminars was that more than half of the five days was spent in small groups in the field under the guidance of skilled leaders observing the effects of ecological forces. The seminar provided a unique opportunity for the interaction of decision makers and interested lay people with technical experts in an atmosphere that was conducive to understanding and a meaningful exchange of views.

The most important outcome of the seminar was the change of attitudes and the dedication to ecological principles that developed in the participants. The environmental experts became aware of the growing concern on the part of members of industry and government about environmental deterioration. The environmentalists, on the other hand, learned about the real and substantial problems involved in rapidly changing some of the unecological policies and practices designed into our society and our economy throughout the 20th century. It was apparent that the changes in attitude of all participants would reach out in a far wider circle in much the same fashion as a ripple spreading over the surface of water.

As a result of our attendance at these seminars, the company gave some support to the Thorne Institute, and Dick and I made efforts to encourage other company executives to attend. Those that did also had a positive reaction:

> I learned that serious ecologists are attacking the grave problems with a balanced view. I focused my thinking to the point where a new dimension, the ecology of the situation, will be added to our decision-making process.
> —Earl L. Barkley, Vice-President and General Manager, Syntex Agribusiness, Inc.

Other corporations across the country that have sent participants are equally enthusiastic:

> The one thing that stood out is that its success was due in large measure to the diversity of the people who participated. This plus the very smoothly run schedule and high caliber staff people made this, for my money, one of the most worthwhile conferences I have ever attended.
> —George S. Caldes, Manager, Environmental and Consumer Affairs, Du-Pont De Nemours

For companies that are trying to increase environmental awareness within their organization, these seminars can serve an important purpose. Information can be obtained from Thorne Ecological Institute, 2336 Pearl Street, Boulder, CO 80302. The institute can also use company contributions to maintain and expand its programs. Many firms have provided financial support, including American Metal Climax, IBM, American Smelting & Refining, Public Service of Colorado, U.S. Gypsum, Utah International, Exxon, Georgia-Pacific Corporation, Sports Illustrated, and Cleveland Cliffs Iron Company.

Sempervirens Fund

In the same year that I attended the Thorne seminar, the company made its first contribution to another environmental organization: the Sempervirens Fund. This first modest contribution resulted from a letter sent to one of our corporate officers by Dorothy Varian, the widow of Russell Varian, a physicist, inventor, and co-founder of Varian Associates, a Palo Alto-based electronics firm. In her letter, Mrs. Varian told us about the plans of the Sempervirens Fund to raise public and private funds for the completion of two neighboring state parks in northern California: Castle Rock and Big Basin Redwoods Parks.

She told us that Castle Rock was a brand-new park that her husband had initiated with a plan to purchase and donate to the state of California about 600 acres in the vicinity of a site known as Castle Rock. Russell Varian died shortly after he obtained an option on the first key property in 1959, but Dorothy told us that she had been working hard for eight years to complete her husband's plans. She told us that the Varian Foundation (funded from the royalties of Russell's invention of the klystron tube and other instruments) had already purchased 1,000 acres of what would eventually be a 2,500-acre park.

Mrs. Varian also told us about Big Basin, a larger park in the same area (destined to be 18,000 acres), which was in some danger. Actually Big Basin is the oldest park in the California State Park system. It was established in 1902, when a group of local conservationists persuaded legislators and the governor that preserving giant redwoods in Big Basin was infinitely more important than felling them for timber. These were the first redwoods preserved in California. The original grove was purchased with an appropriation of $250,000. The land today is worth about $15 million—a real tribute to the foresight of those Californians working for the environment three-quarters of a century ago.

The immediate problem with Big Basin was the 9,000 acres still within the park boundaries that were in private hands and in danger of being logged or their park values lost through resort or subdivision development.

The goal of the Sempervirens Fund, Dorothy Varian said, was to undertake a unique partnership with the state aimed at the acquisition of all necessary lands required for the preservation of the two parks. The plan anticipated that the state would provide a large portion of the funds required for acquisition, while the Sempervirens Fund would seek private gifts and the acquisition of key parcels to block any efforts toward development.

We responded to Dorothy Varian's appeal with a modest contribution and a pledge to take a continuing and meaningful interest in Castle Rock and Big Basin. Our first gift was used to equip a campsite in Castle Rock Park. In 1971, we were able to provide a larger gift to help in the acquisition of a parcel that connected Big Basin with the sea. In the following year, we helped Sempervirens by hosting an all-day meeting of 30 sponsors and members of the organization's board of directors in our new company conference center.

In 1974, Tony Look, the executive vice-president of Sempervirens, sent us an interesting proposal involving the Saratoga Toll Road—an alternate parallel route to the Skyline-to-the-Sea Trail that would eventually connect Castle Rock and Big Basin. The toll road was constructed in the late 1860s for the movement of timber and served as a private thoroughfare until it was turned over to Santa Cruz County. The proposal was to have a study done on the feasibility of using the toll road as a hiking and riding trail. The study would be performed by Kristin Ohlson, an undergraduate student in environmental studies at the University of California at Santa Cruz.

We liked the idea and agreed to provide the modest funding required, and I met with Kristin Ohlson to take a walking tour of part of the trail. Late in 1974, we received a copy of the completed report, which contained a history of the toll road; data on ownership of parcels bordering the road; a natural resource inventory of the area; a number of photographs, maps, and other illustrations; and 10 recommendations for the implementation of a plan to use the toll road as a hiking and riding trail.

In 1975, we provided some funds to help complete the acquisition of the Founders Grove of redwoods, 75 years after this group first met in Big Basin and formed the Sempervirens Club. Also in that year, we helped fund a proposal for two interns from the University of California at Santa Cruz to research and map the entire network of trails throughout the Santa Cruz Mountains.

By 1980, the work of the founders of Sempervirens and the dream of Russell and Dorothy Varian will be a reality. The efforts of many dedicated people will have put together one of the great state park complexes in northern California. It is significant that the tremendous efforts of these environmentalists generated about $4.5 million of state and federal funds in support of their vision and perseverance.

The Nature Conservancy

While we were getting involved with Thorne and Sempervirens in the early 1970s, I read an editorial in the local newspaper about another environmental organization: the Nature Conservancy.

The editorial said that the Nature Conservancy, a nonprofit organization that specialized in acquiring natural lands that it would eventually turn over to a government agency, had obtained an option on some important San Francisco baylands and was looking for funds to complete the purchase. I wrote to the western regional director of the Conservancy, Huey D. Johnson, and enclosed a modest company contribution to assist in the purchase of the 80-acre shorebird area known as the Morse Baylands. This was the beginning of an association with Huey Johnson that has continued and grown in mutual respect to this day.

I later learned from Johnson that the Conservancy was trying to acquire some land in California that was part of a unique ecological staircase. This area was known to me because my wife, Ann, and I had an opportunity to visit at the invitation of John Olmstead of the California Institute of Man and Nature.

It is a unique section of the Mendocino Coast, where five level terraces climb the coastal scarp in 100-foot steps from the ocean's edge. Each succeeding terrace is 100,000 years older than the one below it, and each one displays distinctly different plant communities in an ordered sequence. In Jughandle Creek bottom, below the youngest terrace, Alaska biologically meets Mexico as the Sitka spruce and the bishop pine stand side by side.

I sent to Huey Johnson a copy of a poem, "Jughandle Creek," which I had written after Ann and I spent the day in the area with John Olmstead. Unfortunately, I wasn't able to attach a company check to it.

Johnson told me that the Conservancy was starting a new program to obtain business support for its programs. Up to that point, the organization's funding came from foundations and individuals. Corporate members were being solicited at $1,000 per year. We decided that it was a fine idea, and in 1971 Syntex became the first corporate member of the Nature Conservancy. In 1972, three other corporations came aboard: Equitable Life Assurance Society, General Mills, and State Bank of Albany, New York. Since then, over 180 corporations have become members, providing a substantial amount of annual financial support from the business community.

The Conservancy's successes have been many. Over 1,700 areas of forest, swamps, marshes, prairies, mountains, and beaches, involving nearly 1 million acres through the United States, have been saved from development or destruction through direct Conservancy action and involvement. The Conservancy and its 42,000 members have been responsible for protecting natural lands in 47 states. It also maintains 680 reportedly owned sanctuaries across the nation. For each dollar expended for operations in 1976, the Conservancy preserved land with an estimated market value of $28. That is what businessmen enthusiastically refer to as financial leverage!

The National Science Foundation has contracted with the Conservancy to collect and organize, in one central computerized data base, information on "established scientific ecological reserves." The Conservancy also received a seed grant from Exxon to compile much more comprehensive, but closely related, data on areas to be preserved. Through the collection of these programs, the Conservancy plans to create a national data bank containing information on the existence, status, condition, and distribution of all natural areas and their components. Such a bank will identify valuable tracts of land based upon hard facts that justify the area's importance.

The Nature Conservancy publishes an annual report that can be obtained from the national office, 1800 North Kent Street, Arlington, VA 22209. The locations of 15 regional, field, and state chapter offices are listed in the annual report.

Corporations desiring to participate in the preservation of natural lands can usually find projects in their own areas. This type of local participation is usually the most worthwhile and results in maximum recognition by employees and by the people in the communities where the firm's facilities are located.

The Trust for Public Land

Late in 1972, Huey Johnson sent to me information about a new environmental organization: the Trust for Public Land. He was going to leave Nature Conservancy and launch his new organization early in 1973. The TPL would be based on principles similar to those of Nature Conservancy, with some new approaches and objectives. It would involve the preservation of a worthwhile *urban* lands as well as wilderness areas. It would also concentrate on the development of a new group of professionals—retirees and dedicated young professionals—to become land experts in their own communities throughout the country.

The TPL began with solid financial support, including start-up grants from the Ford Foundation, the San Francisco Foundation, and the Andrew Norman Foundation, and a $10 million line of credit from the Bank of America. Later the TPL would receive broad support, including contributions from Boeing, Equitable Life, Sunset Magazine, Title Insurance & Trust Company, Touche Ross, and Weyerhauser.

One of Huey Johnson's most pressing problems after lining up financing was to start building his staff organization. I recommended my neighbor and friend Bob McIntyre to fill a key financial position. Bob graduated from Stanford and received an MBA from Harvard. After several years with Philco-Ford, he ran his own small manufacturing firm and was involved with a nonprofit organization that assisted minority businesses. Johnson and McIntyre hit it off from the first interview. Bob joined the TPL early in 1973 and was named financial vice-president about a year later.

In 1975, I was invited to become a member of the national advisory council of the TPL, joining an ex-Syntex financial vice-president, Kenneth Davis, whom I had introduced to Huey Johnson when he was establishing the organization.

In its first four years, the TPL got off to a good start. In 39 projects in seven states, 10,800 acres of land were preserved through the organization's land acquisition techniques. The value of these properties was $21.7 million, and $4.9 million in public funds were saved in the acquisition process. TPL regional operations were established in Ohio, Florida, and the New York–New Jersey area.

The TPL devoted a great deal of energy to developing new recruitment and training concepts. It trained retired volunteers, university interns preparing for careers in land conservation, and local citizens interested in organizing community land trusts. This effort was supported in part by a Rockefeller Brothers Fund grant.

The promotion of local independent land trusts emerged as an exciting area for the TPL. The land trust provides an opportunity for a community's participation in the shaping of its own destiny. This is accomplished through acquisition efforts and long-range stewardship of the land. Lands protected by local trusts can be held in perpetuity for a wide range of public uses.

In line with its philosophy of preserving and developing city areas for community use, the TPL started one of its most exciting projects in 1975: the National Urban Land Program.

The objective was to transform the thousands of acres of inner-city vacant land into food-producing gardens, playgrounds, or miniparks —changing them from often cluttered eyesores into attractive neighborhood recreational areas. The program would be based on "bottom-up" community planning involving the local residents in each phase of the development process. This is a critical element according to Peter Stein, director of the project in Newark, New Jersey:

> When you involve people from the beginning in the selection of the site and then in the design of what happens there, then in the maintenance and eventually in ownership, they feel a total responsibility for the project. It's not as if they're building a park or a garden, it's as if they are expanding the background of their neighborhood.[2]

[2]Karin Abarbanel, "The National Urban Land Program: Greening America's Cities," *Foundation News* (November – December 1977): 12.

Other important aspects of the program are its cost-effectiveness and the speed with which things can be accomplished. In an article describing the program in *Foundation News,* Karin Abarbanel points out that city governments have spent $20,000–$60,000, using community volunteers and a variety of nonprofit land-acquisition techniques. She also states that city-hall–sponsored garden projects generally take from three to eight months just to cut red tape before planting can begin, while the NULP has been able to refine its process so that several garden projects took 60 days from land acquisition until the first plants began to break through the soil.

The first project started in Oakland, California, just across the San Francisco Bay from the TPL's offices. Seed funding of $50,000 came from several local foundations (Vanguard, Gerbode, and Laras) with some help also from the National Endowment for the Arts. After the Oakland project was under way, several corporations (Clorox, Safeway, Sunshine Cookies, and the Bank of America) made contributions. The Bank of America's contribution was the "loan" of Arnold Bellow, a professional appraiser who helped put the project on a firm financial and management basis. A number of community groups also got involved, including the San Francisco Community Design Center, the University of California at Berkeley, and several local 4-H and community arts organizations.

As a first step, 940 vacant lots were identified in a 20-square-block area—representing about 250 acres of usable space. Most of these properties in declining neighborhoods were owned by banks and savings-and-loan associations (through tax and loan foreclosures).Karin Abarbanel said that in the first half of 1976, five savings-and-loan firms agreed to sell or contribute 32 properties in the target neighborhoods. Valued at $125,000, the lots were acquired by the NULP for $7,000! Oakland residents subsequently recycled 25 of the 32 lots. About half were turned into food-producing gardens and half into miniparks, and the remaining lots were retained for future community development.

The gardens were divided into family plots, with each garden supervised by a community-elected individual and a committee. Some Oakland community gardeners, Karin Abarbanel tells us, raised from $200 to $500 worth of fruits and vegetables in one year.

Newark, New Jersey, was the second city in which the program was established. Financial support came from the Fund for New Jersey, the Victoria Foundation, the Geraldine R. Dodge Foundation, the Beinecke Trust, and the Florence and John Schumann Foundation. As in Oakland, corporations also helped. New Jersey Bell Telephone and Public Service Gas & Electric gave $10,000 and also donated some of their heavy vehicular equipment to clear some of the lots. These efforts through 1977 resulted in eight miniparks and the same number of community gardens.

Based on the success of the Oakland and Newark projects, the six-member National Urban Land staff has received requests for information and assistance from city governments and community groups throughout the country. It is likely that many other cities will adopt this novel and effective approach. It represents a unique blend of a good program concept; an important and widespread need; broad financial support from government, foundations, and corporations; and the active involvement of the people whom the projects are intended to serve. The Trust for Public Land has been most effective in conceiving projects that combine these interesting characteristics.

The TPL publishes an annual report describing its many innovative programs. It is one of the most attractive and informative distributed by any nonprofit organization. The report lists the names and locations of the regional directors and field representatives. It also includes the names of the foundations, corporations, and individuals that provide financial support. A copy can be obtained from the Trust for Public Land, 82 Second Street, San Francisco, CA. 94105.

California Planning and Conservation League

Another worthwhile environmental organization that the company became involved with is the California Planning and Conservation League. This goes back to 1967, when we were just getting our contributions program in gear. We were looking around for a good environmental cause and someone mentioned the PCL. I was asked to look into the organization.

I found out that the PCL was formed to promote sound environmental legislation in California. The PCL represented 4,500 individuals and over 90 civic and conservation organizations. It had developed a reputation in Sacramento as a solid and objective organization. We decided to forward a check. Needless to say, they were surprised by an unsolicited donation from a business corporation. We received a nice letter from Lew Butler, an attorney and vice-president of PCL, saying that "Syntex is the first corporation to confirm our belief that enlightened business and industry will one day be a major force behind legislation to enhance our environment."

For several years, Dr. Carl Djerassi, then president of Syntex Research, served on the PCL board of directors. When he relinquished that post, I served for a brief period in the same capacity. In 1973, I recommended that our director of environmental health and safety, Bob Spence, replace me as a board member; he served in this capacity several years and was replaced in 1977 by Doug Graham, a Syntex product development manager.

In addition to financial support, the company has helped the PCL in other ways. In October 1975, the company's facilities were the site of a fund-raising event honoring Melvin Lane, president of *Sunset* magazine. A PCL board member, Lane was the first chairman of the San Francisco Bay Area Conservation and Development Commission and was then serving as chairman of the California Coastal Commission.

Marine Ecological Institute

San Francisco Bay is one of the most important estuaries on the Pacific Coast. It directly influences the quality of life in the Bay Area for over 5 million people. It is a natural habitat for many species of fish, birds, and mammals.

Unfortunately a rapidly expanding population and resulting development have caused some problems. The amount of treated and untreated waste flushed into this body of water now exceeds the amount of water that enters the estuary from natural sources. Land filling has reduced the estuary to almost half its original size from 700 to 400 square miles. Finally, the rate of sedimentation is probably the highest of all estuaries in the United States.

Since 1970, the Marine Ecological Institute has been carrying out research and education programs to increase public awareness of this unique natural resource and the dangers that threaten it. Institute scientists have established data on the marine environment of the area. This accumulation of data has enabled local, regional, state, and national agencies and organizations concerned with the bay to make decisions based on scientific knowledge rather than on conjecture.

Another important contribution of the MEI has been the exciting Marine Ecology Discovery Voyages experienced by over 60,000 students from 300 schools, colleges, and universities in the 13 counties around the bay. One young participant suggested a new ecological principle: "I learned a lot about small living things and how we have to care for them because they have no say in what happens to them."

In the summer of 1975, the company co-hosted with the MEI a cruise on San Francisco Bay on the 85-foot *Inland Seas* research vessel. The guests were business executives and the goal was to develop increased corporate support. Also attending was the former astronaut Scott Carpenter, who had developed a keen interest in oceanography. The cruise was the idea of MEI's president, Bob Rutherford, and I felt that increasing the institute's base of support was a worthy undertaking for our company.

In 1976, we began to serve as a corporate sponsor of several Discovery Voyages for local high school students, joining companies such as Pacific Telephone & Telegraph, Mobil Oil, U.S. Steel, Dow Chemical, the Bank of America, Leslie Salt, Stauffer Chemicals, IBM, and Foremost-McKesson. The United Airlines employees' fund has also contributed. These firms, service clubs, and local foundations sponsored over 250 Discovery Voyages in 1976. One of the reasons we decided to do this was the enthusiastic response of the schools to this program. Here are some comments sent to one sponsor by a science teacher:

> Congratulations! My image of Dow Chemical Company has just risen one hundred percent. Your company was the one which sponsored our recent trip on the *Inland Seas*. This was an experience many students will never have a chance to repeat in their lifetime. Some are beginning to gravitate toward a vocation in science, especially the field of oceanography. It is a relief to know that a chemical company is interested in education and the environment.

Over the years, we have been able to support a number of other interesting environmental projects and programs, mostly through cash grants out of the contributions fund:

- Provided funds for the production of a film, "Captain Ecology," which depicted the wilderness experiences of inner-city children.
- Provided funds to obtain equipment for a camp run by the American Friends Service Committee to provide wilderness experiences for underprivileged children.
- Helped the local Sierra Club chapter complete an audioslide film to encourage disadvantaged children to participate in backpacking trips.
- Contributed support to enable California Tomorrow, an environmental organization, to produce and distribute to radio and television stations a series of public service announcements to increase interest in comprehensive environmental planning in the state.
- Contributed funds to the John Muir Institute to sponsor the presentation on public television of a film depicting the diverse activities of an environmental-awareness week at a local high school.

The public and employee reaction to these efforts was most encouraging. In 1971, the company received an honor award from *Environment Monthly,* a leading publication dedicated to the improvement of our physical environment. In commenting on the award, for citizen action, editor Bill Houseman had some nice things to say about our efforts: "You name it and if it involves environmental or social progress, the people at the U.S. headquarters for this pharmaceutical concern at Palo Alto are probably up to their ears in it."

In 1973 we received another honor award from the same publication—for our efforts in environmental education. Again Bill Houseman was generous in his praise: "That's the way Syntex does things—mixes the comfortable with the controversial, the safe with the venturesome, and lets the world make something of it if it will!"

19

Common Ground: A Community Garden on Company Land

To feed the world population, projected to increase to 6 to 7 billion in less than 25 years, food production must be about doubled on the available arable land.[1]

At one end of the Syntex company's land there is a sloping four-acre plot. In 1972, that land was virtually barren; even the weeds had a hard time there. It was sitting in reserve; in time, the company would build on it. Today that land is a flourishing garden and is producing an almost unbelievable amount of vegetables. It is run by Ecology Action, and it is called Common Ground.

It is not simply another company garden (although some 50–100 company employees and 500 community residents do garden there). It is primarily a research garden where Ecology Action is testing the yields of various crops using the biodynamic French-intensive method of gardening.

Ecology Action is a local, nonprofit organization with some 300 dues-paying members and is dedicated, as its name implies, to environmental education and to encouraging ecologically balanced life-styles. In its brief six-year history, it has run a variety of projects, and in the past, these included a highly successful community recycling project and bicycle workshops. At present, in addition to the Common Ground garden, it offers classes in urban homesteading (gardening, raising chickens and goats, canning and preserving, alternative energy sources, etc.) and operates a small store in Palo Alto that is both an organic gardening and supply store (inexpensive seeds, fertilizers, books, herbs, tools, etc.) and a center for the organization's educational activities. Its

[1]David Pimental *et al.*, "Land Degradation: Effects on Food and Energy Resources," *Science* (October 8, 1976): 154.

classes, with attendance of 5–70 persons, often meet there, and the store also contains a circulating library that includes tapes and slides as well as periodicals and books.

What, now, is this biodynamic/French-intensive method of gardening? Its name makes it sound like a rather sophisticated and perhaps even an oddball method. But it is not. Rather it is a relatively simple method based on common sense, and even I, by and large uninformed in agricultural matters, can understand and appreciate it. I only wish I could change its name to something less imposing. Throughout the rest of the chapter, I will refer to it simply as the BFI method.

History of the Biodynamic/French-Intensive Method

There are, of course, good historical reasons why the BFI method has the name it does, and I am sure that the Englishman Alan Chadwick did not think of the image the name would present as he developed the method between the 1920s and the 1960s. Rather, he was working out of two traditions: the biodynamic and the French-intensive, both developed during the late 1800s and the early 1900s.

The French-intensive was a method developed on a two-acre plot near Paris in order to supply high-quality vegetables year round. The essentials of this method were crops planted in 18 inches of horse manure and spaced close together so that their leaves would barely touch. The impotant aspect to Chadwick was the close spacing because, in effect, this created a miniclimate and did the same work as a mulch ordinarily does.

The biodynamic method was more important to Chadwick, and he learned it in the 1920s from the Austrian Rudolph Steiner, who was a philosopher and an educator as well as a horticulturalist. Steiner was concerned with the decline in the nutritive value and yield in crops in Europe, and he traced this decline to the then-new use of chemical fertilizers and pesticides. His method was basically a holistic response to the analytic approach of technology, and he argued, in effect, that a farmer should create an environment for his crops that duplicates, as much as possible, the environment nature would provide. The basics of this environment are compost (which enhances the microbiotic soil life), organic fertilizers (which are less harsh in their effects on plants and longer-lasting), and companion planting (various plants help other plants in a variety of ways). The result, Steiner discovered, was healthier plants that were resistant to pests, thus avoiding the need for chemical pesticides.

It should also be noted that Steiner's answer was one not based on the latest scientific developments. If it sounded new, it sounded new only to the scientific world. In fact, his methods were conservative and often based on folk knowledge: heavy mulches, companion planting, etc. What he did was to organize and refine much of this knowledge.

There is a similar conservative tradition in American farming, in spite of the fact that America is the center of the "green revolution," which relies heavily on inorganic fertilizers, pesticides, and irrigation. Even here, there is a difference between the way farmers treat their large fields and the way they treat their small family gardens. What they do with their cash crops—the fields of grain, cotton, and soybeans—is one matter, a matter of necessity in this technological age. On the other hand, in the family gardens or small truck-farming plots, they use old-fashioned methods, especially heavy composting. On most farms, almost nothing goes to waste; ashes, manure, kitchen waste, and garden trash are returned to the soil.

There is one other technique that Steiner developed that is important in the BFI method, and that is the use of raised beds. This too is old knowledge, in this case as old as the ancient Greeks, who had noticed that plants grew better where landslides had occurred. What this gave was a curved surface that allowed greater penetration of water, roots, and compost. This, in particular, is a technique that Alan Chadwick has refined into the BFI method, and the specifics of his method usually call for beds three to five feet wide (so they can be worked by hand without stepping on them) and "double-dug" to a depth of 24 inches.

The value of the "double-dig" technique is rather obvious when you learn about it, although most of us are rather content to use a rototiller on the top 8 inches or to dig down one shovel depth, and the double dig is the best way to do this. First, of course, you put a goodly amount of compost on top and then dig a trench 12 inches deep (as deep as most spades) along one end of the bed and put the dirt alongside, being careful to disturb the soil as little as possible. The point here is to preserve the natural layering of the soil, and in any case, as you dig, compost will sift down. After the trench is dug, you then loosen (not dig) the soil at the bottom another 12 inches deep. Then you start on the next trench, placing that dirt in the first trench, and so on, until the whole bed is dug. The last step is to add organic fertilizers (aged manure, bone meal, wood ash) and to sift them in to the top 2–3 inches. This prepares the topmost soil for seeds or transplanted seedlings and once again approximates the layering nature would create. The end result of all this is a "raised" bed, since the soil has been loosened and compost has been added. It is now ready for intensive planting.

What Alan Chadwick did between the 1920s and the mid-1960s, as the double-dig method shows, was to refine and combine techniques from each method—taking the principles of deeply prepared beds and intensive spacing from the French-intensive and the principles of raised beds, organic fertilizers, and companion planting from the biodynamic.

Of course, there was much he did not adopt. For instance, he did not adopt the French-intensive reliance on large amounts of manure. Manure is not always available, especially in large quantities, but more important, Chadwick observed that the heavy use of manure created an imbalanced soil, one that was overloaded with nitrogen. In fact, he prefers a compost that is composed of one-third vegetation (preferably still green), one-third kitchen waste, and one-third soil. Manure, along with other organic fertilizers, is added only at the end and on top of the bed.

Thus far, I have noted only the general aspects of the BFI method that Chadwick has developed: deep soil preparation; intensive planting in beds, not rows, which is made possible by the deep soil preparation, thus allowing roots to grow downward, not outward; heavy composting, which improves and "texturizes" the soil, thus allowing the soil to absorb water and retain it longer; organic fertilizers to bring, then keep the soil in chemical and biological balance; and companion planting, which helps control pests and, in some cases, such as strawberries and beans, actively aids growth and yield.

Basics of the Method

At this point, it might be helpful to the reader to summarize the principal aspects of the BFI method.

1. *Double-dug, raised beds,* in which the soil is dug thoroughly the first 12 inches and loosened an additional 12 inches by a simple manual method using a shovel. This loose soil enables roots to penetrate easily and allows a steady stream of nutrients to flow into stems and leaves. Moisture is retained well, erosion is minimized, and weeding is simplified because of the looseness of the soil. Also, since yields are about four times as high, only one-fourth the area need be prepared, dug, watered, and weeded for a given yield.

2. *Intensive planting.* Seeds or seedlings are planted in raised, three- to five-foot-wide beds of varying length using a hexagonal spacing pattern. Grains are often grown in wider areas. Each seed is placed the same distance from all seeds nearest it, so that when the plants mature their leaves barely touch. This provides a miniclimate under the leaves, which retains moisture, protects the valuable microbiotic life of the soil, retards weed growth, and helps provide high yields.

3. *Companion planting.* Many plants grow better near other kinds of plants. Green beans and strawberries, for instance, thrive better when grown together. Some plants are useful in repelling harmful insects, while others attract beneficial ones. Borage, for example, repels tomato

worms, while its blue flowers attract bees. Also, many wild plants and weeds have a healthy effect on the soil. Their deep roots loosen the subsoil and bring up previously unavailable trace minerals and nutriments. The use of companion planting aids the gardener and farmer in producing fine-quality vegetables and helps create and maintain a healthy, vibrant soil. The placing together of symbiotic companion plants itself does not appear to produce significantly increased yields but rather promotes the soil life and health necessary to sustain increased yields.

4. *Compost.* The high yields and lowered water requirements made possible by intensive planting would not be possible without a way of maintaining the health and vigor of the soil. Garbage, vegetation, manure, and many other forms of readily available organic matter, when properly composted, provide most of the elements necessary to maintain the biological cycles of life that exist in the farm or home garden. The texture and microbiotic life of the soil are improved by the compost, which creates better aeration and water retention.

5. *Promotion of microbiotic life.* All biodynamic French-intensive techniques promote healthy microbiotic plant and animal life in the soil. These not only fix atmospheric nitrogen in the soil but also produce antibiotics that help enable plants to resist diseases. Standard farming techniques tend to destroy these life forms.

It is important to note that the biodynamic French-intensive method is a *whole system* and that the component principles of the method intermesh in actual use to create complex living units. Farmers in Europe experimenting with only the intensive-spacing factor in combination with commercial techniques are finding themselves beset with deteriorating soil fertility; nitrate toxicity in plants, soil, and water; lower-quality produce; diminishing populations of beneficial insects; and lowered plant resistance to disease and pests. Chadwick is quite clear about this. The point is to improve the soil in order to develop healthier plants, and different climates, different soils will demand modifications of the technique.

In fact, many of the specific techniques that Chadwick has developed have worked especially well in the San Francisco Bay Area, where we have a heavy clay soil, a long growing season (nine months), and no rainfall for six to nine months. Furthermore, the BFI method has become relatively popular in this area only in the last 10 years, ever since Chadwick transformed a barren hillside on the grounds of the University of California at Santa Cruz into what most observers call a Garden of Eden. (I should note that Chadwick is not only a horticulturalist but also an actor, a writer, and a painter and has not been particularly concerned with popularizing the BFI method.) The BFI method is very much a method in process.

Beginning of the Common Ground Project

This is where Ecology Action comes into the picture. Its members are enthusiastic supporters of the BFI method, and from early on (1972), they wanted to make others aware of it, through classes and/or a gardening plot at Common Ground, and to test and refine the method further. This has been no easy task, and over the past five years, Ecology Action has never had the resources to do the job as adequately as it would have liked. By this, I mean they have not always been able to meet the demands of a full-time research garden (the demands of an educational program are much less). A research garden needs a large staff and the staff needs to be paid. Volunteers for the most part do not have the time or the inclination to do the job properly.

But what need is there for Ecology Action to research the BFI method further? No need, if the BFI method is just another method for backyard gardeners. But if you have any hopes that the BFI method can become a widely used farming method for much of the world, then the need is great. You have to be able to prove that the BFI method can produce crop yields greater than those provided by present methods, that such yields can be sustained, and that it is economically feasible for a farmer to adopt this new method. Chadwick had not addressed these problems in any detail (although it was obvious that he produced high yields), and Ecology Action stepped in.

Still, I can hear my reader wonder why a new method is necessary. Aren't we doing fine as it is? In a sense, the answer is "yes." In fact, most industrially advanced countries are feeding their populations adequately. But all is not well, particularly in the developing countries. Each year, some 10–30 million die of starvation, and a much larger number suffer from malnutrition. On a global scale, there are severe food shortages.

If it were simply a matter of a food shortage, however, then we could probably trust the scientists responsible for the "green revolution" to devise techniques to increase yields. They have succeeded admirably thus far in doing so. But as I noted, their methods rely heavily upon the use of inorganic fertilizers, pesticides, herbicides, machines, and irrigation, and in most areas of the world, these are not abundantly available. In large part, this is a matter of economics; the world's 2 billion simply cannot afford them.

The problem, however, is more than a matter of economics. If so, the industrially advanced countries could, I suppose, help poor countries build dams and supply them with tractors. (And I, for one, would be glad to see the United States increase its foreign aid for such purposes.) No, the problem is that the methods of the "green revolution" rely too heavily on fossil fuels, from which the nitrogen fertilizers and pesticides are made, to say nothing of the gasoline to run the tractors and harvesters. Once again, this is more than a matter of economics (although if all countries could afford unlimited supplies, food shortages could be cut dramatically in the short run); we must also remember that fossil fuels are a limited resource. Quite simply, we cannot rely on them forever (some say for only 30–40 years at the most). Even over the short run, given the nature of international politics today, many countries could suffer severe petroleum shortages, and these would adversely affect food production.

Dr. David Pimentel of Cornell University is widely recognized as an expert on the energy demands of various agricultural systems and has long argued that the strictest limiting factor on man's ability to feed himself is the energy supply. In a 1975 conference on world food problems, he said that if American farming and food processing methods were suddenly adopted worldwide, in order to raise, to the American level, the diets of four billion people, the amount of energy needed would deplete, within eighteen years, the entire known reserves of petroleum.

Company Involvement with Ecology Action

When Ecology Action approached the company for the use of its land in 1972, I must admit that I did not fully understand all the arguments that its members advanced and that I have tried to describe here. I can only say that I had a feel for the rightness of what they were saying and have become more convinced as the years have passed. In fact, the same should be said about the members of Ecology Action. They had a bias in favor of the BFI method, a feel for the rightness of it, but it then existed as a hypothesis, and they were careful not to push their claims for it too far. They were straightforward about their intentions: they wanted to test the method, in addition to providing a community garden.

There were two reasons that the company was willing to listen to Ecology Action's proposal. First, several company employees were deeply involved with the organization and urged the company to become similarly involved. Second, Ecology Action had an excellent record with community programs, and the company had, in fact, supported these programs in small ways.

The most important of these was a metal and glass recycling operation it had run in 1971, and one estimate was that some 50% of the residents of Palo Alto had taken part in it. Ecology Action had also been able to elicit the support of many local companies, which had donated warehouse space, dump trucks, forklifts, drivers, printing services, and bins. My company had donated breathing masks. The project had been, in short, a large one and well run, and it had received several awards, including one from the American Institute of Architects and the "First Community Improvement Award" in Palo Alto. The true measure of the success of the project, however, was the fact that the city had been sufficiently impressed by the program to incorporate it into its own solid-waste management operation, and this is what Ecology Action had been aiming toward all along. From the beginning, it had regarded itself only as a catalyst and had known that the program would grow and become a permanent one only if the city took it over.

Ecology Action had also begun a bicycle education program in late 1971, and the company had contributed money to it. The aim of this program was to increase the public's awareness of the bicycle as an alternative form of transportation and to educate as many as possible in the basics of bicycling safety, repair, and touring. Since Ecology Action did not have its store at that time, it first had to convert a van that would serve as a traveling workshop clinic. Once again, this was a successful project, although it was not as large nor as influential as the recycling operation. Rather, it was part of a general movement that ultimately led to the establishment of bike lanes throughout the city.

In spite of Ecology Action's good record, the company was wary of this audacious plan for Common Ground. The company felt it was a good idea, but also wanted to protect its interests. First, there were a certain number of legal problems: liability, zoning regulations, and the fact that the company only leases its land from Stanford University. In a sense, these were minor problems but still factors that had to be considered.

Second, various departments in the company had to be consulted in order to make sure that nobody had an eye on that land for possible future use. This would affect the term of the company's commitment. At the same time, Ecology Action would need to work the land for at least three years in order to obtain any significant results.

Third, and perhaps most important to the company, was the physical appearance of the garden. The company has always taken pride in its well-kept site, and in this case, the garden plot would be visible to company employees and the many visitors to Syntex. Thus the company and Ecology Action talked about such details as storage sheds, greenhouses, fencing, and a parking lot. Closely related was the question of compost piles: Would they smell and would they be an unwanted source of insects?

Fourth, the company was concerned about the project's financing. It wanted some assurance that the project could continue for three years. Otherwise, why start in the first place? Initially Ecology Action did not have the funds even to begin the project (the storage sheds, fencing, etc.), but soon it did. In fact, I had something to do with this. It so happened that I met Dr. Alejandro Zaffaroni, a former president of Syntex Research, on a plane while returning from a business trip and mentioned the project to him. He was immediately interested, and when Ecology Action contacted him soon thereafter, he personally contributed $5,000. Alza Corporation, the company he founded after leaving Syntex, made a modest contribution. These contributions, although inadequate for Ecology Action's continuing needs, were at least sufficient to persuade our company that the project should begin.

Last, and most important, the company is an international one and understands all too well the related problems of overpopulation and food shortages that exist in many countries. Most here feel that the BFI method may well prove to be of more value in developing countries than in the United States. I know I do, and I remember one lunch at which John Jeavons and Dr. Albert Bowers, president of the company, were discussing the BFI method and came precisely to this conclusion. The crucial point in this case is that the BFI method is labor- and skill-intensive, as is most farming in developing countries. In the United States, on the other hand, farming occurs on a much larger scale and is not labor-intensive.

So the company had a basic sympathy with Ecology Action's proposal. The agreement would not be entirely one-way, however; there would be benefits for the company. First, not all of the garden was to be used for research into the BFI method. One-fourth was to be used as a community garden, and obviously, company employees could participate as members of the community. In effect, Common Ground could also operate as a company garden and become a valuable fringe benefit for those employees who cared to take advantage of it. In fact, three-fourths of the garden has been used as a community garden (simply because Ecology Action never has had enough staff to work more than an acre effectively), and company employees have never had any problem obtaining space.

All these considerations were in the air after Ecology Action came forward with its proposal, and it took several meetings to resolve everything. Those most involved on the company's side were the plant services manager, a representative from the legal department, and of course myself. Those from Ecology Action included Lane Carpenter, its president; Craig Cook, one of the co-coordinators of the garden project; and especially John Jeavons, the other co-coordinator. In fact, John Jeavons has been the moving force behind the garden project over the years, and I have come to respect both his business sense (he was previously business manager for the Stanford University Library) and his understanding of the relationship of the BFI method to established agricultural methods.

The result of the negotiations was a four-page agreement between the company and Ecology Action, and the main aspect of this agreement was that Ecology Action would manage and maintain the garden, while the company agreed to contribute the land and water for a period of three years. Following its expiration in 1975, the contract was renewed for another period.

The land, of course, cost the company nothing extra, but the water was a different matter. In fact, the water had not been part of the original proposal, but during the course of the negotiations, we discovered that it would cost much less for Ecology Action to tap into the company's supply than to connect with the city's mains as a new customer. In this way, expensive installation charges could be avoided, and the cost of water would be less. We agreed to donate the water, and the assumption of this cost has periodically made it possible for the project to continue when funds were low.

This was the only cost to which the company agreed in the contract, but over the years, the company has also contributed over $20,000 because it is convinced that the project is a worthy one. Most often, these contributions have been general contributions to Ecology Action, with the informal understanding that they would be used for the garden project.

The first of these was an apprentice program during the summer of 1973 to which the company made a contribution to sponsor eight high school students. The purpose of the program was to train students in BFI techniques, and the money was used to pay both instructors and students. In addition, the company specified that four of the apprentices were to be minority students, and this is where the problems developed. Ecology Action had no disagreement with this condition, but it did have problems convincing minority students to participate. In fact, it could find only two. The only conclusion we could draw was that minority students found such an activity unattractive because, perhaps, they were more interested in activities more closely related to the mainstream of American life. On the other hand, white students were interested—perhaps because it was something different to do and perhaps they harbored romantic notions about returning to the land.

This problem, however, had little to do with the decision to discontinue the apprentice program. Those students who did participate learned a great deal. No, the basic reason was that Ecology Action had limited resources, in terms of both money and staff, and felt that it was necessary to commit its resources to overall management of the garden and to the research base before expanding into a formal educational program. However, two of the apprentices did decide to go to agricultural colleges as a result of the experience.

The second specific project that the company sponsored was an exhibition booth for Ecology Action at the 1976 World of Plants run by Bill Graham at the Cow Palace in San Francisco. At first, the idea seemed an excellent one because Ecology Action could thus reach a much wider audience. But the audience proved to be disappointing. The show was well attended, but those who attended turned out to represent an uninterested new audience of houseplant growers and an older audience of those inclined to be sympathetic with the BFI method, if they were not in fact already practicing it. In addition, those attending were at most backyard gardeners, and in the end, we concluded that the publicity was not worth the cost. Unfortunately, there does not now exist an appropriate show convention at which Ecology Action can reach the farmers and agronomists it wants to contact.

Some other Ecology Action projects have been quite successful. Since 1972, it has operated an organic gardening store offering inexpensive seeds, a variety of organic fertilizers, books on organic gardening, and free weekly classes and local gardening advice. The organization has also held classes on urban homesteading skills, including such topics as cheese making, blacksmithing, and raising chickens, bees, and goats. A growing reference library includes publications on organic gardening and other alternative living skills.

Publication of Book

One other way the company aided Ecology Action was helping with the design format and printing of 1,000 copies of its 77-page manual written by John Jeavons, *How to Grow More Vegetables Than You Ever Thought Possible on Less Land Than You Can Imagine.* Previously, Ecology Action had produced 500 copies of the manual in photoduplicate form plus 1,000 copies in a simple offset edition, and it was obvious that the manual would sell. How well it would sell was another matter, but John Jeavons argued that an attractively designed, clearly printed book would sell well and thus provide a much needed source of income for Ecology Action. He also noted that the organization lacked the capital for such a project, and so the company agreed to undertake it. One of my Syntex colleagues, Bill Spencer, thought up a catchy title; Tom Lunde, of the graphics department designed the book and in particular created the cover; the company print shop took over; and John Jeavons proved to be right. In a little more than two years, Ecology Action has sold or distributed over 40,000 copies (including hundreds outside the United States), and the over $60,000 net income from these sales has kept the garden project alive.

Two research reports about the garden project have been published; one for 1972 and a summary report for 1972–1975. All of these publications can be ordered directly from Ecology Action, 2225 El Camino Real, Palo Alto, CA 94306.

I should note that my company has not been the only one to contribute to Common Ground Ecology Action. Others, including Alza, Zoecon and Saga corporations, the Luke B. Hancock Foundation, the Wallace Alexander Gerbode Foundation, the Arca Foundation, and several individuals, have contributed at least another $26,000.

Obviously, there has been a large commitment of time, money, and energy to the Common Ground project. What results, however, has Ecology Action achieved there using the BFI method? And what future do Ecology Action and/or the BFI method have?

How Well Does the Method Work?

In spite of limited resources, Ecology Action has achieved results that are quite promising, and some of these are presented in Table 6, which I take from Ecology Action's research report summary for 1972–1975. The percentages are percentages of United States average yields, except in the case of zucchini, where the comparison is with the average yield from our home county, Santa Clara, California.

These are impressive yields and annual increases in yield. They are even more impressive when the original soil quality is considered. Ecology Action found a soil that consisted of one-third rock and one-third stiff clay with almost no plant nutrients, and John Jeavons suspects that the garden plot was, in fact, a place where fill was dumped during the construction of the company buildings. In contrast, good agricultural soil contains about 5% rock and is rich in plant nutrients. In spite of poor soil quality, the BFI method was able generally to produce much larger than average yields even on the initial planting and then to improve the soil so that successive plantings produced successively larger yields. Even now, the soil in the test beds would not be considered good agricultural soil.

John Jeavons, of course, is not surprised by such yields. He points to

Table 6. BFI Yields as Percentages of Average United States Yields[a]

	1972	1973	1974	1975
Beans, snap	390%	520%	—	
Cucumbers	—	360	900%	—
Lettuce, bibb	230	—	560	—
Soybeans	—	25	91	225%
Wheat	—	—	106	190
Zucchini	550	650	164	—

[a] John Jeavons, *1972–1975 Research Report Summary* (Palo Alto, Calif.: Ecology Action of the Midpeninsula, 1976), p. 4.

the fact that intensive planting by itself should increase the yield as much as fourfold when compared with the yields from standard methods (rows), since there can be, quite simply, four times as many plants. (This applies to vegetables, not grains.) In addition, he cites a University of California study that claims that overall root health in United States crops has declined over the years and that a 2–4% increase in root health should give yields 2–4 times larger. Thus, he sees no reason why in some cases yields from the BFI method should not be 8–16 times larger than the present average United States yields.

In addition to increased yields, Ecology Action claims other benefits from the BFI method. These include the use of as little as 1/2–1/16 the nitrogen fertilizer, 1/2–1/16 the water, and 1/100 the energy that standard farming methods currently use. The unit of comparison in these figures is a pound of food.

The energy figure must also be qualified. The figure is accurate, but it is due to the fact that the BFI method substitutes human labor for machine labor.

Many people have described the biodynamic/French-intensive method as labor-intensive. More correctly, it should be described as skill-intensive, because only about 15% of the time expended can be considered moderately hard labor. The initial soil preparation, when a person is changing over to the method, can be difficult. Also, performance of the method is not monotonous because of the varied tasks of soil preparation, compost preparation, fertilization, planting, harvesting, weeding, and watering.

John Jeavons is aware of this problem, and he is attempting to overcome resistance to the BFI method by presenting its possibilities in terms of a "miniagriculture" concept. This concept is basically an extension of the intensive aspect of the BFI method and posits that an adequate yield can be obtained from a small area worked by a limited number of people. But what does *adequate* mean here?

How much land is necessary in order to grow food sufficient to feed one person? Jeavons's initial answer, based on projected yields from the BFI method, is that one person, working 15 minutes a day, could produce a complete nutritively balanced diet on as little as 1,250 square feet (see Figure 3). This assumes a 12-month growing season with or without miniature greenhouses. A 6-month growing season would require double the space (2,500 square feet) and time. If his figures are anywhere near accurate, they contrast favorably with present United States figures (assuming a 6-month growing season) of 21,649 square feet for a typical diet that includes meat and 10,114 square feet for a vegetarian diet. Even in Japan, where reasonably intensive methods are use, the figures are 7,260 and 4,842 square feet, respectively, for typical meat and vegetarian diets.

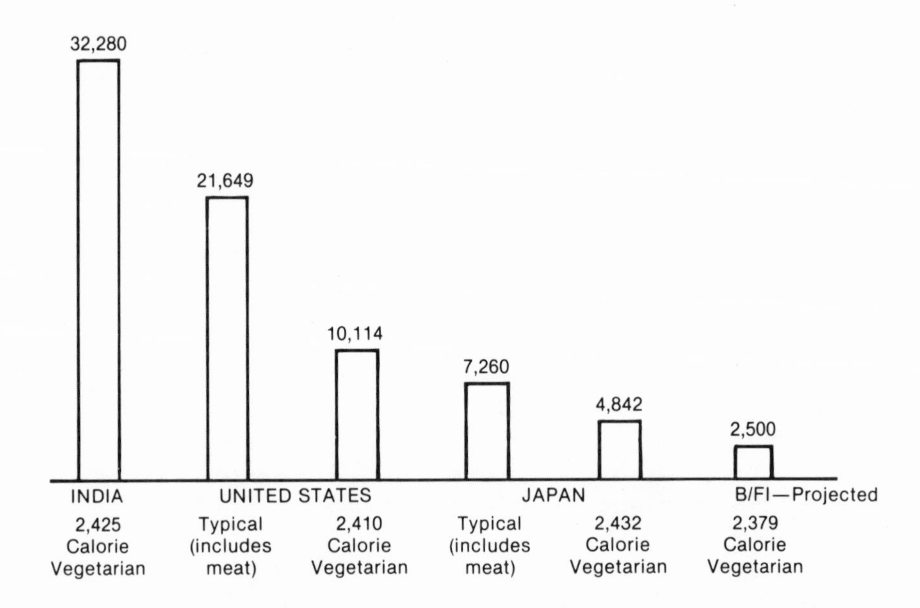

Source: Ecology Action 1972-1975 Research Report Summary

Figure 3. Square footage required to produce nutritional diet (BFI compared to three country averages).

I should also add that in order to arrive at these figures, Jeavons had first to define a complete, nutritively balanced diet. The one he and his colleague, Robin Leler, created is vegetarian and contains 2,379 calories per day. It includes grains, vegetables, tree fruits, and milk. Fodder for the goats or cows is included in all his calculations.

Minifarming

The possibility of using the biodynamic/French-intensive method on a limited acreage with accompanying high yields and low resource-consumption has created a new concept: the minifarm. Ecology Action estimates that a minifarmer, working a 6-hour day, 7 days per week, should eventually be able to grow enough food for 24 people on about three-quarters of an acre. A family working an 8-hour day, 7 days per week, could grow enough food for 32 people on a little less than an acre. For a family of four, this would mean only 2 hours a day of work per person.

These efficiencies will not be reached immediately. Improvements must be made in most soils and the skills of most minifarmers. Much basic information, conceptual and practical, is still to be discovered and delineated about the actual workings of the method. Finally, many countries are experiencing such a shortage of firewood that agriculturally valuable manure is being substituted. In these instances, organic matter for soil improvement will first have to be grown in order for the soil to be properly prepared.

One or more minifarmers working a total of 56 hours per week on a little less than an acre may be able to grow a complete 2,379-calorie diet (grains, vegetables, fruit, and fodder for dairy products) for 32 people, according to Ecology Action estimates. This would be during a 12-month growing season, using inexpensive miniature greenhouses. The food grown in this manner would be worth $9,600 at wholesale prices. (Wholesale prices are about 50% retail costs.) Or, in a 6-month growing season, a four-person minifarming family would be able to grow the same amount of food and income on twice the area, a little less than two acres, without minigreenhouses. Each individual would have to work only 23 hours per week.

The figures for both these kinds of minifarmers assume that the produce would be grown by skilled farmers working in good soil and marketed by them locally and directly. It would probably take three to five years for a minifarm to be operative at peak effectiveness, although more research needs to be done in this area. Both income figures are for gross income. However, the expenses for small-scale minifarming are very low. Not much in the way of land, tools, water, fertilizer, energy, and other materials is required. The method is not capital-intensive.

Additional Research Required

John Jeavons is aware that the results Ecology Action has achieved at Common Ground are encouraging but that further research is needed. To date, some 62 crops have been tested, but not all, by any means, have been thoroughly tested. Replicability is now the most pressing issue. It is clear that the BFI method works well at Common Ground, but will it work equally well in other climates and in other soils? What will happen in areas that depend on rainfall, not irrigation, for water? Is the method necessary in areas with deep, rich topsoil, such as the American Midwest? And is the method, in spite of its seeming simplicity, actually too sophisticated for others to use well? Obviously, the BFI method must extend beyond Common Ground and many others must become involved.

All this will take a large amount of funds. A research garden is not an inexpensive proposition, and even Common Ground, to operate effectively as a full-time research garden, needs some $75,000–$90,000 per year. Most of this goes for staff salaries. At present, John Jeavons estimates that he can find and keep staff members who will work for as little as $25 per day (take-home pay). Even this is not much, but it is enough for those who want to work on and develop an alternative method. Previously, the Ecology Action staff, when it was paid at all, worked for as little as $10 per day, but the staff turnover was high.

Fortunately others are becoming intereseed in the BFI method, and the combined commitment of various groups may very well open up new sources of funding. In 1976, for example, John Jeavons and I attended a conference on family food production in Santa Barbara, and the sole purpose of this conference was to discuss the applicability of the BFI method to developing countries. The conference was sponsored by the League for International Food Education (LIFE), which is a consortium of scientific and professional organizations, including the American Society of Agronomy, whose purpose is to provide opportunities for its members to share their knowledge with those working on the food and nutrition problems of the developing world. Those attending included agronomists from several major United States universities, representatives from volunteer relief agencies, representatives from developing countries, and of course practitioners of the BFI method (including those from the Institute for Man and Nature in Covelo, California, where Alan Chadwick was working).

The conference was a success, largely because everybody decided not to argue about the relative values or dangers of chemical fertilizers and pesticides. Rather, the participants attempted to come to an agreement about the value of the BFI method in the developing countries where such fertilizers and pesticides are not used. And agree they did. Not only did everyone feel that the BFI method is an excellent one for areas where small-scale, labor-intensive farming is practiced, but they also agreed that a project must be started that will scientifically research the effectiveness of the method in various areas of the world, particularly tropical areas.

20

Better Transit Systems for Work Trips

The commuter does not like all those cars on the road that slow him down on the way to or from work. The boss doesn't like the thought that in another few years, there will not be enough room downtown for all the workers, if they each bring a car with them. No one is really pleased with the current state of affairs. But no one is ready to change anything.[1]

Our society has long accepted a philosophy of economic growth, as long as we were growing "bigger" as well. We have seen, since World War II, that a philosophy of "bigger means better" has produced areas of urban sprawl, huge connecting highway networks, industrial parks, population concentration, and a large demand for consumer goods ranging from lawnmowers and dishwashers to automobiles. All this began to change somewhat in the early 1960s, when we noticed that at the same time we had polluted our lakes and riverbeds, littered our land, and created ugly brown hazes that sit like a pall over our cities and urban homes.

Moreover, our energy consumption marched forward unheeded —energy was cheap and available—and gas and electricity gave us tickets to individual freedom and fun, once provided by exploring the uncharted land itself. But our life-style faced a startling awakening in the Great Energy Crisis in 1973–1974 and the escalating shortages of natural gas and oil. Suddenly, our society has been confronted with the concept of finite resources and the need for conservation and consumption cutbacks. Since 1973, industries and homes across the nation have been forced to cut energy consumption.

At Syntex, energy consumption was cut by 35% between 1973 and 1974 and another 6% the following year. Although costs rose dramatically—by more than one-third in gas consumption alone—still by reduc-

[1]Sid McCausland, "Along for the Ride—People, Politics and Transportation: California Style," Assembly Committee on Transportation Report, Sacramento, August, 1974.

ing consumption levels, Syntex saved $125,000 in 1974 and another $163,000 in 1975 at its Palo Alto facilities.

Although conserving energy in buildings and other "stationary sources" is an important mechanism for saving energy consumption, in California the most prolific user of energy and a prime producer of pollution is the automobile. The single-occupant car source of transportation for work and for leisure activities provides twin problems in air pollution and energy consumption. Although, in fact, state regulations and federal requirements have added devices to cars to mitigate some of the pollutant effects, nevertheless these antipollution devices are energy-intensive and require increased gasoline consumption to operate.

Thus, although we have taken initial steps to stop pollution, we are nowhere near solving the other problem caused by the usage of already scarce energy resources.

Furthermore, even with a reduction in pollution and an increase in energy usage, we still have not cut down to any substantial proportion our problems of traffic congestion and parking spaces. The decision to reduce the numbers of cars on the road has been left, in the final analysis, to the individual, to the private citizen, the car owner. Experience has demonstrated that without reasonable incentives or disincentives, the average person is not apt to change his transportation habits.

Growing Interest of Corporations in Transit

Since 1973, however, leaders in the public and private sectors have begun seeking alternative ways to mitigate the unfavorable effects of automobile transportation. As major sources of both employment and thus traffic congestion and revenue, a few private corporations have demonstrated that they have the ability to take some effective initiative in (1) assisting governmental decisions in transportation planning; (2) encouraging employees and the community to join in implementation of new transit systems; (3) sponsoring company "van-pooling" systems; (4) aiding intracompany or intercompany "carpools" or "ride-sharing concepts"; and finally (5) providing other incentives for group travel to and from work.

Planning for mass transit systems and national energy conservation is occurring at all levels of government: the Urban Mass Transportation Administration (UMTA) provides guidance and federal funds for projects. In California, the State Department of Transportation (CalTrans) is working on a statewide car-pooling program. Counties and even individual cities are considering group transportation, such as van pooling, for their employees, as well as improved transit systems for local residents.

Corporations can take some responsibility in the areas of planning, information sharing, and encouraging employees and management to become personally involved in transportation issues.

The Pamtrans Project

In August of 1974, I appeared before the Palo Alto Planning Commission on several issues of direct interest to our company. One option in the city's drafted comprehensive plan would rezone some of the land we lease from Stanford University from commercial to residential use. The rationale was that this would reduce traffic congestion; that is, fewer people would drive fewer cars. I pointed out that the density of our development was 10 people per acre and that most residential areas in Palo Alto exceed that figure. I stated that we should be allowed to proceed with our low-density commercial development and that we would consider steps to decrease automobile use at Syntex.

The tone of that planning-commission meeting was very much antitraffic and protransit. It became clear as the meeting progressed that almost no one was pleased with the increasing congestion in the area and that there was a great deal of interest in the development of a plan that would reduce or slow the rate of growth of traffic in the area. Robert Augsburger, who was then vice-president of business and finance at Stanford, pledged the university's help in the development of such a plan.

One member of the audience who heard Augsburger's remarks with great interest was Professor James Jucker of the industrial engineering department at Stanford. The department had a research group that had been working on transportation-planning research projects for the Department of Transportation since 1970, and Professor Jucker felt that this research group would be the appropriate vehicle for providing the help that Augsburger had pledged.

Another who was especially interested was Naphtali Knox, director of planning for the city of Palo Alto. Both Jucker and Knox contacted Augsburger, and within a very short time, Pamtrans (Palo Alto–Menlo Park Area Transportation Project) was under way. Professor Jucker served as director of the project.

At the first meeting of representatives of Palo Alo, Menlo Park, and Stanford where this project was discussed, it was decided that it was essential that the project have an advisory board comprised of individuals who were knowledgeable about transportation, who were well known and respected in the community, and who could represent the views of the major employers and the various governments and agencies that would be directly influenced by any transportation plan. In addition, a citizens' advisory committee, including senior citizens and handicapped persons, would also be formed as a source of information about the transportation and transit needs of residents of the area.

When Professor Jucker called, we were ready and anxious to join his committee and see what could be done to fulfill our commitment to the city of Palo Alto.

Some local firms and governmental agencies quickly made commitments of financial aid "in-kind" support to supplement the project funds provided by the federal government. During the ensuing year, the board of advisers met regularly with the Stanford study group, offering comments and suggestions. In addition to Jucker, Knox, and myself, the committee members included John Guilhamet, senior civil engineer of San Mateo County and project director for the San Mateo County Local Bus Transit Study; Alva Johnson, transit coordinator of the Metropolitan Transit Commission, the regional transportation agency; Oscar Nelson, Jr., master planner at Stanford University; Ted Noguchi, director of transportation for the city of Palo Alto; Leon Pirofalo, director of community development for the city of Menlo Park; James Pott, then director of the Santa Clara Transportation Agency; and William Powers, director of planning for San Mateo County.

Pamtrans Recommendations

The Pamtrans report issued in November 1975 is primarily concerned with two problems: work trips into the Palo Alto–Menlo Park area and how to alleviate their impact, and how to improve the county bus systems serving the area. Largely, the thrust of the study proceeded from the perceived need of involved members to identify the first problem and help the situation by tailoring the county bus system to satisfy better the needs of those making the daily work commute to the Palo Alto area. Santa Clara County was in the process of reviewing and upgrading the countywide transit system, and the Pamtrans study filled what was perceived locally as a gap in county–city planning and coordination.

The study demonstrated that of the 269,000 local vehicle trips through Palo Alto and the 11,000 "through vehicles each day in the city, more than 46% originated as home-based work trips. Moreover, most of the work trips originated elsewhere—especially in the cities to the south of Palo Alto—where large numbers of Palo Alto industrial firms' employees reside.

The county bus system in operation in the community (as inherited from the city of Palo Alto) had been designed as a "hub-and-spoke" system, with the downtown Southern Pacific Railroad station serving as the hub, and the spokes radiated out to the old residential areas of Palo

Alto. Studies demonstrated that even if the 300 buses operated by the county were to operate with 35–40 passengers in each bus, given the residential patterns of employees and then-accepted bus routes, only 3% of the working commuters needing transportation would be served. The Pamtrans study group investigated several ways to alleviate commuter traffic congestion and better serve the commuter population of Santa Clara County. In short, the Pamtrans report recommended a new expanded and rerouted bus system and alternative paratransit forms of transportation. The proposed bus system would run along a "grid-and-loop" pattern, instead of hub-and-spoke, and would better link areas within Palo Alto and Palo Alto with its neighbors.

The Pamtrans report emphasized the need for paratransit, including car pools, van pools, and commute buses. The report specifically suggested that the cities of Palo Alto and Menlo Park, Stanford University, the Metropolitan Transportation Committee, and the San Mateo County and Santa Clara County transit districts join together with representatives of business and industry to work together to encourage alternatives to the single-occupant automobile, such as van pooling, car pools, and commute buses.

When it was issued in November 1975, the Pamtrans report was widely distributed and publicized in the community.

To promulgate community discussion, we invited area employers to a meeting to discuss the Pamtrans study and its ramifications. Thirty-nine representatives of business and industry and government in the area attended. Prior to the opening of the meeting, all the attendees received information packets that included the summary and recommendations of the Pamtrans report; a copy of a July 24, 1975, *Wall Street Journal* article on van pooling; and information on a proposed sales tax assessment to raise funds for the operation of the expanded county bus system. The members were addressed by James Jucker; Jack Beckett, a Hewlett-Packard vice-president who also served as chairman of the Metropolitan Transportation Commission; and Santa Clara County Supervisor Geraldine Steinberg.

Expanded County Bus System

The Santa Clara County Transit District obtained a grant commitment from the Urban Mass Transportation Administration for the purchase of 516 new buses, and proposed a plan of its own, based on the assumption that the tax assessment would be approved by the voters. The "516 Plan" would use federal and local funds to replace old buses and to increase the number of buses in the county system from 236 to 516.

In March 1976, the voters of Santa Clara County approved the half-cent sales tax. Several months later, the director of transportation for Palo Alto informed the city council that the staff was preparing a modified Pamtrans plan in keeping with the buses to be allocated under the 516 Plan. In June, the city adopted most of the Pamtrans recommendations. To our satisfaction, with the revenue from the sales tax and approval of the plan, the city and the County Transit District agreed to incorporate much of the "grid-and-loop" system as proposed in the Pamtrans study. We corresponded with the city and the county in planning for the routes of the "southern loop" grid proposed in the Pamtrans master plan. We wanted to ensure that the routes best met the needs of employees in the Stanford Industrial Park.

In the interim, before the new bus system was implemented, the County Transit District initiated operation of a commuter bus service called Express One. This bus begins 20 miles to the south and travels on a freeway directly to the Stanford Industrial Park. Running at regular intervals, it provides fast, efficient service and has been enthusiastically received by our employees and employees of other firms in the area. Companies promoted usage by distributing information packets. A flexible working-hours policy of several major employers, including Hewlett-Packard Corporation and Syntex, contributes to the success of the commuter bus route.

Ride Sharing

Assisting in the design and implementation of public transit systems is only one way for corporations to involve themselves in the transit problems of their employees and their communities. An individual firm can also work with its own employees to reduce automobile usage and on-site parking. A reduction of this kind not only alleviates the high costs of constructing new parking spaces but also has a "ripple" effect: less traffic congestion, less air pollution, less gasoline consumption. Federal Energy Administration officials have estimated that if all commuters traveled in pairs, there would be 15 million fewer autos on the roads daily, and the United States consumption of gasoline would drop 500,000 barrels each day. Moreover, the U.S. Department of Transportation's Federal Highway Administration estimates that a driver can save from $281 to $654 a year by car pooling. The more riders in one car, the greater the savings.

Van Pooling

An innovative idea receiving increasing popularity nationwide is van pooling, pioneered by the Minnesota Mining and Manufacturing

Company (3M) in St. Paul, Minnesota. During the energy crisis, in April 1973, the 3M Company began a pilot program using six 12-passenger vans. By September 1975, 73 vans were in operation at 3M, and more than 15 groups of 8–12 people were waiting for vans. In 1977, about 1,000 3M employees traveled to work in vans, representing 12% of 3M's employees at the location. 3M purchases the vans, which cost about $7,000 each, and, in effect, leases them to the drivers. Each van holds 11 people in addition to the driver. The daily fares of the first 8 riders cover the cost of the van. As an incentive, the driver rides free and is able to pocket the fares of the 9th, 10th, and 11th riders. The driver is responsible for the van during nonworking hours and for a "reasonable mileage rate" can use the van for personal use on weekends and during non-working hours.

The van-pooling concept is economically efficient and effective for roundtrips of more than 20 miles, and the fares vary between $20 and $25 per month, depending on the distance. Today, numerous employers across the country—including Conoco in Houston; the Aerospace Corporation in El Segundo, California; Hewlett-Packard in Palo Alto; and the Tennessee Valley Authority in Knoxville, Tennessee—all use van pooling as a method of ride sharing for their employees. In California, van pooling got off to a slow start because of a Public Utilities Commission regulation that appeared to make van pooling illegal. However, because of statewide interest in van-pooling programs, in 1975 a bill was passed (AB 918) that exempted van pools from PUC control.

The Pamtrans report in 1975 strongly endorsed van pooling in the Bay Area and urged area firms to initiate programs. To spur interest, we hosted a two-day conference on van pooling at Syntex on January 28–29, 1976. The conference was sponsored by Congressman Paul N. McCloskey, Jr., and Supervisor Geraldine Steinberg of Santa Clara County.

More than 120 individuals representing the private and public sectors attended. Speakers included Robert Owens from the 3M Company, Leon Bush of Aerospace Corporation, William Fortune of Continental Oil, Robert Hemphill of the Federal Energy Administration, James Jucker of Pamtrans, and David Calkins of the Federal Environmental Protection Agency.

At the meeting, the Federal Energy Administration cited the benefits of van pooling to employers, employees, and the general public:

1. Reduced congestion at the employment site.
2. Reduced tardiness and absenteeism.
3. Increased potential labor pool, particularly in areas having little transit service.
4. Good public relations for employers.
5. Lower automobile insurance rates.
6. Reduced mileage on personal automobiles.

7. Greater reliability of commuting.
8. Reduced commuting costs.
9. Reduced risks and tension of commuting.
10. Freeing car for use by other family members.
11. Reduced congestion on streets and highways.
12. Reduced land use for parking and other automobile-related facilities.
13. Positive effect on the environment—less air and noise pollution.
14. Reduced energy consumption.

A National Association of Vanpooling Operators was formed later in 1976 and includes about 30 companies. David J. Lester, manager of special projects for Atlantic Richfield Company in Los Angeles, was named interim president.

In the Bay Area, van pooling has caught on in both government and private sectors. Freed by recent legislation, Santa Clara County is initiating a van-pooling program for county employees. The program operates similarly to that of the 3M model, but Santa Clara is leasing the vans rather than purchasing them. Syntex has one van operating between Palo Alto and San Francisco and expects several others to be put into operation in 1979.

Revitalizing and Extending Car Pooling

A third vital form of paratransit for employees is a revitalized concept of car pooling or ride sharing. Under a bill passed by the legislature in 1976, CalTrans received $1.4 million to spend on ride-sharing programs in five areas: the San Francisco Bay Area, Los Angeles, San Bernardino, San Diego, and Sacramento. CalTrans has allocated $350,000 for the Bay Area, with $100,000 designated for Santa Clara County.

Utilizing the resources of a computer, CalTrans can match individuals working in an area, according to their census tracts and assigned work zones, or by using a grid system to encourage and assist commuters. CalTrans installed car-pool information signs along freeways and is distributing information about this program to large companies. According to Merle Johnson of CalTrans, his San Francisco office receives about 40–50 calls daily, requesting ride-sharing information. CalTrans distributes an application that interested individuals can fill out and return to CalTrans to be matched. The application requests name, address, work telephone number, hours worked, whether hours are flexible, and preference for driving or riding and asks for a predesignated work zone number, specified on the back of the application form.

Responses take approximately two weeks. Officials at CalTrans estimate that they have successfully matched 84% of their requests —6,500 as of January 1977.

The CalTrans car-pooling program was originally begun in February 1974, sponsored by a consortium of public and private agencies during the energy crisis. Although the ranks of ride-sharers swelled during the energy crisis, the program lacked funds for promotional activities until a new bill was approved in 1976.

A second but tangential program run by CalTrans is more specific in area. If requested, CalTrans will run an "on-site" or "in-house" program, matching only the employees of a single organization. Both programs are offered free of charge. Several local organizations, including the Veterans Administration Hospital and Kaiser Aerospace, are requesting the on-site program.

In October 1976, we told our employees how to apply for the statewide computer-matching program. They were asked to fill out an application that we would forward to CalTrans. Of the approximately 100 employees who responded, about 80 were "matched" in the state computer.

In conclusion, it is the responsibility of both the private and the public sectors to work together to reduce the undesirable effects of single-occupant automobiles in a commuter–urban-based society. Our air quality must be preserved and our energy resources must be conserved in a harmonious effort to protect and enhance our living and working environment.

21

Support of the Arts: Fastest Growing Area of Corporate Philanthropy

As our country moves toward its third century, away from a century of extraordinary material growth and scientific development, perhaps we can look to the arts and public attitudes toward them to assure us of a national life that has more joy, more human fulfillment, and more ordered grace.

John B. Hightower, former President,
Associated Councils of the Arts

Over the years, business interest and involvement in the arts has advanced, although sometimes in a sporadic fashion. The turning point was signaled in a 1966 address by David Rockefeller, president of the Chase Manhattan Bank, at the 50th anniversary conference of the National Industrial Conference Board. In this address, Rockefeller pointed out that there was an increasing cultural interest abroad in the country and that business had a stake in nourishing it:

> This is a situation that should concern us all, both as businessmen and as citizens. For the arts are a vital part of human experience, and surely our success as a civilized society will be judged largely by the creative activities of our citizens in art, architecture, music and literature. Improving the condition of the performing and visual arts in this country calls, in my judgment, for a massive cooperative effort in which business corporations must assume a much larger role than they have in the past.

Rockefeller then went on to enumerate the various tangible benefits that would accrue to the business community from greater participation in the arts:

> It can provide a company with extensive publicity and advertising, a brighter public reputation, and an improved corporate image. It can build better customer relations, a readier acceptance of company products, and a superior appraisal of their quality. Promotion of the arts can improve the morale of employees and help attract qualified personnel.

He explained that the sources from which the arts have traditionally drawn their support—primarily wealthy individuals and foundations—were no longer able to cope with the growing needs, and not enough companies had moved in to take up the slack. He said that only a tiny fraction of direct corporate giving—less than $25 million or a mere 3% of business gifts—was then going to meet cultural needs.

Business Committee for the Arts

Rockefeller recommended the establishment of a new organization to do for the arts what the Council for Financial Aid to Education had done to increase business support for educational institutions. The Business Committee for the Arts (BCA) was founded in the following year. Financed by four major foundations (the Rockefeller Brothers Fund and the Andrew W. Mellon, Ford, and Rockefeller foundations), its first chairman was C. Douglas Dillon, a well-known Wall Street businessman and government figure.

The goals of the new organization were (1) to gather and disseminate information on corporate support of the arts; (2) to provide counseling for business firms seeking to initiate new arts programs or to expand existing ones; (3) to carry on a public information program to keep corporations informed of opportunities for support of the arts; (4) to work to increase the effectiveness of cultural organizations in obtaining support from business; and (5) to increase the personal involvement of business executives with cultural organizations.

As chairman of the BCA, one of Dillon's first moves was to call upon the business community to increase the level of its direct contributions from 3% to 10%. He asked that this increase come from an overall *enlargement* of corporate giving rather than by diversion from other needy causes. He commented on the amazing growth of corporate support for education, which rose from $24 million in 1947 to $325 million in 1967:

> Business in this country has a way of rising to new challenges as they are recognized. I am confident that the challenge posed by the growing needs of the arts will be no exception to this tradition, and that the business community will join hands with government and with private givers in lending the arts the support they will require over the years that lie ahead.[1]

The dedicated efforts of business leaders such as David Rockefeller, who proposed the formation of the BCA, and Dillon, who served as its first chairman, began to make corporate executives more aware of the importance of the arts and the need for substantial support from the business community.

[1]From an address to the friends of City Center of Music and Drama at the New York State Theatre, December 9, 1968.

The presence of an organization devoting its entire efforts to this challenge was also significant. The BCA's quarterly and monthly newsletters were started. They now have a combined circulation of almost 15,000 company heads and civic and arts leaders across the nation. The BCA organized national and regional conferences to bring leaders of business and the arts together. It organized an annual national awards competition in collaboration with *Esquire* magazine to ensure that the outstanding programs of corporations directed at support of the arts would be made known and recognized throughout the country. In recent years, this awards program has been carried out in collaboration with *Forbes* magazine.

All these efforts had their impact. Shortly after the BCA was founded, it conducted a survey that disclosed that total corporate philanthropic support was $22 million, and by 1970, this had increased to $56 million. These sums were about equally divided between cash contributions and other types of support, such as "in-kind" contributions and the underwriting of programs on public television, as well as direct sponsorship of art projects and programs as institutional promotion. By 1973, a Touche Ross and Company survey commissioned by BCA revealed cash and other business support of the arts totalled $144 million. A Conference Board study disclosed that between 1972 and 1975 the percentage of the business cash contributions dollar going to the arts nearly doubled—from 4.1% to 7.5%—making the arts the fastest growing field of corporate philanthropy in recent years. The 7.5% allocation to the arts in 1975 represents cash contributions of over $100 million, so total support now is probably over $200 million.

Gideon Chagy, BCA vice-president, offers a good reason why everyone, including business leaders, should take a vital interest in the arts:

> While art is not a panacea for society's problems, it is a restorative for the sense of community; it helps us keep open and responsive; it connects us with our past and gives us intimations of a better life.[2]

Certainly, the modern business executive is necessarily concerned about design in his day-to-day activities. Print advertising, broadcast and television commercials, product brochures, annual reports, audio slide training presentations, employee publications, and packaging—all involve artistic forms, including drawing, graphics, music, acting, photography, and typography.

Paradoxically, while some business executives are concerned about design in commerce and industry, they may be indifferent to art in other forms and find it difficult to understand the need to support painters, museums, theater, ballet, or opera. Even more paradoxically, this myo-

[2]Gideon Chagy, *The New Patrons of the Arts* (New York: Harry N. Abrams, Inc., 1972), p. 83.

pia is prevalent in the communications, publications, and advertising industries of our country. This point was made by Eric Larrabee, executive director of the New York Council on the Arts, at the 1972 conference of the Associated Councils of the Arts:

> Can anyone imagine the $12.5 billion advertising industry without a continual supply—from independent writers, painters, musicians, and filmmakers whom it presently does not pay—of the verbal, graphic, musical and cinematic raw material which it insatiably consumes? If the advertising industry alone were to assess itself one percent for art research and development—for the replenishment of the fresh and the imaginative—it could contribute $125 million a year which would be more than double the amount now estimated to be given the arts by all of American business under the label of philanthropy.

On the other side, there is evidence of the alienation of many artists from the mainstream of everyday existence and certainly from the day-to-day life of business and commerce. Gideon Chagy explains it this way:

> [The artist's] skepticism is often expressed in the assertion that businessmen and corporations are incorrigibly crass, philistine, and incapable of actions that do not serve their own self-interest, narrowly conceived in terms of maximum possible profit. If business is inherently egocentric and grasping it follows that any act of philanthropy on the part of business must be suspect, and its "real"—and therefore reprehensible—motive must be exposed. For some artists it also seems to follow that acceptance of help from business or from a businessman must corrode their artistic integrity, and acceptance of such patronage will show up in their art as a visible reminder of their fall from grace.[3]

There is another factor that affects the relationship of the businessman and the artist in our society. Culturally enlightened business executives, along with other artistically interested professional people, often have a fairly sensitive antenna to detect the specious statement, the false or inflated values, the pompousness that too often masquerade as art. Chagy says:

> Life enhancing as they are, the arts are not always and inevitably the most important things in the world, particularly when they foster neglect or contempt for the more prosaic elements that are necessary to survival.[4]

This feeling was illustrated by the tongue-in-cheek comment of a director of the Bay Area Rapid Transit System when he was asked to approve a $58,000 commission for each of two major artworks that would grace one of the San Francisco entrances of the subway transit system. "My idea of a work of art," he said, "is a train entering the station every two minutes."

There are several characteristics of art and related cultural activities that are important for the businessman to understand. Artistic and

[3]Ibid., p. 73.
[4]Ibid., p. 31.

cultural activities cut across all boundaries—religious, economic, ethnic, geographical, and political. There is no business or community environment in which *some* appropriate type of artistic activity cannot be successfully developed or supported. Also, as a form of communication, art is successful in circumstances where other means of communication are not only less effective but frequently useless.

J. Irwin Miller, former chairman of the board of Cummins Engine Company, addressed this aspect of art at the 1972 annual meeting of the Business Committee for the Arts:

> Art is best understood as attempts at human communication at the most intense level. This is transparent in the art of today. At its best, contemporary art is often the best preacher, and the visible prophet among us. At its shabbiest it is simply propaganda—but in nearly every case it represents a desperate need of one human to express a personal feeling to other humans. . . . So, in this society which is already so rich in things, the single legacy which we might best hand on to our posterity is a legacy of the spirit and mind, a flourishing of all the arts in our time such as would truly give release to the creative potential within us, that would permit us to reach out to each other in expression of our deepest thoughts and needs, and in the release and the expression would help us find a new sense of community such as might make our lives rich and not empty, and might change our view of the future from fear to excitement.

In my experience, I have seen the wisdom of Mr. Miller's words worked out in real life. Again and again, I have observed that successful art projects and programs have developed extraordinary responses and have generated strong positive attitudes toward sponsoring firms that no amount of corporate propaganda could have elicited.

Columbus: "Athens of the Prairie"

One of the most vivid and persuasive examples of this concept is the work of J. Irwin Miller and his company in Columbus, Indiana.

In a 1964 *Saturday Evening Post* article, this quiet country town of 30,000 in the southeastern corner of the state, was called the "Athens of the Prairie"—and with good reason. Columbus is the location of more than two dozen outstanding buildings by some of the world's leading architects.

The man responsible for what the *New York Times* in 1971 called "the finest architecture per capita of any city in the United States" is J. Irwin Miller, an extraordinary person. He has degrees from Yale and Oxford; is a Republican who helped lead the March on Washington for Jobs and Freedom in 1963; is a former Sunday school teacher who relaxes by playing the violin. Mr. Miller is a fourth-generation member of a family that made its fortune in Columbus in real estate, banking, electric railroads, corn-starch refining, and diesel engines. (Cummins Engine

Company is the world's largest independent producer of diesel engines.)

In 1941, the Miller family arranged for Eliel Saarinen to design the new First Christian Church, whose most striking feature was a rectangular tower the height of an 18-story building. It was also the first contemporary church building done by Saarinen.

In the early 1950s, Miller selected the late Eero Saarinen—Eliel's son and a former classmate—to design new quarters for Irwin Union Bank & Trust Co., which his family controls.

About the time the bank was being built, Columbus completed a new high school, and Miller decided, according to the *New York Times*, that "better things could be done." He implemented his idea by establishing the Cummins Engine Foundation in 1954. The foundation offered to pay the architect's fee for any new school building if the board of education would select the architect from a list compiled by experts in the field. The result has been the construction of 11 new schools of innovative design by well-known architects since 1965.

Along the way, other new public buildings and churches benefited from the creative talents of well-known architects. The Cleo Rogers Memorial County Library, built in 1968, was designed by I. M. Pei, architect of the proposed John F. Kennedy Memorial Library. The Pei design was not funded by the foundation, but Cummins contributed $800,000 to help pay the $22 million construction costs of the new library. Perhaps the most impressive example of contemporary architecture in Columbus is the North Christian Church. It was the last work of Eero Saarinen, completed in 1964. Its spiral pinnacle rises 192 feet out of the hexagonal slope of the main structure.

Columbus has averaged two architectural masterpieces a year, according to an eight-page review in *The Architectural Forum*, and the *New York Times* has called the result "a stunning pot pourri of creation." Not all of these projects involved support from the Cummins Engine Foundation. Nevertheless, the foundation's contributions over the years of $2.7 million in architectural fees and $3.2 million for construction have been instrumental in making Columbus the "Athens of the Prairie."

"A Look at Architecture: Columbus, Indiana," a 100-page brochure on the city's architecture, was published in 1974 by the Columbus Area Chamber of Commerce. It is available for $3 from the Visitors Center, 506 Fifth Street, Columbus, IN 47201.

Strong Public Support for the Arts

In 1973, the National Research Center of the Arts, an affiliate of Louis Harris and Associates, Inc., made the first in-depth survey of the public's attitudes toward the arts. The survey was updated in 1975. The public's evaluation of the arts is high indeed. Ninety-three percent said that museums, theaters, concert halls, and like facilities are important to the quality of life in a community. Eighty-five percent believed that arts and cultural facilities are important to the business and economy of the community. The survey indicated time and again the common belief that the arts are central to life in America today.

Support of the arts is also something that can contribute substantially to better employee relations. This benefit was cogently expressed by Edward L. Steiniger, the retired chairman of Sinclair Oil Corporation:

> There is some irony in the reluctance of many business corporations to apply their rationale for supporting education to the arts. They may well find in the near future that the education they have helped to provide has made their support of the arts inevitable. The people who make up most of the audiences for the performing arts, are also the best educated—and it is this group which provides industry with most of its managerial and professional personnel. They want to work for companies and in communities that satisfy their very discriminating standards.[5]

There is no question that the public and company employees are looking for more opportunities to enjoy a wide range of artistic and cultural experiences. The opportunity is present but there are also significant problems.

The problems were predicted in 1966, when Baumol and Bowen published their study, *Performing Arts: The Economic Dilemma*.[6] They pointed out that the rise in demand for the arts would mean that arts organizations would have to provide many additional services. That would mean more perfomers and staff since arts organizations are labor-intensive. But since there are no labor-saving devices in the arts—no mechanization, no technology, no mass production—there was no way that was possible to meet higher costs just through greater box office receipts.

New sources of financial support, including significantly greater government subsidies and private support, would have to be tapped. Corporate financial support, which has lagged substantially behind business gifts to education, health, and welfare, would have to be dramatically increased to help fill the growing gap between box office receipts and inexorably rising operating costs.

These new sources are being found. Corporate executives are learning that the arts are so basic that they fit into the company's activities in a natural way. These projects and programs don't have to be something apart from the firm's ordinary business activities but can be integrated and assimilated with excellent results both for art and for the corporation.

[5]From an address to the Second State Conference for the Arts in Topeka, Kansas, on March 22, 1969.

[6]William J. Baumol and William G. Bowen, *Performing Arts: The Economic Dilemma* (New York: Twentieth Century Fund, 1966).

One excellent example is the Levi's Denim Art Contest—an idea of Bud Johns at Levi Strauss. Johns is my counterpart there and a colleague whose creativity and competence I greatly admire.

Johns observed that young people were decorating their Levis in extraordinary ways. He decided to sponsor a contest for everyone, artists included, to see how much creativity could be poured into the decoration of jeans and jackets. The result was the fabulous Denim Art Contest. An immediate sensation, it appeared in museums in New York, San Francisco, Los Angeles, Tucson, Madison, Memphis, and Cincinnati. Then it went abroad to Toronto, Dusseldorf, Amsterdam, and Brussels. The original contest led to other contests in Europe and Japan also. Harry N. Abrams, Inc., published a book, *American Denim*, based on the competition, and Warner put out a paperback version.

The Art of Learning Medicine

There is an experience of my own that also illustrates the compatibility of art and business. The involvement of the company began in mid-1973, when Dr. Alister Brass, then a Syntex physician, suggested that we go down to Southern California to visit an artist working in the medical field. Dr. Brass had become familiar with May Lesser's work when, as an editor of the *Journal of the American Medical Association*, he had featured several of her works as cover illustrations.

We visited Lesser shortly thereafter at her home in Newport Beach. She took us into her storeroom, the garage of her house, and began to pull out of wooden and cardboard boxes an amazing collection of beautiful etchings, pastels, and drawings. As she did so, she explained their origin.

Because she was part of a medical family (her father, brother, and husband are physicians), she could pass through the initial response of guilt or frustration or abhorrence for the sick and resentment of the physician to find a beauty in the training of people to care for other people.

Raised in New Orleans, she graduated from the H. Sophie Newcomb College, Tulane University, in 1947, with honors in drawing, and she earned a master's degree in painting from the University of Alabama. In addition to studying etching over the years, she also taught graphics at the University of California at Irvine.

In the fall of 1967, Lesser wanted further experience in sketching anatomy and audited an anatomy course at UCLA School of Medicine attended by first-year medical students. And when these first-year students went to their graduation ceremony in the summer of 1971, Lesser was still with them. She did not complete the four years with a degree but with hundreds of drawings and color etchings that captured the experiences of the students, the professors, and herself. In this period, she had also written a personal narrative of these experiences.

During our visit, Lesser told us that she wanted to publish these illustrations and her narrative in a book called *The Art of Learning Medicine*. She said that she had a publisher lined up and that UCLA would support the project with a $15,000 loan against future royalties but that additional funds were needed to subsidize the high cost of preparing the plates for the many color illustrations that would be used in the book.

I was able to convince Syntex to provide the funds, and the book was published in 1974 by Appleton-Century-Crofts. It includes 90 color illustrations and 206 black-and-white plates within its 416 pages. *The Art of Learning Medicine* is divided into four parts—one for each year of medical school.

The book was reviewed extensively in the medical field because of its subject matter. Dr. George L. Fite made these comments in a review published in the *Journal of the American Medical Association* in June 1974:

> This remarkable record succeeds in capturing the heart of the educational process in almost an effortless manner; the atmospheres, the intensities of the students, the inner earnestness inspire her drawings. Lesser becomes the soul of the student, always serious, always intense, and physicians who review these drawings, etchings, and paintings will recognize, sometimes painfully, the accuracy of her observations.

The reception of the book in the art world was not nearly as dramatic. May Lesser was prepared for this response. She saw medicine as an ideal subject for art but most of her artist friends were appalled by the project. One art professor, after her first year of work, told her, "Enough is enough! Now go back and do the landscapes and flowers, the gentle, lovely work you have been doing. This experience will ruin you. Who cares about wounds and blood?"

Obviously May Lesser knew that medicine was not just wounds and blood. It was "the loveliness in the function of human beings helping one another," and it was a student in an immunology lab who recalled to her one of Rembrandt's models in *Women with the Arrow*.

Our support of the book presented several worthwhile opportunities. In our agreement to provide support, we stipulated that the company could purchase copies of the books at a good discount from the retail price. We did so and distributed copies to medical libraries and related institutions. These gifts were well received, and the company's involvement became known and appreciated.

The company also purchased 50 original prints from the series to add to its permanent collection. Physicians visiting the offices of our medical group in Palo Alto have been intrigued to view the collection. The company's pharmaceutical marketing group later decided that it wanted to exhibit the collection at major medical meetings throughout the country. It turned out to be excellent institutional promotion for the company over the two years it was exhibited at 20 meetings.

The company's total investment in *The Art of Learning Medicine* was about $40,000 over several years. This amount included the subsidy to get the book printed, the purchase of a large quantity of books, the acquisition of 50 pieces of original art, the cost of making shipping crates for the collection, and the printing of a brochure describing the series.

It was an excellent investment and was handled as a regular business expense rather than as a contribution. Our involvement paid good returns in the form of better professional relations with physicians as well as employee and visitor appreciation of the collection as part of our permanent art collection. The BCA thought it was a worthwhile project and bestowed an honorable mention award on the company in 1973.

The Syntex Gallery

Another major involvement of the company in the arts is the Syntex Gallery. This story began in the late 1960s, when the company was planning about $17 million of new facilities at its 100-acre site in the Stanford Industrial Park of Palo Alto. These included an auditorium, conference rooms, a food service facility, offices, and laboratories.

I had had the idea of a company gallery in my mind for several years, and this seemed to provide an opportunity to see if one could be established. I asked to see the architect's drawings for the conference center. In the midst of the conference center was 3,500 square feet of space. I asked, "What is that?" The architect said, "That is the lobby." I replied, "No, that's the art gallery ." He got the point and was as enthusiastic as I was to see what could be done.

My first move was to contact Bernard Hern, who was formerly director of the Lytton Centers of the Arts in California. I gave plans of the space to Hern and asked him to figure out what was required to develop it into a first-class gallery area. The major additions he recommended were a system to permit art to be displayed on freestanding panels as well as on the walls; electrical outlets in the tile flooring; overhead track-lighting systems; and the installation of venetian blinds on the large window surfaces on both sides of the area. The costs for these designs, equipment, and installation were under $25,000. Surplus lighting equipment was purchased from one of the Lytton Centers.

Before the gallery space was completed, we had our first taste of the exhibition business in the summer of 1971. We displayed "The Magic Machines" of Robert Gilbert in our newly completed food services building. Our employees and visitors thought it was terrific, and we were off and running. Our first formal exhibition in the Syntex Gallery opened in September of that same year. It was a display of resist textiles by Lois Brooks, an artist from Southern California.

In 1972, we had four shows capped by "The New Masters"—an idea of Hern's, who was now hanging the shows and helping to select art for our gallery. The pieces in "The New Masters" exhibit were by 22 outstanding young California artists who were working toward or had recently earned their master of fine arts degrees. Hern looked at more than a thousand works of art in California colleges and universities for the selection of the 42 works of art in the show.

Here is what Alfred Frankenstein said about it in his review in the *San Francisco Chronicle,* November 2, 1972:

> We don't ordinarily review exhibitions in business houses, but the show in the art gallery at Syntex in the Stanford Industrial Park in Palo Alto is something very special. It is devoted to paintings and sculpture by 22 Californians who have recently earned their master's degrees. Syntex has long demonstrated that capitalism and The Pill both work. Now art is added to the team. The exhibition demonstrates a good many things that the younger generation of Bay Region artists is thinking about. It is the kind of show we should have had at the San Francisco Museum as part of its reopening festivities; it ought to be brought to San Francisco in any case. [It wasn't.]

The highlight of the 1973 season at the Syntex Gallery was the "Circles of Light" exhibition by J. Alfred Anderson, Steven R. Carlson, and Michael Ashford Cooper. It was a display of lighted and kinetic sculpture that was a real mind blower. Then the show closed, we purchased five pieces by Cooper, and they have been in the lobbies of Syntex buildings since that time, contributing to the amazement of visitors to the site.

In 1974, we had five exhibitions. The first was an exhibition of the works of May Lesser, using for the name of the show the name of the book she had published with Syntex support: "The Art of Learning Medicine."

Another popular show that year was "Beyond Illustration: The Art of Playboy." Conceived by *Playboy's* art director, Arthur Paul, "Beyond Illustration" consisted of the work of 43 nationally known artists, including such diverse talents as Salvadore Dali, Roy Schnackenberg, Dave Packard, and Andy Warhol. Getting this show was quite a coup for Syntex. It was the first northern California exhibition of "Beyond Illustration" after a three-year tour overseas.

In 1976, an exhibition titled "Nineteenth Century Painters of the California Landscape" was held in the Syntex Gallery. The idea for the show came from a local environmental organization, the Committee for Green Foothills. The Committee wanted to tie the exhibition into the production of an original American opera.

The first president of the Committee for Green Foothills was Wallace Stegner, who wrote *Angle of Repose,* a Pulitzer-prize–winning novel about the struggles of an American family in the West in the latter part of the 19th century. On November 6, 1976, the San Francisco Opera premiered a new and original opera based on Stegner's book, with music by Andrew Imbrie and lyrics by Oakley Hall.

The Committee for Green Foothills planned a reception for Stegner and the creators and producers of the new opera to be held the day after the premier in conjunction with a preview of the show in the Syntex Gallery. The purpose was also to raise funds for the committee, and in this they succeeded—about 500 people made a contribution to attend. U.S. Senator Alan Cranston gave a nice introduction to Stegner, and it was an extremely enjoyable evening.

In the first five years of the gallery's existence, it had 26 exhibitions, which featured the works of several hundred artists. The gallery established itself as a place where good contemporary art was displayed. Public acceptance was immediate, and support grew as each succeeding show added a new dimension to the art scene in the area.

Let me mention a few benefits of the gallery. First of all, it provides an additional place for artists to exhibit their works in a business environment. There are many fine artists in northern California, but the opportunities for displaying the works of all these talented people are still limited.

If the artist desires (and most do) that the works in the show at Syntex be offered for sale, this is feasible. A price list is displayed and public visitors contact the artist or the artist's representative. Syntex does not become involved in such sales. In the case of purchases by the company for its permanent collection or purchases of artworks by employees, we deal directly with the artist. This is quite a benefit, since it generally means a substantial savings from the same artist's prices in commercial galleries—as much as 40%.

Finally, the gallery is a major point of interest at the site for large numbers of people. These include 1,600 employees; Syntex visitors from other company locations; the many business, professional, and other outside visitors to the site; and the several thousands who annually visit the facility as part of the company's organized tour program for professional, school, and community groups.

The gallery is also a major attraction for nonprofit groups, which are permitted to use, in the evenings and on weekends, our facilities for fund raising or other purposes. About 25 such events are held each year, and the exhibitions in the gallery are an important part of the attractiveness of having such gatherings at Syntex.

Some outside groups have tied directly into the art exhibitions for fund-raising functions. These have included UNICEF, Big Sisters of the Bay Area, the Service League of San Mateo County, and the California

Youth Symphony Association. These events have generally taken the form of a special preview of a new show.

The company has also acquired its own collection of art. In addition to the works of contemporary California artists, the collection embraces a diversity of art forms by prominent artists from nine countries. Major works in the collection include a sculpture by Sir Henry Moore and a commissioned oil painting by the Mexican artist David Alfaro Siqueiros. Bronzes cast by Cristos Capralos and Kenneth Armitage, a 16-foot serigraph by Robert Rauschenberg, and tapestries designed in Abusson, Portalegre, Poland, and the USSR are part of the collection.

It is interesting how involvement in the arts at one company location is picked up at others. Our chemical manufacturing subsidiary, Arapahoe Chemicals, opened a new headquarters and research facility at its plant in Boulder, Colorado. Designed by A. M. Kinney, Inc., of Englewood, Colorado, it was selected the "Lab of the Year" by *Industrial Research* magazine in 1976. Part of the new space proved to be suitable for the display of art. In October 1977, it housed the annual membership exhibition of the Boulder Artists' Guild. Ina Posey, art critic of the Boulder *Sunday Camera,* commented on the unusual but effective space:

> Imagine a space three stories high, awash with light, through which plunge massive golden and mandarin pipes, tracking after the shapes made by their own colors; envision a long, winding handrail of lemon yellow for the dancing accent line; suppose this place to be a shelter for immaculate walls, and what do you have? You have a place to hang pictures, obviously. The Boulder Artists' Guild found this place, and have placed 61 pictures on the walls, and it is a sight to see. (October 16, 1977)

The point of this story is twofold. First, a good example is frequently imitated. Second, art is compatible with many company locations: office buildings, research laboratories, manufacturing facilities—just about any open and pleasant environment in which people work. Firms should take advantage of appropriate spaces already available and, if new construction is planned, include some area that might serve as a fitting location for the display of art.

Special Performances

One of the attractive aspects of the arts is that they involve people in meaningful and enjoyable ways and the possibilities of such involvement are unlimited.

In the early 1960s, I was on the board of directors of the Masterwork Music and Art Foundation, which funded and organized the Masterwork Chorus directed by David Randolph. He was also conductor of the Randolph Singers in New York and radio commentator for the Metropolitan Opera and the Little Orchestra Society.

The Masterwork Foundation itself began in 1955, when 28 persons met in the Morristown, New Jersey, living room of Shirley May—a former schoolteacher with an intense interest in music—to form a local choral group. Five years later, they had grown to 200 members and were performing Bach's *Christmas Oratorio* in Carnegie Hall.

It was during this period that I was in charge of public relations for CIBA Pharmaceutical Company, the United States subsidiary of the large Swiss firm. CIBA Pharmaceuticals began its activities in this country in May 1937, and 1962 marked its 25th anniversary. As part of the anniversary celebration, it was decided to engage the Masterwork Chorus to present a special performance on May 24 for employees and prominent community people. The concert, held in the auditorium of Summit High School, featured Beethoven's *Eroica* and Brahm's *German Requiem.* The concert was well received, and CIBA (now CIBA-Geigy) has continued its sponsorship of community concerts.

Stanford Summer Festivals

During the early 1970s, Syntex was able to participate in a novel way in the Stanford Summer Festivals organized by Steve Baffrey, who now covers the performing arts for radio station KCBS in San Francisco. Baffrey is a capable producer and was able to line up a fine collection of talent to perform at Stanford University. He brought to the area for the first time the Joffrey Ballet, the Preservation Hall Jazz Band, and many other outstanding artistic groups and individual performers.

Like most producers, however, Steve had one persistent nightmare. He had to stretch his potential resources to line up an exciting performance, but without a sell-out house, he was going to get a sharp dose of red ink in his ledger. Baffrey came up with an idea to solve his problem. How would Syntex like to serve as a corporate *guarantor* of a specific performance? It would work like this. The company would agree to purchase all tickets still unsold one week before the performance. If the performance was sold out, the company would have no obligation. In either case, the Stanford Festival would be protected from financial disaster. For this commitment, the company would be listed in the program as the guarantor of that performance.

We liked the idea and tried it for the first performance of the Joffrey Ballet. We wound up with some tickets but made them available at a discount to our employees. Buoyed with this success, the next year we became a corporate guarantor of the opening festival performance of *Jacques Brel Is Alive and Well and Living in Paris.* Again we wound up with some tickets, but the box office sales for the subsequent performances in the run were well above breaking even. Our guarantee, in both cases, had enabled Steve to take a limited risk and gave him a "sold" evening on which to build his audience for the remaining performances in each series.

Commissioning Artworks

The commissioning of artworks is another area where corporate support can be worthwhile and exciting. Syntex has had several such experiences. When the company was in its early years in Mexico, it commissioned David Alfaro Siqueiros, one of that country's outstanding artists, to paint a scene showing peasants gathering barbasco root—the plant that was then the principal starting material in the production of steroid hormones. This strong and beautiful painting now hangs in the lobby of the main research building of Syntex in Palo Alto.

In 1977, another special opportunity presented itself. Dr. Ralph I. Dorfman, president of Syntex Research, and a company director, was retiring. He and his wife, Peggy, were enthusiastic music lovers and were active supporters of the San Francisco Symphony Orchestra. It was decided to commemorate Dorfman's loyal and productive service to the company by commissioning in his honor a new work by Toru Takemitsu entitled *A Flock Descends into the Pentagonal Garden.* The new work had its world premier by the San Francisco Symphony Orchestra under the direction of Edo de Waart on November 30, 1977.

Philip Morris Incorporated

There is one corporation that I feel has surpassed all others in the extent and quality of its support for the arts: Philip Morris. Like most creative corporate efforts, it stems directly from the commitment of its top officers. Here is the company's philosophy of artistic involvement as stated emphatically by George Weissman, vice-chairman of the board of directors:

> There is something called corporate responsibility and it's both altruistic and in our enlightened self interest. What you will hear is some down-to-earth observations of why and how one company undertakes to integrate art in its business operations—and why we regard such an effort as worthwhile investment in our own future and in fostering a positive environment in the communities in which we operate, and an investment in the free enterprise system in America, as well.[7]

The effects of this enlightened philosophy can be seen in hundreds of specific programs, projects, and events that have been supported by Philip Morris. These include the purchase and commissioning of art-

[7]Remarks at the corporate patrons' luncheon at the Dallas Museum of Fine Arts, March 25, 1977.

works; financial support for arts organizations; the organization of a united arts fund among company employees; the funding of art exhibitions; providing financial support for performing arts events; the sponsorship of art films; funding of public television; and the creation of an advertising campaign in national publications to underscore the importance of corporate support of the arts. Additional information about this firm's activities can be obtained by writing to Philip Morris, 100 Park Avenue, New York, NY 10017.

BCA Materials

For an idea of the many other possibilities of company involvement, an annual booklet, "Examples of How BCA Companies Supported the Arts," can be obtained without charge from the Business Committee for the Arts, 1700 Broadway, New York, NY 10019. The BCA also distributes another worthwhile information piece, "Approaching Business for Support of the Arts." This is designed for arts organizations that want business support but don't know how to go about getting it.

One interesting part of the brochure explains "How *Not* to Raise Funds." Two examples are relevant:

- The manager of a touring theatre company rushed into the BCA offices one Friday afternoon. His group of Equity actors was to leave Sunday for the West Coast. He needed to find a businessman to write a three thousand dollar check for immediate expenses by the bank closing time!
- A large corporate foundation, just getting involved in support of the arts, sent twenty checks for $1,000 each to arts organizations asking in the covering letter that the recipients write back to report on the use of the funds and to indicate whether they were interested in this type of support. Although all twenty checks were cashed, only four arts organizations bothered to reply.

Needless to say, artists and cultural organizations have to do their homework to achieve a better understanding of the attitudes and activities of the corporation and to offer interesting and feasible proposals on how a specific business can best get involved.

One encouraging development in the continuing involvement of art and commerce is the growing awareness and determination of arts organizations to operate in a businesslike manner as far as nonartistic operations are concerned. For many years, it was accepted that there was some inherent organizational gene that made it impossible for arts organizations (including some of the most impressive and well-known professional groups in the country) to operate with any degree of managerial skill or efficiency.

This era seems to be passing, and it is encouraging to hear the presidents of performing arts organizations discuss the quality of their management skills with the same enthusiasm that they praise their artistic accomplishments. It's a truism that one can't get along without the other, and, in fact, there is considerable synergy when both managerial and artistic skills are operating at a high level of performance.

22

Public Television: Vital Communications and Cultural Need

We offer programs that entertain, stimulate and inform. Our purpose is to help you cope better with the world and your own life.

WGBH Boston Public Television

Until very recently, a discussion of public television and corporate support for it could have been relegated to one page in the chapter on corporate support of the arts. However, with more interconnected television stations (over 275) than any other network (more than ABC, NBC, or CBS), the Public Broadcasting Service has become unique in the world. It deserves a separate chapter as well as the serious consideration of every corporation, foundation, or agency attempting to commit funds to responsible, effective, and worthwhile causes either locally or nationally.

PBS has brought to our homes such high-quality and richly diverse programming as "Sesame Street," "Masterpiece Theatre," "Nova," "Wall Street Week," "Theater in America," "Evening at Symphony," "The Electric Company," "Zoom," "Mister Rogers' Neighborhood," "The Ascent of Man," "Evening at Pops," "Julia Child," "The Adams Chronicles," "The Advocates," and more.

All this has been made possible only through grants and contributions, large and small, from corporations, foundations, government, and individual viewers. There are no commercials and therefore no advertising revenues. It is the purpose of public television to satisfy the educational, cultural, public affairs, or sporting interests of one segment of the populace or another not otherwise sufficiently dealt with on commercial television.

Alternative broadcasting is a term aptly used to describe this unique local and national asset, and most recent figures show that more than

40% of the nation's television households are now watching at least once a week and 60% at least once a month. That seems to be a good indication that the goal of public television is being realized, a goal perhaps most aptly, if broadly, described by the simple credo at the beginning of this chapter that starts and ends each broadcast day on Boston's station WGBH.

History and Structure

The first noncommercial television station in the United States went on the air in May of 1953. It, and the 80 that followed in the next nine years, performed valuable educational services for limited audiences and received financial support mostly from state and local governments, schools and colleges, and private foundations (particularly the Ford Foundation).

In 1962, Congress recognized the growing desire and necessity for expanded noncommercial broadcasting operations and authorized $32 million in matching funds to aid in the acquisition and installation of new educational television broadcasting facilities. Five years later, based primarily on the recommendation of the Carnegie Commission Report, Congress enacted the Public Broadcasting Act of 1967. That act provided both for the continuation of facilities grants and for the establishment of a nonprofit educational broadcasting corporation through which to funnel grants for the development of new and innovative programming.

Educational broadcasting had steadily broadened its scope and reached beyond classroom use originally conceived of as instructional television. To a great extent life *is* the classroom, and public television, as the Carnegie Commission had suggested it should more aptly be called, was beginning to recognize its responsibility to broadcast programming of drama, public affairs, cultural events, and alternative sports.

Accordingly HR 6736 had been labeled the *Public* Broadcasting Act of 1967, and the nonprofit entity created thereby was called the Corporation for *Public* Broadcasting. CPB was authorized to make its funds available primarily for local stations' program acquisition and production but also to help establish effective interconnection services among the stations and to aid the stations with audience and other research, professional training, and experiments with new technology. CPB does not itself produce programs for distribution to the stations. It is governed by a 15-member board of directors appointed by the President (with the advice and consent of the Senate) but is sufficiently independent of Congress to serve as a buffer between the source of funds and the program producer, thereby providing protection from undue interference or control.

Just as CPB is an outgrowth of Congress serving as a conduit to public broadcasting stations, so is the Public Broadcasting Service an outgrowth of the stations themselves. Created in 1969, PBS was reorganized in 1973 with ownership transferred to the stations. PBS is governed by a board of 35 distinguished citizens and 15 station executives. PBS is not a network in the familiar sense, for it does not own any of the stations and does not produce any programming; it merely interconnects the stations technically and serves the stations professionally.

Funding Sources

The initial funding for public broadcasting came from schools, colleges, and local and state governments, later encouraged and matched by federal dollars. Thereafter, enormous aid in programming efforts came from large private foundations, most notably the Ford Foundation, without whose $250 million over 20 years public broadcasting would not likely have survived. But both Congress and the Ford Foundation recognized that public television would have to generate support from other sources. A broader base of support would not only be necessary to continue growth and expansion and improvement of facilities and programming but would also be the only real proof that a public service was indeed being provided that was important enough to the public to warrant its support.

Now public television enjoys rising support from every sector of the American society: corporations, foundations, all levels of government, and most impressively, more than 2 million contributors who keep this extraordinary service alive and growing.

The total national annual cost of operating and programming public television was $333.3 million in 1976. According to the Public Broadcasting Service, it came from the sources in the amounts (in millions) given in Table 7.

Table 7. Sources of Funding for Public Television[a]

Federal government	$ 73.0
Local government	22.7
State government	77.4
State colleges	15.8
Private colleges	1.9
Members	38.0
Auction	11.6
In-kind support	40.9
Foundations	15.6
Corporations	17.4
Other	19.0
Total	$333.3

[a]Source: Public Broadcasting Service.

Government funding not only comes through CPB for programming (as described earlier) but is granted also by HEW and various federal agencies mostly for specific program development and production. Also, many stations are licensed to school boards or to state authorities or commissions and accordingly receive most of their support from these state and local coffers.

Private foundation funds are most often granted either for local programming or capital needs (generally not operations) or for specific national program development or production. In addition to the Ford Foundation, leaders have been the Rockefeller Foundation, the Lilly Endowment, the Carnegie Corporation of New York, the Markle Foundation, the Andrew W. Mellon Foundation, and the Arthur Vining Davis Foundation.

Individual viewer support is growing the most rapidly of all sources now that viewers are pleased by the quality of programming they see, which was made possible only from prior support by government, foundation, and corporate funds (see Figure 4).

Approximately 2 million families are now regular contributors to their local stations and provided in 1977 over $46 million through their contributions. Every year brings a larger number of new contributors, and public television people hope to have 3 million individual or family contributors by 1980. This would be a clear indication that the American people want public television in their communities and will contribute directly to its support.

It is an important asset of public broadcasting that funding comes from such diverse sources for two reasons. One is that if any one source dries up, fades away, or becomes disenchanted, the entire bottom will

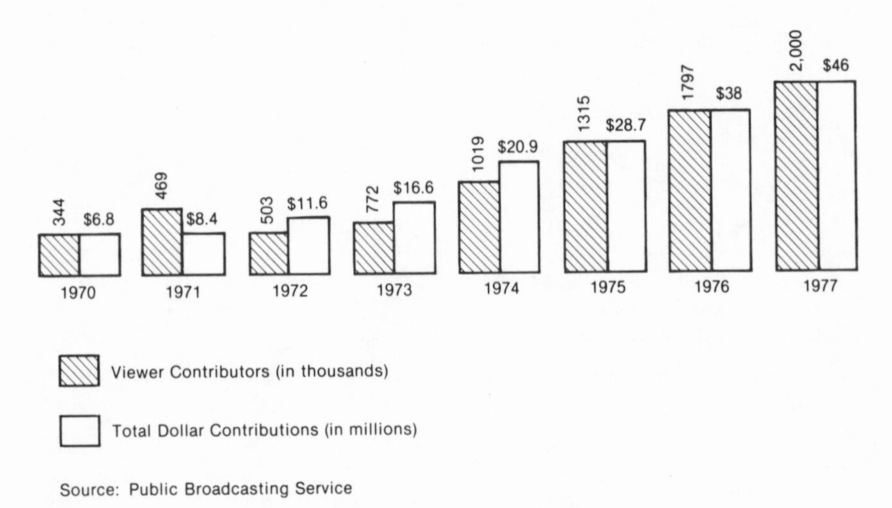

Figure 4. Public television viewer support.

not have fallen out. The other is that no one benefactor can exercise a significant enough amount of pressure to control programming content or direction. Ideally, perhaps, the entire cost of public broadcasting would be underwritten by contributions from the viewers, but that is not a likely possibility, and even if possible it would be unreasonable, if not irresponsible, to fail to take advantage of the money available through the generosity of foundations, corporations, and the government to maximize the quality and quantity of public television programming.

Corporate Support of Public Television

Enough has been said now of public television's origins, goals, and funding patterns to provide a perspective from which all the options for corporate support can be understood and contemplated. Let's first run through the various options and then relate the many good reasons for a corporate decision to support public television and the ways to make that support even more worthwhile.

Corporate support (to which the rest of this chapter will be devoted) can be directed toward a local station's operating, capital, or programming production expenses. Or it may more heavily be granted for a specific program idea intended for national distribution, most often produced by one of the stations in a large metropolitan area for obvious reasons having to do with availability, accessibility of talent, creativity, technical expertise, equipment, facilities, related services, etc.

It should be remembered at the outset that programs are generally produced or acquired by one of the 275 independent public television stations, not by PBS or CPB, and then sold or offered free (if paid for by an outside funder) to all the rest of the stations within the Public Broadcasting System.

It should also be noted that not all of the following options for corporate support are utilized by every public television station. These are the options most widely recognized, but every station has the freedom to exercise its own discretion.

Large-scale underwriting by major corporations of nationally distributed programs has become an increasingly important factor in the success of public television. It is generally the most distinguished and highly acclaimed programs that have really caught the public's attention, and these are so expensive that without at least partial corporate support they may never have been produced or acquired at all.

Imagine the loss to television viewers nationwide if public television had been without the following program series, each of which has been dependent upon at least partial corporate support: "Evening at Symphony" (Raytheon); "Nova" (Exxon); "Evening at Pops" (Martin Marietta);

"Adams Chronicles" (ARCO); "National Geographic Specials" (Gulf); "Great Performances" (Exxon); "Masterpiece Theatre" (Mobil); and "The Thin Edge" (Bristol Myers).

And don't forget the many specials or documentaries underwritten periodically by IBM ("The Belle of Amherst"), AT&T ("Black Filmmakers' Hall of Fame"), 3M ("The Puzzle Children"), and others. These companies don't spend as much as Mobil and Exxon, perhaps, but they make regular and important contributions to the fare of public television. And *all* the aforementioned companies have spent much additional money to promote awareness of the programs, thereby attracting viewers in a way public television could not afford to do itself.

Corporate support in the form of national program underwriting has increased dramatically to nearly $14.5 million in the 1976–1977 season, representing about 25% of the total funding for national programming (see Figure 5).

More than 40 companies provided these funds. Table 8 lists the 10 largest corporate contributors during the 1976–77 year. These numbers include not only grants for 1976–77 season programming but in some cases for programs to be produced and broadcast within the following year of even two.

A corporation may choose to underwrite all or part of the production or acquisition costs of a program or series to be distributed nationally. If the complete costs are underwritten by an outside funder, corporate or otherwise, then that program or series is offered by the producing or acquiring station free to the entire system. Any and all stations may elect to telecast it or not, and they may telecast it either at the network feed time or at a time of their choosing. Hardly a station in the system will let slip the opportunity to telecast a worthwhile program of no cost to themselves.

If, however, a corporation wishes only to underwrite a portion, say

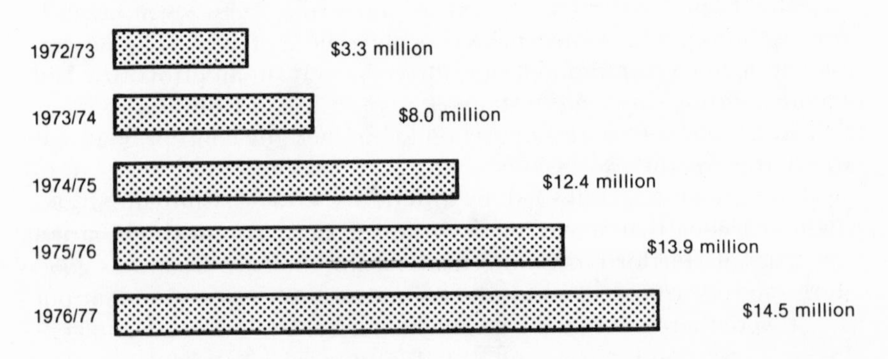

Figure 5. Public television national program underwriting.

Table 8. Ten Largest Corporate Contributors to Public Television Programming, 1976–1977[a]

Mobil Oil Corporation	$3,679,000
Exxon Corporation	3,031,000
Atlantic Richfield Company	2,280,000
Gulf Oil Corporation	1,390,000
McDonald's Corporation	1,172,000
Martin Marietta Corporation	1,046,000
Prudential Insurance Company of America	625,000
Raytheon Company	400,000
Polaroid Corporation	400,000
General Foods Corporation	360,000

[a] Source: Public Broadcasting Service.

half, of the costs, then the producing station must find the other half from another source: corporate, foundation, government, or the system's stations themselves chipping in to accumulate the total amount needed. WGBH Boston's "Evening at Symphony" has in recent years been underwritten half by the Raytheon Company and half by the stations. WNET's "The Adams Chronicles" was made possible by grants from the National Endowment for the Humanities, the Andrew W. Mellon Foundation, and the Atlantic Richfield Company. Credit is given to all funders before and after each telecast, with audio similar to the foregoing sentence and video consisting of the complete funder name in nonlogo typeface.

Local Underwriting and Other Support

There are several ways for a company to underwrite programs in its own local area. Annually, local public television stations join with other stations in the system to fund series not wholly underwritten by outside funders through a national program-purchasing mechanism called the Station Program Cooperative (SPC). In the case of programs purchased through the SPC, a local company may underwrite the station's costs of acquiring and broadcasting the series for local telecast. Standard audio and video credits to the company will be made within the local viewing areas as provided for by FCC regulations and PBS policies. Examples are "Wall Street Week," "Washington Week in Review," and "Evening at Pops," all paid for through the cooperative effort of those stations wanting the program enough to vote their monetary support.

Local stations provide one of public television's most important services to the local community by covering local cultural, sporting, or political events, by producing programs that deal with timely concerns and issues of local importance, or merely by satisfying the tastes and interests of various segments of the community. These productions, whether they concern the local busing issue, the community youth orchestra, or the city hockey championship, can often be underwritten by (with credit again given to) a local company—and at very little cost relative to the costs of the more complicated and sophisticated national programming.

Many of the nation's public television stations use annual televised auctions as one of their fund-raising techniques. WNET in New York, which had its first auction in 1975, grossed over $1 million in 1977. Two of the larger stations had gross revenues from auctions in 1977 that were in excess of $700,000: KQED in San Francisco and WGBH in Boston.

Donated products or services are sold to the highest bidder calling in, with proceeds going to the station. Companies can benefit from the on-air thanks for their donations; viewers benefit from the fun and opportunity to get a real bargain; and the station benefits from all the proceeds above and beyond the costs of producing the auction in the first place.

If a large company wants to help in a major way, it can make a special donation, such as the newest automobile in its line, the latest computer to hit the market, or a family trip to Europe. Or it can make a cash grant in many cases to help pay for the auction's production cost directly, thereby being credited on air much as with a standard programming grant.

One of the reasons so many viewers contribute to their local station is that they are stimulated to do so by live on-air appeals called *pledge nights.* Not all stations make use of this fund-raising vehicle, but those that do find it especially successful. The opportunity for a company in this situation is to supply the phone volunteers who receive the viewers' pledges. The participating company is thanked on the air for supplying its employees.

Additionally, the company should consider a large cash contribution to be announced on the air (during the night its employees are on the phones) as a matching incentive to new donors. In this way, the station receives many more pledges than it otherwise would, and the company receives televised recognition both for its employees and its matching grant.

Public Relations Benefits of Corporate Support

The corporate public relations benefits are more immediate and varied than from support of just about any other nonprofit entity or service In the case of program underwriting, the rules applying to funder credits are strict and enforced, as they should be. Public television is noncommercial, and while disclosure of funding sources is required for the benefit of the viewer, those credits can neither represent the logo of the corporate underwriter nor mention the company's products or services. Furthermore, a company is not allowed to underwrite a program if it has a direct and immediate interest in the program's content. However, beyond these limitations, there is much direct and valuable public relations benefit and potential from underwriting.

If a company's name adequately stands on its own and represents its product or service clearly, then recognition and appreciation by the millions of viewers tuned in nationwide will be considerable. Who among us has not seen the front and back credits to Mobil, Exxon, 3M, Xerox, IBM, Gulf, Bristol Myers, ARCO, and many others—not to mention all those smaller companies underwriting local productions or acquisitions?

And there are ways to promote the program and thereby a company's funding relationship to that program that are not only allowed but encouraged by PBS and producing stations alike. Underwriters may take out "tune-in" advertisements in print media promoting the program and its air date, and they may even use a corporate logo in those ads inspite of logo prohibition on the air. Generally ads are purchased (when affordable) in *TV Guide,* major metropolitan newspapers, and selected national special-interest magazines related to the program content. Press kits bearing funder credits can be sent to television critics at the major newspapers and to all public television stations. Notices can be stuffed into a company's monthly billing statements. Posters can be prepared for use within the company and its branch offices.

Proper and creative promotion is important for all concerned, and since public television stations don't have the funds to promote sufficiently a program or series, it is usually recommended that a corporate underwriter (local or national) spend as much on promotion as on the production grant itself. It is certainly in the interest of the underwriter to be recognized for its contribution and to attract as many viewers as possible. The funding of programming and promotion for a major series requires a substantial corporate commitment. Gulf Oil's five-year commitment for the National Geographic specials is about $15 million.

In short, the public relations benefits are significant and the effect on employee relations is just as real. Whether underwriting locally or nationally or participating in auctions or pledge weeks, not only are the viewers cognizant of a company's support, but the grantor's employees feel proud of and a part of their company's role, perhaps even more so because they can watch the results at home with family and friends.

It is clear that I favor corporate financial support for public television. I realize that there are thoughtful people who do not share my view. Among them is Charles S. Steinberg, former vice-president of CBS Television, who is a professor of communications at Hunter College, City University of New York. He expressed his concerns in an article, "Has Public TV Become Corporate TV?" which appeared in the September–October 1977 issue of the *Columbia Journalism Review.*

Steinberg objects to corporate underwriting of public service programs on several grounds. He feels that it violates the prohibition against any advertising on public television. My feeling is that public television viewers seem to express little discomfort at the occasional mention of a corporate underwriter's name at the beginning or end of an hour-long program. It takes a very sensitive viewer, I would say, to be made very uncomfortable after experiencing continually the omnipresent commercials touting products and services that adorn commercial telecasts. Besides, it is an FCC requirement that all major funders be listed *so that the viewer will be aware of* the source of funds.

Steinberg also states that

> few, if any of these [corporate underwritten] programs have been of a documentary, public affairs, or investigative nature dealing with such issues as the economy, the environment, the defense establishment, or other so-called controversial areas.

I agree that corporate underwriters have tended to support cultural rather than political or other controversial subjects. But that's not at all surprising and doesn't diminish the value of what they *do* support. Corporations have large and varied constituencies, including employees, shareholders, suppliers, distributors, and customers. Corporations have not been known to prosper by unnecessarily alienating those groups whose support is vital for business survival. My own concept of corporate responsibility does not include the requirement that General Motors sponsor a program on automotive recalls with Ralph Nader as the narrator.

Steinberg's final concern is that "Corporate underwriting carries with it not only the stigma of commercialism, but the always implicit problem of control." He backs up this concern with the statement that "from an original outlay of about one million dollars in 1970, corporate underwriting has increased each season until its current investment may now have reached fourteen million dollars." This figure for corporate underwriting represents about one-fourth of all direct program underwriting and amounts to less than 5% of the total national cost of operating and programming public television in one year. It is certainly appropriate to be vigilant about undue influence in public television from any source, but I don't see any evidence of serious problems in this area emanating from the corporate community. There are important safeguards, Steinberg himself points out, including rules that forbid any direct connection between the underwriting corporation and the products or services of that corporation.

The principal effect of corporate underwriting of public television to date has been a proliferation of excellent programs that have achieved enthusiastic and widespread public response. I believe that this public response is the best guide for corporations to follow in determining their support of public television, either through general contributions or through program underwriting grants. In a pluralistic society such as ours, in which companies cannot afford to remain isolated, support of public television results in positive public recognition by the people who buy a company's products and services, by its employees, by its shareholders, and by its neighbors in the community.

23

International Assistance: Several Projects in Latin America

If there were one major change I would like to see in the villages of the barrancas, it is the same I would wish upon humanity as a whole: namely, that each man assume a greater responsibility for the welfare of his fellow man.[1]

At first glance, it might seem that corporate giving for international projects might be misplaced and unrealistic. There are so many questions and unknowns involved. The problems of hunger, inadequate health care, and poverty are so big and various. Isn't this an area best handled by the big foundations and by federal government agencies? And now that so many countries have expressed distrust of "foreign aid," isn't such giving apt to be unwanted by the very people it is designed to help?

I don't pretend to have answers to these problems, but I can speak out of my own limited experience in this area. And I believe we have had some success.

First, I want to repeat my earlier advice: you can't solve all the problems at once. You have to chip away at them. And there are many small organizations in the international field that desperately need corporate support. In fact, in our experience, some of the most realistic and effective programs are modest ones.

Not only are corporations generally large organizations, but many are also international. Certainly this is true of those firms with whom I have been employed. In these firms, we have encouraged our local subsidiaries to get involved in local projects. They know what needs to be done and what resources are available. But the more complex problem is what type of international giving can be effectively directed from the United States.

[1]David Werner, director of Project Piaxtla Sinaloa, Mexico.

In our case, we decided to focus our efforts in two ways. First, we give priority to projects that take place in Mexico, and it is rather simple why we do so. The company began there in the mid-1940s. We still have people and facilities there, and thus we know something about that country.

Second, we give priority to those international efforts that are based or receive substantial support from individuals or groups where our United States offices are located. This way we can stay in close contact with the organizations and be more responsive to their needs. In general, there has been no need to go looking for projects that are both oriented toward Mexico and supported by people and groups in our area. It so happens that many persons in the San Francisco Bay Area are knowledgeable about Mexico and are involved with organizations that work there.

These organizations are apt to be less visible and less fashionable today than they were in the mid-1960s, simply because much of our attention now is directed toward domestic issues, but their work is still important. Their projects may appear more risky, more marginal than they once did, but they are probably not more so than they ever were. Particularly with the smaller organizations, your risks can't be very great. The rewards for those on the other end can be substantial. At least, this has been the case with three of the local groups we have supported: CREO, the Hesperian Foundation, and Neighbors Abroad.

CREO

CREO is an acronym for the rather ponderous title of the Chiapas Relief and Encouragement Organization. I myself had not remembered that until I was going through the files a while back, and when I asked Rob Manson about it (he is a past president and has been one of the group's prime movers over the last five or six years), he laughed and added that nobody in the group, as far back as he could remember, ever thought of it as anything but CREO. So CREO it shall be. I only mentioned the longer name because I find the fact that CREO members use the shorter one to be revealing about their intentions and dedication. Throughout their 10-year history, they have attempted to divert attention away from themselves as a charitable organization (relief and encouragement indeed!) and toward the Indians of Chiapas, Mexico. CREO has become increasingly self-effacing as the years have passed, and I find this admirable. This is how they described their philosophy in their 1969 annual report:

> CREO means "I believe" in Spanish, a name adopted to emphasize the founding premise that the Indians of Chiapas, Mexico, deserve a better life

and have the right to choose for themselves that alternative mode which will insure not only their well-being but preserve their dignity as individuals.

CREO may be dsecribed as a people-to-people program working with, for and at the invitation of the Indians of Chiapas.

As the years have passed, I have become more and more convinced that such a people-to-people approach is crucial, and I find that this approach characterizes each of the three groups discussed in this chapter. Perhaps this attitude also explains why we prefer to support locally based groups. It is a way to avoid the more denigrating aspects of charity. (In fact, is *charity* really a word we want to use anymore?) Nobody likes to be given something by a faceless organization, and more practically, probably the only way to discover what people want and can use is to talk to them and get close to their needs. Then it is important to discover to what extent they take part in the decision-making process and to what extent they work in the project.

But enough about the people-to-people aspect. I hear my reader asking just what CREO actually does. At present, it is rather simple. Its members are helping the Indians around San Cristobal (the second largest city in Chiapas) to build systems for potable water. They primarily give technical advice and sometimes materials. This was not always, however, the CREO's direction.

In 1965, three young women from Stanford University were invited to Chiapas for the summer by Bishop Samuel Ruiz Garcia. They surveyed the area generally to see where they might be of some help. Immediately, they were struck by the area's health problems, and upon their return to California, they organized CREO in order to supply medical assistance. The next year, a group of 10 returned for the summer, and in 1967, 30. All paid their own transportation. These groups included several doctors (in particular, Dr. Donald Prolo, then a resident in neurosurgery at Stanford), nurses, premed students, and many others with a variety of skills, and they quickly decided to operate as a traveling clinic in order to bring medical care to outlying Indian villages. Basically, their work was of a paramedic nature, administering inoculations and dispensing medicine for worms (one of the major problems, especially for the children), but they also handled as well as possible the variety of illnesses that inevitably came their way. The response to their clinics was large, sometimes overwhelming.

About this time, our company became interested in the organization. Obviously we were attracted by the medical nature of its projects, as were several other pharmaceutical firms, which contributed generous amounts of drugs and medical supplies. Western Airlines contributed shipping as far as Mexico City. At first, we gave a small cash contribution but quickly became more involved when it became apparent that CREO had excellent community support in both Palo Alto and San Cristobal.

The Camera Junior there and the Jaycees here joined with CREO to create Focus San Cristobal, which was largely a fund-raising organization. It did, however, help channel community involvement, and soon people began to work toward a mobile medical unit that would cost some $50,000. George Dueker, a local architect, drew up plans. We gave another cash contribution.

This mobile medical unit was seen as a possible answer to several problems that CREO was meeting in the field. Most important, it would allow the volunteers to deliver to the villages the quality medical care that they felt was necessary and that they were then unable to supply. The plans called for an X-ray unit, facilities for dental and ophthalmological care, a small analysis station, and of course ample storage space for whatever medicines and supplies they would need.

At the same time, CREO hoped the unit could operate, in cooperation with the Mexican government and private Mexican physicians, year round in Chiapas. It had become apparent that many of the medical problems were of a chronic nature and that one disease, even if cured, would be quickly followed by another. The summer programs were inadequate. In one particularly frustrating case, several of the volunteer doctors and nurses performed a rather sophisticated operation, a thoracic laminectomy, under primitive conditions on a young girl who couldn't walk. (She was suffering paralysis in the lower part of her body due to tuberculosis of the spine.) The operation was successful: four months later, the girl walked again, but two months after that, she died of whooping cough.

Unfortunately, not enough funds were raised to finance the mobile unit. Of course, the funds that Focus San Cristobal did raise were not wasted, but in any case, we would have regarded whatever we had contributed as well worth the investment. The idea was an excellent one and the planning careful. In the end, the funds were used to purchase a four-wheel-drive pickup for CREO, and this at least solved some of the minor transportation and supply problems. CREO also rented and renovated a house in San Cristobal, which they could use as a year-round base. They still hoped for a better medical program, and the summer clinics continued.

In 1970, we also began "in-kind" support for CREO by printing their annual report (for 1969), and we have done so ever since (except when they did not issue one). I must admit, however, that when they returned with the next one (1972), we decided to help them organize the report a bit better. The previous report was longer than it needed to be and had too many pictures. They took our suggestions with good grace.

As I said, the summer medical programs continued, but CREO was also branching out. From as early as 1967, they had analyzed water samples in hopes that they might help villages find sources of potable water. This was a natural complement to their medical clinics, and many felt that this would be more beneficial than any short-term medical care they might bring. Finally, in 1969, they built a system for potable water, and another in 1970. And this was fortunate, because the summer clinics were coming to an end.

CREO still could not create a permanent structure in Chiapas through which they could supply year-round medical care. During the summers after the unsuccessful efforts to acquire a mobile medical unit, CREO gradually abandoned the traveling clinics and instead concentrated on specific villages. One such village was Amatenango, and in 1968, several volunteers, and Dr. Robert Firpo in particular, drew up plans for remodeling an existing building into a medical clinic. The hope was that CREO and the Mexican government could pool their efforts and supply year-round care. Something, however, went wrong in the planning process, and during the summer of 1970, CREO discovered that the Mexican government was already in the process of building a clinic and had adequate staffing plans for it.

This was an unusual mistake for CREO to make, and one that I would not dwell on, except that it is an informative one. In general, potential contributors to international projects should ask about the requesting organization's relations with local governments. The organization, if it has planned carefully, should be sure that its efforts complement and do not compete with existing official projects. If it has not carefully cleared its projects with local authorities, not only does it run the risk of duplicating services, and thus wasting its efforts, but it may also offend those authorities and, at worst, be asked to stop its efforts. CREO had previously been very careful about this, particularly during the planning stages for the mobile medical unit. And it has been ever since, often being able to obtain supplies and services from local governmental agencies.

After the summer of 1970, the members of CREO sat down and carefully rethought their programs. They decided to discontinue their medical programs and concentrate instead on the water systems. They also decided to support only a few full-time members in the field (expenses only, no salaries) and to abandon their larger summer programs, which were larger only in the sense of the numbers of volunteers involved. I, for one, was happy with their decisions. They showed they were able to change directions and to put their resources to effective use. We continued to support them with cash contributions (which we increased during the year when they needed a new truck) and with in-kind support.

Their program has proved to be highly successful. From 1971 through 1975, they helped plan and construct some 40 water systems, and they were able to do so on a budget of approximately $6,000 per year. Also, in 1974, they received a grant of $29,000 from the Catholic Relief Agencies to be used solely to help villages finance the water systems. Part of the money is intended to be a revolving loan fund. I understand that CREO is now committed to projects for the next five years.

The secret of their success lies in the simplicity of their projects and in the way they work closely with the villages. Typically, they wait for a village to invite their help, and only then do they spend any appreciable amount of time there (often, in fact, they have never even visited the village before). All planning is done with the villagers. They must agree to the location of the water tank, pipes, and faucets, and at least several villagers must understand how the system works. All this is a time-consuming process, but it is the only way, CREO feels, to make sure that the system will be used and maintained.

CREO also attempts to keep the system as simple and inexpensive as possible. The fewer the faucets, the better. And they use almost exclusively hand pumps or hydraulic rams (a gravity-fed pump), hardly ever motors. This approach results in less severe maintenance problems and enables local people to handle the upkeep of the system with readily available materials.

In 1973 and 1974, Josh Smith and Perry Keen of CREO also developed a ferrocement process for constructing holding tanks. This reduced not only the amount of materials needed (a major problem when a village is not accessible by road) but also the cost of both materials and labor. Previously, a stonemanson had to be hired; now CREO members and the villagers can build a tank themselves.

CREO has continually impressed me by its ability to adapt its resources to local needs and to innovate where possible—as the ferrocement process shows. I have a great respect for these people, who dedicate two to three years (and sometimes more) to the Indians of Chiapas, and I told Rob Manson so one day. In turn, he made two interesting comments about our support. First, he said our in-kind support was more important than our cash contributions. This surprised me, since our cash contributions are more than double the dollar value of our in-kind support. He explained that CREO could probably have raised the cash—by knocking on doors, if necessary—but that the annual report was their basic contact with their supporters and potential contributors. It was something they could not have done nearly so well without our help. And, he added, he was referring to more than just the printing of the report; he was also referring to our advice about how to put it together and our advice about various fund-raising ideas.

He also paid us a large compliment. He said that our relationship with CREO has been analogous to CREO's relationship with the Indians of Chiapas. He explained that we had never imposed an *a priori* set of conditions for our giving and that we had been willing to sit down and talk with them about their needs. I am sure that we do not entirely deserve the compliment, but it does express an ideal toward which all donors should work. CREO's address is Box 1143, Los Altos, CA 94022.

The Hesperian Foundation

This is a locally-based foundation that was created originally to sponsor Project Piaxtla in the state of Sinaola, Mexico. The project, more specifically, is located in the Las Barrancas area, a mountainous terrain of cliffs and ravines where there are almost no roads, only burro trails. Piaxtla is the name of the area's main river.

The project, like CREO, began primarily as a medical one, and as in CREO's experience, most of the medical problems are of a basic nature and can be handled by paramedics. Its field-workers spend most of their time administering innoculations, treating worm infestations, assisting in childbirth, giving advice about nutrition, and so forth. The project provides medical care for 10,000 people in an area of 5,000 square miles and does so on a budget of $12,000 per year. At present, it operates a main clinic and training center at Ajoya and 12 health outpost clinics in the surrounding countryside.

Also, like CREO, the project has recognized other health-related problems. For example, it too has helped construct a potable-water system (at Ajoya) and has even involved villagers in experimental agricultural projects in hopes of increasing the nutritional value of the local crops. But it has reserved its main efforts for the health outposts.

The project, however, ran into a problem that CREO did not, and that is the lack of other medical care that it cannot provide. At least CREO was working around San Cristobal, where adequate medical facilities existed. Project Piaxtla is working, on the other hand, in a remote area that the country's public health program has yet to reach: This means that the project had first to set up the central clinic as a training and referral center at Ajoya and to supply it with some basic equipment—an X-ray unit, a small laboratory, and dental facilities. Only then could it work on the problem of bringing care to the even more remote villages, and because of the rugged terrain, it could not pursue, as CREO did, the idea of a traveling clinic. The health outposts have, however, proved to be effective, and they refer the more difficult medical problems to the main clinic.

There are, of course, many problems that even the clinic cannot treat, and when this happens, it refers the patients to the hospitals in the coastal cities. In some of the more special cases, it has even been able, through the Hesperian Foundation, to send those with orthopedic problems (e.g., infantile paralysis or tuberculosis of the spine) to the Shriner's

Hospital for Crippled Children in San Francisco and those with birth defects (e.g., hare lip or cleft palate) to the Stanford Medical Center. In the latter case, the children are treated through the Interplast Program, which began in the early 1970s and which is composed mainly of Stanford physicians. At first, this program worked mainly in the field, and it even worked for a while in Sinaloa, with Project Piaxtla, but after various problems, it has tended to provide treatment in the United States. We have also supported Interplast with cash contributions.

Project Piaxtla has been operating successfully for some 12 years now. This success is due to a variety of reasons. The most important of these is the dedication and energy of one remarkable individual, David Werner. A few years back, the Hesperian Foundation sent out a summary of the project and described him and the beginnings of the project in this way:

> Project Piaxtla is essentially a personal venture, founded on friendship, dedication and trust. It has evolved, little by little over the years, ever since 1963, when David Werner, an American biologist and high school teacher, first hiked through the Barrancas in search of interesting birds and plants. Struck by the beauty of the landscape, the friendliness of the people, but also by their health problems, David later returned with six of his students, armed with much needed medical first aid supplies. For three weeks, they traveled from village to village, coping with medical emergencies as best they could. Overwhelmed by the response of the villagers and the difference in human suffering which ever so brief a venture could make, David determined to return alone for a year. After consulting with many doctors, poring through medical texts and "apprenticing" in a hospital emergency room, David went back to the Sierra Madre, where he lived with the villagers and cared for the sick and injured as best he could. At the end of the year, David found he was too committed to leave. He decided to stay on and try to help the people develop ways of better coping with their own health problems.

To this, I would only like to add a bit of emphasis. The fact is that David was in Sinaloa for reasons other than establishing a medical clinic, and the project emerged out of his deep concern for the people and only in response to their needs. In no sense did he impose the project on them.

Over the years, he has also spent most of his time in Sinaloa, often 10 months out of the year, returning only to raise funds or gather supplies. It is safe to say that without him, the effort would not have been successful. But at the same time, I think it is fair to ask if there is some danger in such a project's being dependent upon one person.

David Werner himself agrees that there is, although I would like to add that such projects rarely get started and then survive the first five or so years without the enthusiasm of somebody (or two or three others) like him. In fact, I look for such leadership when evaluating programs. Still, there are dangers, and David is quick to point out that it is all too easy to play the gringo here in Mexico. This, of course, undermines the trust and cooperation that is essential to projects such as his.

The larger problem he has faced is how to ensure that the project will be an ongoing one, and from the beginning, he has tried to direct it toward self-sufficiency and self-help. His motto is "Never do for others what you could be helping others do for themselves." In particular, one of the main functions of the clinic at Ajoya has been to train local villagers as paramedics and to train them to operate by themselves. The Hesperian Foundation writes:

> Here [at Ajoya] we have trained young villagers who function, unsupervised when necessary, as medics, dentists, and lab and X-ray technicians. The primary role of visiting doctors and dentists, when the clinic is fortunate enough to have them, is not so much to practice their respective skills, but to teach the subprofessionals who provide the continuity of care.

At this time, the clinics are close to self-sufficiency. All the health outposts are staffed by project-trained villagers, and even the clinic at Ajoya is completely staffed by local personnel. In addition, the locally trained staff at Ajoya is doing much of the training. There are now no American volunteers in Ajoya, except for short-term teaching visits. The village health program is also exploring methods for achieving financial self-sufficiency. David Werner feels that the Hesperian Foundation can phase out financial support of Ajoya in the next few years. He also hopes that the clinic will serve as a model for future clinics elsewhere and that the clinic can train Mexicans to staff them.

So far, no mention has been made of our contributions, and the reason for this is simple. We made none until 1973. I have spent as much time as I have, however, because the story of Project Piaxtla is an interesting and informative one. There should be more projects like it. In fact, I wish we had been involved from the beginning, but we were only vaguely aware of its existence before 1973, and I can find no record that they had asked us for support! Then, David Werner had a rather specific need, and only after a local doctor prepared the way did he finally come forward. What he needed was some help on his book, *Donde No Hay Doctor* ("Where There Is No Doctor"), which is a rural health handbook originally written in Spanish and intended to be used by both paramedics and villagers with as little as three years of primary schooling. The book was then in rough manuscript. We had some medical people in the company take a look, and everybody thought it excellent. We knew the book would be used at least in Project Piaxtla, and we were glad to pay for the printing of the first 1,000 copies.

I should be more specific about the book. Not only is it written in simple Spanish, but it also makes ample use of descriptive drawings, and much of the text is oriented toward preventive medicine and health care in the home. For example, it looks at both good and bad uses of the medicines that can be obtained from rural drugstores in Mexico without a medical prescription (many more medicines, such as antibiotics, are available over the counter in Mexico than in the United States), and it explains the importance of a balanced diet and adequate hygiene in preventing disease. Other chapters deal with injections, vaccinations, maternal child health, midwifery, family planning, and most of the common diseases of Mexico (and thus, of most of Latin America).

The book has been well received, and the initial printing was quickly exhausted. It was soon reprinted with the help of a $5,000 grant from the Sunflower Foundation and was finally taken up by a commercial publisher in Mexico. At present, some 25,000 copies have been either sold or distributed free, and it looks as if it will be around for quite some time. The book is in use in 14 Latin American countries, and such organizations as Amigos de las Americas, the American Friends Service Committee, the University of London–Institute of Child Health, and the California MediCorps use it in the field and or in their training programs. It has been translated into Guajivo (the primary Colombian Indian language) and English, and it is in the process of being translated into other languages. Copies of the Spanish and English versions of *Donde No Hay Doctor* (2nd rev. ed.) can be obtained from the Hesperian Foundation, P.O. Box 1692, Palo Alto, CA 94302.

I am pleased with the part we were able to play in publishing this book, but I am also sure it would have been published by someone —eventually. What we did was to give the book its start and make it easier for David Werner and the Hesperian Foundation to find a commercial publisher (where it rightfully belongs).

What direction does the Hesperian Foundation now take? Will it cease to exist once it phases itself out of Ajoya? I doubt it—at least, knowing David Werner, I doubt it. He has plans for more handbooks in such areas as dentistry and agriculture, and if he does not in fact write them himself, I am sure that he will at least be involved in them and give generous support. More immediately, however, he is helping to bring together many of the rural health projects, both government and private, that now exist in Latin America, and he hopes that they can both exchange information and pool their efforts. It is the only way, he feels, to begin to solve that area's challenging health problems.

Neighbors Abroad

Neighbors Abroad is a local nonprofit organization, with a membership of approximately 200, that is in charge of Palo Alto's Sister City Program. The Sister City Program had its origins in President Eisenhower's People-to-People Program of the last 1950s, and many cities around the country now participate. It is a program—or perhaps *concept* is a better word, since this program involves no large bureaucracy—through which cities from the United States establish informal relations with cities from other countries. In a sense, they adopt each other. In the early 1960s, Neighbors Abroad organized in Palo Alto and quickly established Sister City relations with two other cities: Palo, Philippines, in 1962, and Oaxaca, Mexico, in 1964.

Neighbors Abroad describes the purpose of the Sister City Program in this way:

> The objective of the Sister City program is to further international understanding at all levels on a continuing long-term basis through affiliations between cities in the United States and cities in other countries. Within this program, cities and their citizens exchange things, ideas, and people in a wide variety of cultural, youth, educational, municipal, professional, and technical projects. The Sister City program gives focus to community interests as evidenced by the cities and their institutions, toward building a better climate for world understanding.

These are fine words, but I sometimes worry that they may be too fine. They are words that we have heard before and, unfortunately, ones that we are apt, in the late 1970s, to distrust. Good intentions and fine words only do not create the kind of contact between peoples that promotes international understanding. Something more specific is needed. And let me say from the outset that Neighbors Abroad has found these more specific somethings.

First, let me backtrack a bit and note that throughout the 1960s Neighbors Abroad existed primarily to sponsor student-exchange and scholarship programs between the various cities. This remains an important aspect of its activities, but this aspect, although worthwhile, is not particularly noteworthy—there are many other similar programs. (And parenthetically, let me add that I fear that all too often the only contact Americans have with those from other countries happens during their student years.) In 1971, however, Neighbors Abroad embarked on the first of two projects that have created deep ties between many Palo Alto citizens and many in Oaxaca: the construction of first an observatory and then a planetarium in Oaxaca.

Neither project could have happened had it not been for one individual, Marvin Vann, an astronomer who manages the observatory and planetariums at Foothill College in Los Altos, California. Over the years, he had spent a great deal of time in Mexico, and during one visit, he was in charge of a scientific party to observe a full solar eclipse from Mitla, the famous archaeological site near Oaxaca. One night, while his party was observing the stars from the town square, people from all over the area gathered. They were fascinated with the telescopes, and astronomy in general, and I'm sure Marvin Vann let many of them take a look. He immediately felt that this area should have an observatory and wanted to help build one.

His desire to help build an observatory in this area was not, however, based simply on the response of the people. He was also aware that some 2,500 years ago an observatory existed at Monte Albán, which also lies in the mountains above Oaxaca and is even more famous than Mitla. Only now are archaeologists beginning to understand the full extent of these ruins and to reclaim them from the vegetation. Many also feel that the Zäpotecs, who then ruled Monte Albán, originated the earliest Indian calendar and time system, and to support their argument, they point to the fact that much of the city was laid out in accordance with basic principles of astronomy. The Great Plaza, for instance, was built on a north–south axis, and the building that must have been the observatory points due southwest toward the winter solstice. In addition, at the top of this building, there are slits in the masonry wall that offer a line of sight along the azimuth of the meridian.

A third reason to build an observatory in this region was that there were only two others in all of Mexico at that time, both of them run by the Mexican government and neither of them anywhere near Oaxaca. This would be the third, and there is now, I believe, a fourth. Marvin Vann is a teacher, and he was quick to understand the educational possibilities of another observatory. He might even say that there was an educational necessity for another.

For another year, however, his idea remained only an idea, and an audacious one at that. There seemed to be no way to implement it. Then he contacted Neighbors Abroad, everyone responded enthusiastically, and the project began.

The immediate problem to solve was simply who would provide what, and this took a great deal of careful planning. Obviously the people of Palo Alto could not do it all, nor did they want to. Fortunately the then mayor of Oaxaca, Jorge Martinez Gracida, was deeply committed to the project and, after land was donated, was able to allocate government funds for construction of the observatory building and site. Neighbors Abroad then assumed many of the technical responsibilities and, in particular, assumed responsibility for the telescopes. Marvin Vann was delighted to oversee this part of the project and spent many hours designing and actually constructing the telescopes. These included the main six-inch refracting telescope, a solar-prominence telescope (which Vann privately donated), and a five-inch photographic telescope, and all were accompanied by the necessary accessories, eyepieces and cameras appropriately mounted and electrically driven.

In a sense, everybody had to take a backseat to Marvin Vann (his energy was incredible), but many tried hard to keep up with him. There was, first of all, money to be raised, and I convinced the company to contribute. By the end, more than $5,000 was raised, but when all the donated materials and labor were counted, the total was something like $21,000. At least, that was one estimate; I would estimate a higher figure. A goodly number of professionals (engineers, architects, and artists) donated their services, and these services do not ordinarily come cheap. The contribution of Neighbors Abroad to the observatory was not simply a matter of telescopes. Here are some of the other contributions:

- After Oaxacan architect Rafael Ballesteros made preliminary drawings, based on the design of Zápotec tombs, Palo Alto architect Wayne Rossiter drew up a full set of working plans. He also constructed a scale model and persuaded his friend Bert Larson to do a set of color renditions.
- Artist Ed Jacobsen used the facilities at Foothill College to paint a lively and handsome 10′ × 18′ mural, depicting mythological views of the major constellations, for the curved wall of the observatory foyer.
- Our company provided the resins and fiberglass cloth needed to construct the shell of the observatory dome and shipped these materials to Mexico.
- Ballesteros supervised the construction of the building.
- Western and Mexicana Airlines shipped the telescopes and their accessories to Mexico without cost.
- Marvin Vann and John Babcock went to Oaxaca to help construct the dome and to install the telescopes.

Many others helped coordinate activities, and construction of the observatory went quickly. It was finished in early 1973, and in February some 60 Palo Altans, including me, went down for the dedication. It was quite a time, and I was impressed by the open friendliness of the Oaxacans. It was obvious that they were proud of the observatory and would use it. In fact, Marvin Vann later reported that within three months more than 16,000 people had visited it and looked through the telescopes and that 90% of them walked three to five miles to do so. Later that year, Neighbors Abroad also received an award from the parent Sister Cities organization, the Town Affiliation Association, for the "Best Single Project" by a town with a population between 25,000 and 75,000.

I would like to add a personal note to all this. One day, during the dedication trip, I visited Monte Albán and was so impressed by the site that I was forced to write a poem, one that I would like to share. It is titled, "Monte Albán," and there are only two facts a reader needs to know: first, Cocijo was the Zápotec lord of rain; and second, the Spanish conquerors (incredibly) never knew about the existence of Monte Albán.

MONTE ALBÁN

By November
Lord Cocijo had dispensed
His silver grey bounty in mist and torrent
Blanket spreading leafless morning glory
Over the white mountain treasure
Viewless to the arriving conquerors

The avalanche of snowy petals and vegetation
Stuccoed the native cement and stoneworks
Arranged for the first time in Meso America
With symmetry, order and epic design
Not of nature's programmed mind

The great plaza, temples and platforms
Red reflecting to the heavens the color of the sacred oval
Annealed to the turquoise sky

Within the tombs and pyramidal vaults
Were safely stored
Gold, silver, rock crystal, coral and jadeite
And the obsidian engraved history of 2000 years

On the twelve terraces
Surrounding the sacred mountain
Fifty thousand kept the secrets
Which stelae and jamba silently portrayed
Birth, life and death
Natal cries, laughter, injury, the last tears
Of timeless years: for which the priest astronomers
Sought mathematical formulas
To set the magic heavens in order

And in the gallery of dancers
The Gods covertly communed
With the high priests and stone messengers
Of civilization

So the observatory was built and we all congratulated ourselves, and Marvin Vann in particular, for a job well done. Then, in the late summer of 1973, the mayor of Oaxaca asked when we would be willing to help with a planetarium! It seems that Marvin Vann, during the construction of the observatory a year earlier, had jokingly commented that a planetarium was next. The mayor knew him well by that time and knew that even when he was joking he was serious. The mayor had in fact already received commitments of $20,000 for the construction of the planetarium from various sources in Oaxaca. He proposed that, as before, Neighbors Abroad would assume responsibility for the technical aspects and Oaxaca responsibility for the building. Rafáel Ballesteros would again be the architect of the project.

The planetarium would be, however, more expensive and more

complex than the observatory. A planetarium is, after all, designed to put on a show and thus needs to be larger than an observatory. The dome, for instance, would be 40 feet in diameter, whereas that of the observatory was only 12 feet. Also, nine kinds of projectors would be needed, plus a sound system, and all these needed to be hooked into a master control panel.

I approached my colleagues on the company contributions committee and persuaded them to pledge a contribution early in November of 1973. The contribution, however, was contingent upon a final commitment to the project by Neighbors Abroad (which was not given until the summer of 1974) and upon a certain amount of other funds' being raised and this worked out well for both sides. This pledge gave a psychological boost to the fund-raising efforts and was an important factor in the final decision to go ahead with the project. In fact, I doubt that without this particular pledge, Neighbors Abroad would have continued with the project. Later, the company was able to make another grant and designated that the funds it had contributed were to be used to purchase the 14 peripheral projectors.

During the summer of 1974, the planetarium project also ran into some administrative problems in Mexico. Mayor Gracida had been appointed to an important post in Mexico City, and nobody was sure if the commitments he had made were still in effect. Marvin Vann decided to take matters in hand and, during a trip to Mexico, stopped in Oaxaca. He obtained an audience with the governor of the state, Manual Zarate Aquino, and, to his delight, found the Governor enthusiastic, so enthusiastic in fact that he made commitments on the spot! There was one further bit of luck, and this was that the governor's son, Dr. Renato Zarate, lived in the Bay Area and worked as a researcher at the University of California. Marvin Vann contacted him upon his return, and soon a friendship developed, and this made future negotiations about modifications to the planetarium (in order to accommodate a larger main projector than expected) much easier.

But I am getting ahead of the story. There was still the major problem of the acquisition of the main projector, and in this case, everybody had to trust that Marvin Vann could do enough wheeling and dealing to acquire it at the cut-rate prices that Neighbors Abroad could afford. And of course he was able to do so. In late 1974, he just happened to be at a professional meeting, delivering a paper on the Oaxaca observatory, and just happened to mention the planetarium project. Right away, the people at Olivet Nazarene College in Kankakee, Illinois, were interested and offered their used projector for $10,000, substantially below its market value. This projector new would have cost $65,000 in 1973; today, in 1976, it would carry a price tag well over $100,000. Neighbors Abroad was quick to accept the offer and increased its fund-raising efforts.

When these were not fully successful, several members made up the difference with personal loans.

After the acquisition of the main projector, everything was, in a sense, downhill. That is, it was obvious that the job would be done. Oaxaca could begin constructing the planetarium building, and Marvin Vann could begin his seemingly endless labors—adapting the main projector for the Oaxaca planetarium and fitting it with accessories, designing and constructing some of the smaller projectors, and in general making sure that everything was integrated. And of course he had to make several trips to Oaxaca (with three assistants) to install the complex system.

There was, however, one further contribution that the company made toward the end. Marvin Vann has several friends at the Itek Corporation, and one day they were showing him a series of eight lunar-transformation serigraphs. At that time, the planetarium was virtually completed; the dedication would occur shortly, and Marvin was worrying about a blank wall in the entrance hall. He immediately suggested that Itek donate the serigraphs to the planetarium, and Itek quickly agreed. There was, however, no money budgeted by Neighbors Abroad for displaying them properly. Marvin then came to us and hoped that we too would feel that these fascinating serigraphs would be an excellent final touch to the project. We did and were glad to arrange for their framing.

It is hard to estimate the value of Neighbors Abroad's total contribution to the Oaxaca planetarium. The last figures I saw (in late 1975) estimated the value of the equipment alone at some $92,000, which Neighbors Abroad was able to supply for only $15,000! I know, however, that these figures did not include the serigraphs and their framing nor the increased value of the projector. On top of that, there was the large contribution of time and labor.

The planetarium was dedicated in July of 1976, and once again, a large group of Palo Altans made the trip. This time my wife, Ann, was able to come along. We had a marvelous time. I regret to say, however, that this time I did not write a poem. Soon, perhaps? And what will the next project be? There will be others, I am sure. The relationship between Palo Alto and Oaxaca is a strong one, and the two cities recently received another award (for the planetarium project this time) from the Town Affiliation Association for the "Best Overall Program in 1975" for cities in the category of 50,000–100,000 in population.

The Sister Cities Program is a good one. Information can be obtained from the Town Affiliation Association, Suite 206, City Building, 1612 K Street, N.W., Washington, DC 20006.

In the case of CREO, the Hesperian Foundation, and the Oaxaca projects, corporate involvement was generally limited to Syntex and a few other local corporations. Obviously many corporations are doing a great deal in the international area. In closing this chapter, therefore, I would like to describe an effective program that is supported by many business firms and company foundations.

ACCION International

ACCION began with the idea that young, idealistic, and dedicated north Americans and Latins could make a difference by working directly with the poor in the urban and rural areas of Latin America. The effort began in 1961 with 30 volunteers, who went to work in the Caracas barrios. Here is the mandate of the organization:

> We dedicate our efforts to improving the quality of life for Latin America's poor. We work hand in hand with the private and public sectors, acting as liaison, catalyst, facilitator for needed cooperation. Our target is the poor. Our hope, to assist in integrating into the economic mainstream those Latin Americans at the lowest economic levels.

The ACCION approach stresses self-help and self-development. It does not develop projects *for* the poor. It develops projects *with* the poor. It works with them in defining *their* problems and charting solutions. ACCION makes it easier for the poor to help themselves. It is a cooperative venture in maximizing human potential and dignity.

The UNO credit project in Brazil is an example of this working philosophy. (We were well aware of ACCION's efforts in Brazil because Paulo Ayres Filho, president of Syntex's pharmaceutical subsidiary in that country for many years, serves as one of the vice-chairmen of ACCION.) ACCION initially contacted local banks and secured their commitment to open credit lines for the very small businessmen, who desperately need credit but have never before been able to receive it through the commercial banking system. ACCION worked with the small businessmen to tighten up their business practices so that they were in a strengthened position and better able to utilize the credit when it was granted.

The typical recipients of such loans are shopkeepers with two or three employees. One recipient runs an ice-making shop. He sells his ice to the local fishermen, who are then better able to transport their catch safely to market. The ice manufacturer used the loan to upgrade his capacity and in turn to become more efficient—making more ice available to the local community and indirectly stimulating the economy.

A further benefit of the UNO credit project—and one of vital importance in the economically depressed northeastern region of Brazil—is the job-generating effect of the credit. Thus far, over 1,040 new jobs have been created, which are being filled by the previously unemployed.

Many of the recipients are paying taxes now for the first time; others are providing benefits to their new employees. They are active participants in the process of improving their own economic status; they are not merely passive receivers.

In its development work, ACCION stresses the importance of replicable models. It analyzes a problem, devises a solution, tests it in a given locale, and then attempts to repeat its application in other areas. This means that ACCION is able to keep the cost of its projects down to a modest level while responding in a meaningful way to problems endemic to Latin America's poor.

Another basic tenet of ACCION's philosophy is the concept of training local personnel to carry on the work it has begun. This approach avoids the creation of a cumbersome bureaucracy in the United States monitoring all projects. On the contrary, ACCION keeps its staff small and concentrates its efforts on hiring local people, training them to perform the services required, and then helping them to become independent of ACCION.

One of the most important functions that ACCION performs is to serve as a leverage mechanism for further funding to Latin America's poor. ACCION enters a project with limited funds. Its intent is to use those funds most advantageously in terms of developing other support for each dollar it "invests." In Ecuador, for example, ACCION's studies on slum renewal were used by the Inter-American Development Bank in deciding to invest $20 million for a community infrastructure project. ACCION has also been instrumental in mobilizing substantial health and nutrition projects to be sponsored by UNICEF. The multiplier effect of ACCION dollar inputs is also seen in the UNO credit program where its investment of $60,000 has resulted in $600,000 from local Brazilian sources for operational and programmatic expenses.

ACCION receives support from over 60 business firms and company foundations, including the original donors (Chrysler, Exxon, PepsiCo, and Price Waterhouse) that have been making contributions for 15 years. For further information about this worthwhile organization, contact ACCION International AITEC, 10-C Mt. Auburn Street, Cambridge, MA 02138.

I come now to the conclusion of the chapter, but I find that I have no large generalizations to make about international giving. I have tried to describe the work of four organizations—three of which have been supported by our company. My feeling is that the quality of these efforts must be paramount—then we should try to accomplish the most good that our resources will allow.

I would like to see more companies supporting nonprofit organizations that work internationally, and to accomplish this, I think that companies need only to let it be known that they will consider supporting such groups. Once the word is out, these groups will come forward with proposals and ideas. Many of the organizations are not particularly well geared toward fund raising, and if they know where to ask, their job will be that much easier. They will also have just that much more energy to devote to their projects in the other countries—and that, of course, is where it will do the most good.

24

Human Rights and a Peaceful World

No matter who initiated the first involvement [in the Vietnam War] or subsequent expansions, the rest of us have gone along pretty supinely. If anyone is to blame it is people like me for not speaking out sooner.[1]

The civil rights crisis of the 1950s and 1960s and our country's long and destructive involvement in the conflict in Vietnam turned our world on a new course, and the compass needle has been swinging wildly ever since. We seem to have lost the sense of direction that was once taken for granted. People are now better characterized by what they don't believe than by the uncomplicated certitude of the past.

It is my own belief that the civil rights movement initiated the major societal changes of the past quarter century. The beginnings of this movement, however, were in World War II. The war effort involved the recruitment and induction of many minorities into the armed forces. I saw this firsthand during my own tour of duty with the 82nd Airborne Division in 1946–1948. Although this occurred after the war had ended, the draft was still operative, and a large number of my comrades at Fort Bragg in North Carolina were blacks, Mexican-Americans, Puerto Ricans, and American Indians. Service in the armed forces took many people out of their communities and exposed them to situations not influenced by the social mores in those places they left. The war economy also provided jobs to many minority workers who previously had no hope of entering the industrial world. This too involved, in many instances, leaving rural areas or small towns and moving to urban industrial areas, where social conditions and attitudes were quite different. Finally, in the political arena, the leaders of our country began to understand that the wrongs of several hundred years had to be righted;

[1]Louis B. Lundborg, testimony before the Senate Committee on Foreign Relations, April 1970.

or at least, a strong legislative effort had to be made in that direction because the majority of people in the country felt that they no longer wanted to live with a system that discriminated against millions of the country's citizens.

March on Washington

My own first contact with the civil rights movements was in the organization of a fair-housing group in West Orange, New Jersey, in the 1960s. I also participated in the 1963 March on Washington for Jobs and Freedom as a member of the Catholic Interracial Council. That experience made a profound impression on me.

The march started early on August 28 for those leaving from the metropolitan New York area. Our group met for 3:00 A.M. mass at the Chapel of the Rockland State Hospital in Orangeburg. Appropriately, it was the feast day of St. Augustine, great doctor and father of the church and Bishop of Hippo in Africa. Monsignor James Cox, CIC chaplain, and the Reverend Petty McKinney of the American Methodist Episcopal Zion Church, Nyack, led our group. The latter's church had joined with the CIC to arrange bus transportation.

We drove to Manhattan, where two buses were waiting at Lexington and 42 Street. We left there about 5:30 A.M. Most people tried to sleep until our stop in Delaware. There we got our first impression of the march. Hundreds of buses could be seen. People got on and off with great patience despite the waiting for food and crowded restroom facilities.

When we got back on the bus, someone passed song sheets around. We began to sing the freedom songs: "We Shall Not Be Moved" and "We Shall Overcome." The men and women from the AME Zion Church sang with a conviction and a beauty that came deep from the heart.

As we neared Washington about 11:00 o'clock, the Reverend McKinney instructed us to maintain order and dignity under all circumstances. We were given envelopes that contained badges, programs, and other necessary information. They even gave each of us a brown paper bag for refuse! We took out our food baskets and ate lunch.

As the bus entered the city, we were moved by the presence of hundreds of black families waving to us from porches and sidewalks along the route. The same people would be there to wave a "farewell' later in the day.

We parked at Pennsylvania Avenue and 18th Street and the group walked over to the assembly point at the Washington Monument. The quiet and order were unbelievable with the thousands around us. Temporary restrooms and drinking fountains had been set up. People got in line and waited; there was no confusion or pushing. I did not see during the entire day one single person who was not well behaved. Except for the speakers, we rarely heard anyone raise his or her voice. This was the most fascinating thing about the whole march. It was later summed up by Russell Baker of the *New York Times*: "The sweetness and patience of the crowd may have set some sort of national highwater mark in mass decency."

We unfurled our CIC banner and began to march along Constitution Avenue toward the Lincoln Memorial. Television cameras were everywhere. We saw groups from every part of the country: clergymen, professional people, trade unionists, businessmen, students, teachers, housewives; Protestants, Jews, Catholics; black and white—all with a common commitment to justice for all. The placards and banners heralded the demands of the gentle army: "Freedom Now!" "Freedom and Justice" "Jobs and Freedom." Some struck an amusing note: "No government dough to support Jim Crow" or "Wait—Like Forget It."

When we reached the Lincoln Memorial, the seating had been taken, so we stood to listen to the program. It was a combination of speeches and entertainment—mostly gospel singing and folksinging. The climax was the speech of Martin Luther King, Jr. He spoke like a great prophet of the Old Testament, making every sentence a prayer and a protest at the same time. A quarter of a million people hung on every word. Then it was over.

The buses left as quietly as they came. The historic March for Jobs and Freedom had ended. The national conscience was exposed to public view. The unfinished work of our great democracy was set forth for all to see and ponder.

During the late 1950s and early 1960s, I had contact as a corporate public relations executive in New Jersey with minority groups seeking company support for their efforts directed toward housing, employment, educational opportunities, and other essential needs. These contacts reinforced my belief that the redress of past discrimination would require some fundamental attitudinal changes and substantial alterations in the ways all of our institutions were operating.

Business Executives against the Vietnam War

The beginning of the involvement of the United States in the Vietnam War in the 1950s was another starting point that would eventually spawn a strong and active peace movement and sensitize our young people toward their government in a way that my generation had never experienced. I can't imagine the counterculture's emerging in this country without the trauma and anguish that this conflict created.

This unfortunate war, however, did not affect only the youth of our country; people of all ages, sooner or later, had to take a stand—for or against the policies of the administrations in power in Washington, Democrat or Republican.

My own feelings toward the war eventually led me to take personal action. In November 1969, I joined 10 other businessmen in forming a local chapter of a national organization, Business Executives Move for Vietnam Peace (BEM). Soon our midpeninsula group would combine with the San Francisco–Oakland group to form a Bay Area chapter. Some of the other organizers of our group were Vernon R. Anderson, president of Vidar Corporation; Armin Elmendorf, president of Elmendorf Research; Martin Gerstel, financial vice-president of Alza Corporation; Daniel Lazare, vice-president of Zoecon Corporation; and Robert M. Ward, president of the Ultek Division of Perkin-Elmer Corporation. Although we were speaking only for ourselves and not for our companies, public support for an end to the conflict in Southeast Asia by business executives was a certain sign that opposition to the war had broadened and deepened.

From that point to the withdrawal of our forces from Indochina, the Bay Area chapter of BEM was involved in a number of peace projects, some organized by ourselves and some organized by others:

1. In December 1969, we arranged a luncheon meeting for business executives to hear Harold Willens, a founder of BEM and president of Factory Equipment Supply Corporation in Los Angeles, talk about the work of BEM and the urgency of ending the war.

2. In May 1970, we raised funds from business people to help sponsor a three-page advertisement in the *Washington Post* requesting members of Congress to exercise their constitutional power to stop the spread of the Asian war. The ad, which cost $10,000, was signed by 2,600 citizens of the Palo Alto area, including Arjay Miller, former president of Ford Motor Company and later dean of the Stanford Graduate School of Business.

3. In August 1970, the BEM chapter sponsored the world's longest billboard message—254 words for peace—a reprint from an editorial in *The New Yorker* magazine decrying the chaotic moral and economic results of the Indochina war. Sylvain Heumann (chairman of the Bay Area chapter), other officials of the organization, and I were on hand for the ceremonial paste-up of the first billboard at the corner of Kearny and Washington Streets in San Francisco. It would be followed by 90 other billboards in the Bay Area. The idea was conceived by Bud Arnold of the Maxwell Arnold Advertising Agency in San Francisco, who donated his firm's services to the project.

4. In February 1971, I testified on behalf of BEM at the Hearings on Ending the War in Indochina held in Caifornia by Senator Alan Cranston of California. Here is part of what I said:

> Our BEM members feel that the Indochina War makes no moral, political, social, or economic sense. The war is confusing and dividing citizens of this nation. It is draining away resources which are desperately needed for serious problems we face in this country—inadequate housing, lack of adequate health care and nutrition, the need for better education, the obsolescence of our cities, the pollution of our land, air, and water, and the dishonor of several hundred years of discrimination. This heavy military burden is responsible for a devastating inflation, an international balance-of-payment's deficit, confiscatory taxes on individuals and businesses, and an upcoming federal budget deficit estimated at $18.6 billion.

5. We participated in the April and November peace marches in San Francisco during 1971. The April march marked the first time the BEM participated in a Bay Area peace event as a group, and I recall that the appearance of our members was soundly cheered all along the route of the march from downtown San Francisco to Golden Gate Park.

6. In May 1971, BEM sponsored a public meeting to enable its members and the public to get a firsthand report from Congressman Paul N. McCloskey, Jr., on his visit to Vietnam and to hear his recommendations on steps that should be taken to bring the fighting to an end. In that same month the U.S. Supreme Court affirmed in an 8 to 1 decision (Justice Douglas dissenting) the conviction of Vincent F. McGee, BEM's national executive director, on four counts of noncooperation with the Selective Service System. In a letter from McGee one month later, he appealed to each of us to continue the work that he would shortly leave for a two-year prison term. His last words to us were "What a joy it would be for me to leave prison in a time of peace!"

7. BEM was one of several local sponsors of a peace rally in the Stanford University Memorial Church in May 1971, featuring Navy Lieutenant John F. Kerry, a leader of Vietnam Veterans against the War.

8. We encouraged broad television viewing of the documentary film "Eight Flags for 99c" by placing BEM-paid advertisements in the newspapers of the San Francisco Bay Area. The film, produced by the Chicago chapter of BEM, exploded the myth that the "silent majority" was in favor of continuing the war.

I'm convinced that the efforts of BEM under the direction of Henry Niles, retired chairman of the Baltimore Life Insurance Company, and Bernard Weiss, vice-president of Gimbel Brothers, played an important part in forming the strong public attitudes against our continued involvement that eventually led to the winding down of the war in Indochina. Other business leaders, speaking on their own, increased the public's awareness of the moral deficiency of our government's position in Southeast Asia.

One of the earliest voices from the business community and one of the most effective was that of Louis B. Lundborg. In April 1970, while serving as chairman of the Bank of America, he testified before the

Senate Committee on Foreign Relations, whose chairman was William Fulbright:

> We do have more than adequate data to demonstrate that the escalation of the war in Vietnam has seriously distorted the American economy, has inflamed inflationary pressures, has drained resources that are desperately needed to overcome serious domestic problems confronting our country, and has dampened the rate of growth in profits on both a before and after tax basis. . . . The fact is that an end to the war would be good, not bad, for American business.

Edward Gelsthorpe, president of Hunt-Wesson Foods, appeared before Senator Fulbright's Committee a month later and repeated what Mr. Lundborg had said about the war being a bad influence on the economy. His testimony ended with this interesting exchange:

> *Chairman Fulbright:* We have invited a number of businessmen who have said they didn't feel that they were competent or for one reason or another declined to come before the committee. What inspired you to take a public position?
> *Mr. Gelsthorpe:* Well, at the expense of seeming emotional about it—just a sense of patriotism. I feel the whole business of corporate good citizenship means businessmen acting as businessmen but as citizens and being concerned about the things that are unhealthy for this nation. This country was wounded deeply by the conflict that endured through three presidencies of our country. The scars of that war are still with us and will be with us for long in the future.

Amnesty International

The war in Southeast Asia finally ended, but a new threat to peace and human rights suddenly loomed into view. This threat had been earlier identified by British lawyer Peter Benenson, who wrote an article, "The Forgotten Prisoner," which appeared in *The Observer* in 1961:

> Open your newspaper any day of the week, and you will find a report from somewhere in the world of someone being imprisoned, tortured or executed because of his opinions or religion are unacceptable to his Government.

Benenson was not content just to observe this dangerous phenomenon—he decided to do something to fight it. Together with Sean MacBride (who later shared the 1975 Nobel Peace Prize) and a few others, he founded Amnesty International—an organization that was to be awarded its own Nobel Peace Prize in 1977. It was to be a movement independent of any and all governments, political factions, ideologies, economic interests, and religious creeds, working for the release of "prisoners of conscience"—men and women imprisoned anywhere for their beliefs, color, language, ethnic origin, and religion, *provided that they have neither used nor advocated violence*. This proviso has been one of the core strengths of AI together with the principles of political balance, neutrality, and impartiality.

One of the principal concepts of Amnesty International is the idea of individuals working directly for individuals through "adoption groups"—and there are now more than 2,000 such groups in 31 countries around the world. Each adoption group is assigned three prisoners who have been "adopted" by AI after a determination that the individual is a prisoner of conscience within the definition of AI's statutes. Each group has considerable autonomy within general guidelines to urge as polite and diplomatic an approach as possible in working for the prisoner's release. The adoption groups use many techniques, including letters to officials of governments and international organizations, embassy visits, meetings with traveling government officials, publicity, and contact with the prisoner and the prisoner's family.

Amnesty International carries on its rolls the names of about 4,000 persons who have been adopted as prisoners of conscience or whose cases are under investigation. Of these, 18 are Americans in American prisons. These 4,000 are only a fraction of the 500,000 political prisoners in the world today, according to AI estimates. "This decline—or if you will, this increase in man's bestiality toward his fellow men . . . has become a world-wide scourge, a sickness of the soul of our time," according to Thomas Jones, board member of Amnesty International USA.[2]

One of the notable achievements of the organization, apart from its direct involvement with individuals, was its role in initiating and obtaining unanimous adoption on December 9, 1975, by the U.N. General Assembly of the Declaration on the Protection of All Persons from Being Subjected to Torture and Other Cruel, Inhuman, or Degrading Treatment of Punishment: "the U.N.'s most important human rights document since the adoption of the Universal Declaration on Human Rights in 1948," Jones said.[3]

There are over 168,000 individual members of Amnesty International in 107 countries. Their efforts have played a part in the release since 1961 of more than 13,000 prisoners of conscience.

My first knowledge of Amnesty International came from Ginetta Sagan, who with her husband had organized a local chapter in 1972, and was looking for advice for ways to raise money. She told me that she herself had been imprisoned and tortured during World War II as a member of the anti-Nazi resistance in Europe. I was much impressed by her integrity and dedication to the cause of human rights.

I advised her that I did not think that corporations or foundations would be the best source of funds but rather individuals that wanted to support personally the cause of human rights with their own efforts or contributions. I told her that individual businessmen should be solicited as well as other professional people, and I now understand that over

[2]Thomas Jones, address to United States foreign service officers in Washington, D.C., in October, 1976.

[3]Ibid.

60,000 individuals in the United States now support AI with personal contributions.

I would hope that eventually some corporations would recognize the need and benefit of supporting Amnesty International and similar groups that are working for basic human rights in a fair and effective manner. In the meantime, it is important for individual business executives to be aware of such organizations and to consider personal support. Amnesty International USA is at 2112 Broadway, New York, NY 10023.

In closing, I would like to point out that my involvement with the various civil and human rights organizations mentioned in this chapter represented my own personal involvement as an individual and a business executive. I was not representing the company that employed me. The reasons for this are not hard to comprehend. Fair housing, civil rights, the Vietnam War, and prisoners of conscience are controversial subjects, and not all executives or employees of any firm would be expected to have the same point of view on such subjects.

That is the principal reason I have been careful in not giving the impression that my personal involvement carried along any company endorsement—which I would never request nor expect. It is clear that this is the best approach. Individuals in business, government, universities, and other institutions, however, have the same rights of free expression as other citizens. I also feel that business executives have a strong obligation to express their beliefs and positions, because often they have knowledge and experience that give credibility to their views. Also, in our pluralistic society, it is imperative that in questions of public policy, we have a broad expression of public views—and that includes the views of executives and all employees of business firms.

Index